Video Coding for
Emerging Multimedia Services

Video Coding for Emerging Multimedia Services

Edited by **Anna Sanders**

LANRYE
INTERNATIONAL

New Jersey

Published by Clanrye International,
55 Van Reypen Street,
Jersey City, NJ 07306, USA
www.clanryeinternational.com

Video Coding for Emerging Multimedia Services
Edited by Anna Sanders

International Standard Book Number: 978-1-63240-516-6 (Hardback)

Printed in the United States of America.

Contents

Permissions

List of Contributors

Preface

This book has been an outcome of determined endeavour from a group of educationists in the field. The primary objective was to involve a broad spectrum of professionals from diverse cultural background involved in the field for developing new researches. The book not only targets students but also scholars pursuing higher research for further enhancement of the theoretical and practical applications of the subject.

This book presents an in-depth study of video coding and elucidates its applications. It targets to bring together latest developments and applications of video coding. This book can be beneficial for researchers, engineers, graduate and postgraduate students, experts in this field, and hopefully, also for people who hold interest in video coding. The book talks about error resilient algorithms for H.264/AVC, wavelet-based coding, concerning latest video coding standards, high efficiency video coding (HEVC), multiple description coding, developed compression techniques for multimedia applications, shape compensation, region of interest (ROI) coding, facial video coding, and hardware implementations. Also, it provides many helpful ideas for your own research and aids to bridge the gap between basic video coding techniques and practical multimedia applications. We hope this book will make for a good read and help in contributing to video coding.

It was an honour to edit such a profound book and also a challenging task to compile and examine all the relevant data for accuracy and originality. I wish to acknowledge the efforts of the contributors for submitting such brilliant and diverse chapters in the field and for endlessly working for the completion of the book. Last, but not the least; I thank my family for being a constant source of support in all my research endeavours.

Editor

Advanced Video Coding Techniques

Differential Pixel Value Coding for HEVC Lossless Compression

Jung-Ah Choi and Yo-Sung Ho

Additional information is available at the end of the chapter

1. Introduction

High efficiency video coding (HEVC) [1] is a new video coding standard developed by Joint Collaborative Team on Video Coding (JCT-VC) of ITU-T Video Coding Experts Group (VCEG) and ISO/IEC Moving Picture Experts Group (MPEG). Currently, most of coding techniques are established and HEVC version 1 will be released in January 2013 [2]. We expect that HEVC is widely used in various applications for recording, compression, and distribution of high-resolution video contents [3].

Lossless compression is useful when it is necessary to minimize the storage space or transmission bandwidth of data while still maintaining archival quality. Many applications such as medical imaging, preservation of artwork, image archiving, remote sensing, and image analysis require the use of lossless compression, since these applications cannot allow any distortion in the reconstructed images [4].

With growing demand for these applications, JCT-VC included the lossless coding mode in the HEVC test model (HM) software in consequence of the Ad Hoc group for lossless coding [5]. In lossless coding, no distortion is allowed in reconstructed frames. To achieve lossless coding, transform, quantization, their inverse operations, and all in-loop filtering operations including deblocking filter, sample adaptive offset (SAO), and adaptive loop filter (ALF) are bypassed in the encoder and decoder since they are not reversible in general [6]. Also, sample-based angular prediction (SAP) [7][8] is used to replace the existing intra prediction method.

In the 7th JCT-VC meeting, many lossless coding solutions were proposed. Mode dependent residual scanning (MDRS) and multiple scanning positions for inter coding are suggested [9]. Also, SAP and lossless transforms [10] are proposed. Among these proposals, SAP is adopted in the HEVC standard. In the next 8th JCT-VC meeting, efforts to find the efficient lossless coding solutions continued. Joint proposal that combines SAP and the lossless coding signaling method was submitted [5] and a simplified context-based adaptive binary arithmetic coding (CABAC) structure without last position coding [11] was introduced. Since the development of the HEVC lossless mode is not yet finished, many experts are actively researching efficient algorithms for lossless coding [12][13].

In this chapter, we have tried to design an efficient differential pixel coding method for the HEVC lossless mode. One caution in developing the HEVC lossless mode is that the coding performance of the HEVC lossy mode would not be impacted or compromised. In lossless coding, the residual data is not quantized transform coefficients but differential pixel after prediction. As a result, the residual data in lossless coding has different characteristics than that in lossy coding. Thus, we analyze characteristics of the residual data in lossless coding and propose efficient mode dependent differential pixel scanning and entropy coding using the modified binarization. Note that the proposed method does not require any modification of syntax elements in HEVC, so it can be easily applied to the current standard. Moreover, the amount of complexity increase is negligible.

The chapter is organized as follows. In Section 2, we briefly present an overview of the HEVC lossless mode including its structure, SAP, scanning, and entropy coding. In Section 3, after we analyze characteristics of residual data in lossless coding, the proposed method for differential pixel value coding is explained. In Section 4, the performance of the proposed method is compared to the performance of the HEVC lossless mode in terms of bit saving and complexity. Finally, conclusions are presented in Section 5.

2. Overview of the HEVC lossless mode

The basic approach for lossless coding is to bypass transform and quantization in the encoder and the decoder. Without transform and quantization, SAP can be incorporated to improve coding efficiency of the lossless mode. It replaces the general angular intra prediction method in the HEVC lossy mode.

When the lossless mode is applied, all the in-loop filtering operations including deblocking filter, SAO, and ALF are also bypassed. Since there is no distortion existing in the reconstructed frame in the lossless mode, in-loop filtering operations will not help either picture quality or coding efficiency. The overall structure of the HEVC lossless mode is shown in Figure 1. In Figure 1, dashed lines represent the bypass and all bypass operations are activated in the HEVC lossless mode. Main coding modules are explained in detail in following sub-sections.

2.1. Sample-based angular prediction

In order to explore spatial sample redundancy in intra-coded frame, SAP is employed instead of general HEVC intra prediction. As shown in Figure 2, 33 angles are defined and these angles are categorized into two classes: vertical and horizontal angular prediction. Each prediction has both negative and positive angles.

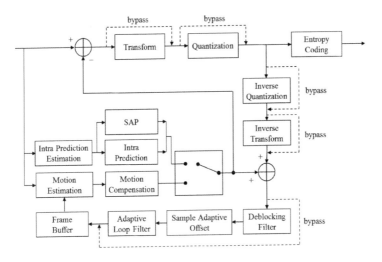

Figure 1. Encoder structure of the HEVC lossless mode

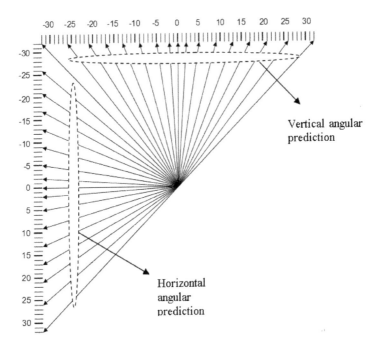

Figure 2. Intra prediction angles (vertical and horizontal angular prediction)

In lossless coding, reference samples within the current prediction unit (PU) as well as neighboring samples of the current PU are available. Thus, prediction can be performed sample by sample to achieve better intra prediction accuracy. All samples within a PU use a same prediction angle and the signaling method of the prediction angle is exactly same as that in lossy intra coding.

In SAP, samples in a PU are processed in pre-defined orders. The raster scanning and vertical scanning processing order is applied to vertical and horizontal angular prediction, respectively. In addition, reference samples around right and bottom PU boundaries of the current PU are padded from the closest boundary samples of the current PU.

Figure 3 presents the reference sample locations a and b relative to the current sample x to be predicted for horizontal and vertical angular prediction with negative and positive prediction angles. At most two reference samples are selected for each sample to be predicted in the current PU. Depending on the current sample location and the selected prediction angle, reference sample a and b can be neighboring PUs, padded samples, or samples inside the current PU. The interpolation for prediction sample generation is exactly same as that in lossy coding.

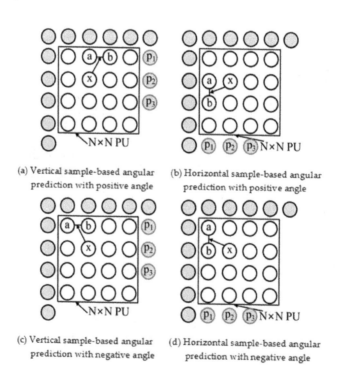

(a) Vertical sample-based angular prediction with positive angle

(b) Horizontal sample-based angular prediction with positive angle

(c) Vertical sample-based angular prediction with negative angle

(d) Horizontal sample-based angular prediction with negative angle

Figure 3. Reference sample locations relative to the current sample for sample-based angular intra prediction

2.2. Mode dependent coefficient scanning

In HEVC intra coding, mode dependent coefficient scanning (MDCS) [14] is used. There are three scan patterns: diagonal [15], horizontal, and vertical, as shown in Figure 4. The each scanning pattern is represented by the scan index. Index 1 and index 2 are assigned for horizontal and vertical scans, respectively. For diagonal scan, index 3 is assigned. Scanning pattern for the current transform unit (TU) is determined by the intra prediction mode and the TU size using a fixed look-up table.

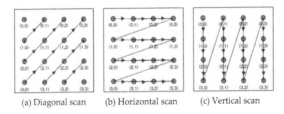

(a) Diagonal scan   (b) Horizontal scan   (c) Vertical scan

Figure 4. Three scanning patterns: diagonal, horizontal, vertical scans

Table 1 shows the look-up table that is used for the scan index selection. The look-up table is changed from the earlier version of MDCS. That is because the defined intra prediction mode number is changed in consecutive order. Here, the first row of the table indicates the intra prediction mode. The first column of the table represents the TU size. According to information of the intra prediction mode and the TU size, we can find the appropriate scan index using Table 1.

	0	1	2	3	4	5	6	7	8	9	10	11	12	13	14	15	16	17	18	19	20	21	22	23	24	25	26	27	28	29	30	31	32	33	34
32x32	3	3	3	3	3	3	3	3	3	3	3	3	3	3	3	3	3	3	3	3	3	3	3	3	3	3	3	3	3	3	3	3	3	3	3
16x16	3	3	3	3	3	3	3	3	3	3	3	3	3	3	3	3	3	3	3	3	3	3	3	3	3	3	3	3	3	3	3	3	3	3	3
8x8	3	3	3	3	3	3	2	2	2	2	2	2	2	2	2	3	3	3	3	3	3	3	1	1	1	1	1	1	1	1	3	3	3	3	
4x4	3	3	3	3	3	3	2	2	2	2	2	2	2	2	2	3	3	3	3	3	3	3	1	1	1	1	1	1	1	1	3	3	3	3	

Table 1. Look-up table for the intra coefficient scan index selection

2.3. Entropy coding

2.3.1. Syntax elements of CABAC

HEVC employed context-based adaptive binary arithmetic coding (CABAC) as an entropy coder. The syntax elements employed in CABAC are shown in Table 2. The gray shaded syntax elements are encoded in TU level and others are encoded in 4×4 sub-TU level.

last_significant_coeff_x_prefix
last_significant_coeff_y_prefix
last_significant_coeff_x_suffix
last_significant_coeff_y_suffix
significant_coeff_group_flag
significant_coeff_ flag
coeff_abs_level_greater1_flag
coeff_abs_level_greater2_flag
coeff_sign_flag
coeff_abs_level_remaining

Table 2. CABAC syntax elements for a transform unit (TU)

Last Significant Coefficient Position Coding: Since HEVC employs big coding unit up to 64x64, the location of the last significant coefficient in a TU is encoded by the column and the row position. For a TU larger than 4x4, the syntax element is separated into two parts: prefix and suffix. Prefix and suffix parts are encoded using truncated unary code and fixed length code, respectively. Table 3 shows the codeword structure for syntax elements of last significant coefficient position. In Table 3, (1) only exists when the TU size is greater than the largest last position that the code can represent and X means 0 or 1.

Magnitude of last coefficient position	Prefix (Truncated Unary Code)	Suffix (Fixed Length Code)
0	1	-
1	01	-
2	001	-
3	000(1)	-
4-5	00001	X
6-7	00000(1)	X
8-11	0000001	XX
12-15	0000000(1)	XX
16-23	000000001	XXX
24-31	000000000	XXX

Table 3. Codeword structure for syntax elements of last significant coefficient position

Significance Map Coding: After encoding of the position of last significant coefficient, significance map is encoded. There are two syntax elements, significant_coeff_group_flag and significant_coeff_flag. sgnificant_coeff_group_flag indicates that a 4x4 array of 16 transform coefficient level within the current TU has non-zero transform coefficient level. Then, for non-zero significant coefficient group, one bit symbol significant_coeff_flag is encoded in scanning order. If significant_coeff_flag is one, the transform coefficient level at the corresponding location has a non-zero value.

Level Information Coding: After the encoded significance map determines locations of all significant coefficients inside the TU, level information is encoded by using four syntax elements, including coeff_abs_level_greater1_flag, coeff_abs_level_greater2_flag, coeff_sign_flag, and coeff_abs_level_remaining. First two syntax elements indicate whether the quantized transform coefficient level value at the corresponding scanning position is greater than 1 and 2, respectively. Then, coeff_sign_flag is encoded. It specifies the sign of the coefficient. After this, the syntax element for the absolute value of the coefficient level minus three (coeff_abs_level_remaining) is binarized and encoded.

2.3.2. Binarization of level information

In order to binarize level information, the codeword is assigned as follows. Given a particular parameter k, an absolute transform coefficient n to be coded is consists of prefix part and a suffix part. The prefix is coded using a truncated unary code and the suffix is coded using a variable length code, as shown in Table 4. As shown in Table 4, the length of the variable length code depends on the unary code and the parameter k. That is, the parameter k controls the length of the codeword structure. Table 5 shows the binarization of coeff_abs_level_remaining when the parameter k is equal to 1.

Value	Prefix	Suffix (in bits)
$0 \sim 1 \times 2^{k}-1$	0	k
$1 \times 2^{k} \sim 2 \times 2^{k}-1$	10	k
$2 \times 2^{k} \sim 3 \times 2^{k}-1$	110	k
$3 \times 2^{k} \sim 4 \times 2^{k}-1$	1110	k
$4 \times 2^{k} \sim 5 \times 2^{k}-1$	11110	k
$5 \times 2^{k} \sim 6 \times 2^{k}-1$	111110	k
$6 \times 2^{k} \sim 7 \times 2^{k}-1$	1111110	k
$7 \times 2^{k} \sim 8 \times 2^{k}-1$	11111110	k
$8 \times 2^{k} \sim 9 \times 2^{k}-1$	111111110	k
$9 \times 2^{k} \sim 11 \times 2^{k}-1$	1111111110	$k+1$
$11 \times 2^{k} \sim 15 \times 2^{k}-1$	11111111110	$k+2$
$15 \times 2^{k} \sim 23 \times 2^{k}-1$	111111111110	$k+3$
...	...	...

Table 4. Binarization method for level information

Value	Prefix	Suffix
0	0	0
1	0	1
2	10	0
3	10	1
4	110	0
5	110	1
6	1110	0
7	1110	1
...	...	...
18	1111111110	00
19	1111111110	01
20	1111111110	10
...	...	...

Table 5. Example of binarization for level information when $k = 1$

The update of the parameter based on the magnitude of the previously encoded absolute level value. After encode one level value, the update mechanism is conducted, as shown in Eq. (1).

$$\text{If } |x| > 3 \cdot 2^k, k' = \min(k+1, 4) \tag{1}$$

Here, x indicates the previously encoded level value, k is the parameter, and k' is the updated parameter. The parameter k ranged from 0 to 4. Based on the pseudo code, we can summarize the selected parameter according to the absolute level range.

Parameter	Absolute Level
0	0, 1, 2, 3
1	4, 5, 6
2	7, 8, ..., 12
3	13, 14, ..., 24
4	25, 26, ..., ∞

Table 6. Absolute level range for determining the parameter

In level information coding, the absolute value of each non-zero coefficient is adaptively encoded by a codeword structure with the selected parameter k. The codeword with certain parameter is designed to encode efficiently in a specified range of the absolute level, as described in Table 6. We can note that the parameter monotonically increases according to the previously encoded absolute level. That is because level coding in CABAC is based on the expectation that absolute level is likely to increase at low frequencies.

4. Efficient differential pixel value coding

In this section, we introduce an efficient differential pixel value coding method. The proposed method consists of two parts: mode dependent differential pixel scanning and level information coding with modified binarization.

4.1. Mode dependent differential pixel scanning

In the HEVC scanning method, the horizontal scan is used for a vertically predicted block. In the similar way, for a horizontally predicted block, the vertical scan is used. Undoubtedly, SAP significantly improves coding efficiency of intra prediction in lossless coding. However, since the current sample cannot exactly predicted by reference samples and there is no transform and quantization processes, correlation in the prediction direction still remains. Thus, the conventional scanning index mapping in HEVC cannot provide the best coding performance for lossless video coding.

In lossless coding, intra predicted residuals do not show the same behavior as transformed coefficients. Instead, it is observed that for relatively small TU, e.g. an 8x8 or a 4x4 TU, when intra prediction is in vertical direction, the residual will often appear in vertical direction. Thus, a vertical scan will often result in better performance. Similarly, when the intra prediction is in horizontal direction, a horizontal scan will often be better. It is motivation of MDRS [16] and we follow this observation.

We assign the vertical scanning pattern to the vertically predicted block and the horizontal pattern to the horizontally predicted block. However, MDRS is proposed for the HEVC test model (HM) 4.0 and the current HEVC standard uses the different intra prediction mode number. Hence, we change the scan index selection to fit the current HEVC intra prediction mode number, as shown in Table 7.

	0	1	2	3	4	5	6	7	8	9	10	11	12	13	14	15	16	17	18	19	20	21	22	23	24	25	26	27	28	29	30	31	32	33	34
32x32	3	3	3	3	3	3	3	3	3	3	3	3	3	3	3	3	3	3	3	3	3	3	3	3	3	3	3	3	3	3	3	3	3	3	3
16x16	3	3	3	3	3	3	3	3	3	3	3	3	3	3	3	3	3	3	3	3	3	3	3	3	3	3	3	3	3	3	3	3	3	3	3
8x8	3	3	3	3	3	3	1	1	1	1	1	1	1	1	1	3	3	3	3	3	3	3	2	2	2	2	2	2	2	2	3	3	3	3	3
4x4	3	3	3	3	3	3	1	1	1	1	1	1	1	1	1	3	3	3	3	3	3	3	2	2	2	2	2	2	2	2	3	3	3	3	3

Table 7. Modified look-up table for the scan index selection

In lossless coding, these differential pixel values are likely to be the end of the PU. As mentioned in Section 2, padded samples are produced and used as reference samples in the prediction process. Figure 5 shows an example that a padded sample is used as reference sample. Here, the padded samples are copied from the closest neighboring sample s. Strictly speaking, these padded samples are not actual neighboring samples of the current sample x and samples that uses these padded samples as reference samples might provide poor prediction performance. It results in the increase of the residual data.

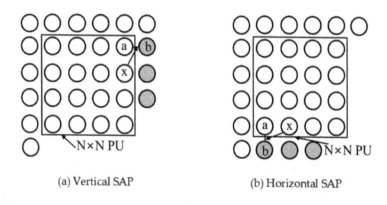

(a) Vertical SAP   (b) Horizontal SAP

Figure 5. Two types of padded samples in the sample-based angular prediction

Since syntax elements in the entropy coder are encoded in the reverse order, the beginning part of the scanned coefficient sequence has a higher probability of having non-zero coefficients compared with the ending part. In this way, the resultant scanned sequence is more suitable for the entropy coding method and experimental results verify that considerable bit saving is achieved. Thus, we change the scan order. For each scanning pattern, we change the scan order in the opposite order of the conventional scanning method.

4.2. Level information coding with modified binarization

As mentioned, in lossless coding, the residual data is the differential pixel values between the original and the predicted pixel values without transform and quantization. Main difference between differential pixel values in lossless coding and quantization transform coefficients of lossy coding is the magnitude of the level information. Figure 6 shows the magnitude distribution of coeff_abs_level_remaining in lossy and lossless coding. We can observe that differential pixel values have much bigger level information than quantized transform coefficients in lossy coding. In other words, differential pixel values have a wide range of magnitudes.

Hence, in our binarization, we extend the parameter range from 0 to 6. The parameter is initially set to zero. The parameter monotonically increases based on Eq. (2).

$$If \ |x| > 3 \cdot 2^k, \ k' = \min(k+1, 6) \tag{2}$$

It contributes the coding performance of the proposed method since it provides appropriate binarization code for bigger level values. The construction method of codeword is same with conventional HEVC coding, as described in Section 2.

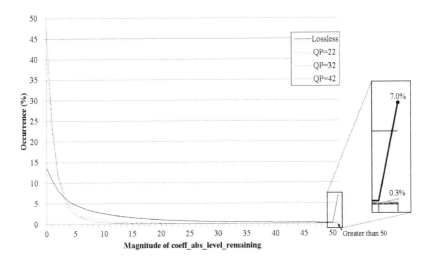

Figure 6. Magnitude distribution of coeff_abs_level_remaining

5. Experimental results and analysis

In order to verify coding efficiency of the proposed method, we performed experiments on several test sequences of YUV 4:2:0 and 8 bits per pixel format [17]. Two UHD (2560×1600) sequences, five HD (1920×1080) sequences, four WVGA(832×480) sequences, and four WQVGA(416×240) sequences with 100 frames are used. Specifically, the sequences that we used are summarized in Figure 7. The proposed method is implemented in HM 7.0 [18]. Table 8 shows the encoding parameters for the reference software.

Parameter	Value	Description
CUWidth	64	Largest CU size = 64x64
CUHeight	64	
IntraPeriod	1	Intra only coding
QP	0	Lossless coding
InternalBitDepth	8	8 bit per pixel
LosslessCuEnabled	1	Lossless coding
LoopFilterDisable	1	No deblocking filter
SAO	0	No sample adaptive offset
ALF	0	No adaptive loop filter

Table 8. Encoding parameters

In order to evaluate the efficiency of the proposed method, we include two sections based on the following settings.

- *MethodI*: Mode dependent differential pixel scanning

- *Method II*: *MethodI* + Entropy coding with modified binarization

5.1. Coding performance comparison

To verify the performance of the proposed method, we evaluate the compression results using bit saving. The definition of the measure is shown in Eq. (3). In the bit saving, negative value represents higher compression efficiency.

$$Bit \ Saving(\%) = \frac{Bitrate_{Method} - Bitrate_{HEVC-LS}}{Bitrate_{HEVC-LS}} \times 100 \tag{3}$$

(a) Traffic (UHD)   (b) PeopleOnStreet (UHD)   (c) Kimono (HD)

(d) ParkScene(HD)   (e) Cactus (HD)   (f) BasketballDrive (HD)

(g) BQTerrace(HD)   (h) BasketballDrill (WVGA)   (i) BQMall (WVGA)

(j) PartyScene (WVGA)   (k) RaceHorses (WVGA)   (l) BasketballPass (WQVGA)

(m) BQSquare (WQVGA)   (n) BlowingBubbles (WQVGA)   (o)RaceHorses (WQVGA)

Figure 7. HEVC common test sequences

Sequence	HEVC lossless mode (bytes)	Proposed Method		Bit Saving of Method I (%)	Bit Saving of Method II (%)
		Method I (bytes)	*Method* II (bytes)		
Traffic	292043389	289021760	288978917	-1.03	-1.05
PeopleOnStreet	285283752	279453835	279453835	-2.04	-2.10
Kimono	135252302	135252302	134976664	-0.20	-0.21
ParkScene	162834309	162834309	161872833	-0.59	-0.60
Cactus	165415216	165415216	164741620	-0.41	-0.42
BasketballDrive	142954441	142954441	142590363	-0.25	-0.26
BQTerrace	159248773	159248773	158651984	-0.37	-0.43
BasketballDrill	29015828	29015828	28759282	-0.88	-0.90
BQMall	31047873	31047873	30892776	-0.50	-0.52
PartyScene	38443400	38443400	38237571	-0.54	-0.54
RaceHorses	31042618	31042618	30855443	-0.60	-0.59
BasketballPass	6938810	6938810	6853810	-1.22	-1.24
BQSquare	8940364	8940364	8893462	-0.52	-0.83
BlowingBubbles	9009542	9009542	8975937	-0.37	-0.37
RaceHorses	8309686	8309686	8249459	-0.72	-0.79
Average				**-0.69**	**-0.72**

Table 9. Comparison of bit savings for the HEVC lossless mode and the proposed method

Experimental results are presented in Table 9. It can be seen that the proposed method gives additional compression efficiency about 0.72% bit savings on average and 2.10% bit savings at maximum compared to the HEVC lossless mode. From Table 9, we confirmed that the proposed method provided better coding performance, compared to the conventional HEVC lossless mode.

5.2. Encoding time comparison

To verify the complexity of the proposed method, we check encoding time of the proposed method and the conventional HEVC lossless mode. Then, we calculate the encoding time change ($\Delta EncodingTime$), as defined in Eq. (4). Here, negative value means the complexity reduction and positive value means the complexity increase.

$$\Delta EncodingTime(\%) = \frac{EncodingTime_{Method} - EncodingTime_{HEVC-LS}}{EncodingTime_{HEVC-LS}} \times 100 \quad (4)$$

The complexity comparison results are presented in Table 10. In general, the most time consuming part in intra lossless coding is not the prediction part, but residual data coding. However, since the proposed method follows the statistical results of lossless coding and consists of simple operations, the variation of the complexity is typically small. It is shown that all encoding time increases are less than 0.65%. In some cases, the encoding time is rather decreased. The amount of decreased encoding time is 1.96% at maximum, compared to the HEVC lossless mode.

Sequence	Proposed Method	
	Method I	Method II
Traffic	+0.10	+0.05
PeopleOnStreet	-0.10	-0.78
Kimono	-0.31	-0.79
ParkScene	+0.65	-0.01
Cactus	-0.20	-0.01
BasketballDrive	-0.30	-0.06
BQTerrace	+0.51	-0.22
BasketballDrill	+0.33	-0.16
BQMall	+0.35	+0.18
PartyScene	-0.08	+0.23
RaceHorses	-0.05	-0.05
BasketballPass	-1.96	-1.16
BQSquare	-0.44	-0.39
BlowingBubbles	+0.18	-0.05
RaceHorses	-0.17	+0.50

Table 10. Encoding time change (%)

6. Conclusions

In this chapter, we proposed the improved differential pixel value coding method for HEVC lossless intra coding. Considering statistical differences in residual data between lossy and lossless coding, we designed new scanning and context-based adaptive binary arithmetic coding (CABAC) binarization methods. In the proposed scanning method, we used vertical scan for vertical prediction and horizontal scan for horizontal prediction. Besides, we changed the scan order in the reverse order. In the proposed binarization method, we extended the range of binarization parameter based on the observed statistical characteristics of residual data in lossless coding. Experimental results show that the proposed method provided approximately 0.72% bit savings without significant complexity increase, compared to HEVC lossless intra coding.

Acknowledgement

This work was supported by the National Research Foundation of Korea (NRF) grant funded by the Korea government (MEST) (No. 2012-0009228).

Author details

Jung-Ah Choi* and Yo-Sung Ho

*Address all correspondence to: jachoi@gist.ac.kr

Gwangju Institute of Science and Technology (GIST), 261 Cheomdan-gwagiro, Buk-gu, Gwangju, Republic of Korea

References

[1] ITU-T SG16 WP3 and ISO/IEC JTC1/SC29/WG11. High efficiency video coding (HEVC) text specification draft 7, JCT-VC document, JCTVC-I1003, Geneva, CH, April 2012.

[2] Ho Y.-S., Choi J.-A. Advanced video coding techniques for smart phones," Proceedings of the International Conference on Embedded Systems and Intelligent Technology (ICESIT) 2012, 27-29 Jan. 2012, Nara, Japan.

[3] ISO/IEC JTC1/SC29/WG11. Vision, application, and requirements for high performance video coding (HVC), MPEG document, N11096, Kyoto, JP, Jan. 2010.

[4] Sayood K., editor. Lossless Compression Handbook. San Diego: Academic Press; 2003.

[5] ITU-T SG16 WP3 and ISO/IEC JTC1/SC29/WG11. AHG19: A lossless coding solution for HEVC, JCT-VC document, JCTVC-H0530, San José, CA, Feb. 2012.

[6] ITU-T SG16 WP3 and ISO/IEC JTC1/SC29/WG11. AHG19: A QP-based enabling method for lossless coding in HEVC, JCT-VC document, JCTVC-H0528, San José, CA, Feb. 2012.

[7] ITU-T SG16 WP3 and ISO/IEC JTC1/SC29/WG11. AHG22: Sample-based angular prediction (SAP) for HEVC lossless coding, JCT-VC document, JCTVC-G093, Geneva, CH, April 2012.

[8] ITU-T SG16 WP3 and ISO/IEC JTC1/SC29/WG11. AHG19: Method of frame-based lossless coding mode for HEVC, JCT-VC document, JCTVC-H0083, San José, CA, Feb. 2012.

[9] ITU-T SG16 WP3 and ISO/IEC JTC1/SC29/WG11. AHG22: A lossless coding solution for HEVC, JCT-VC document, JCTVC-G664, Geneva, CH, April 2012.

[10] ITU-T SG16 WP3 and ISO/IEC JTC1/SC29/WG11. AHG22: Lossless Transforms for Lossless Coding, JCT-VC document, JCTVC-G268, Geneva, CH, April 2012.

[11] ITU-T SG16 WP3 and ISO/IEC JTC1/SC29/WG11. Simplified CABAC for Lossless compression, JCT-VC document, JCTVC-H0499, San José, CA, Feb. 2012.

[12] ITU-T SG16 WP3 and ISO/IEC JTC1/SC29/WG11. JCT-VC AHG report: Lossless Coding (AHG13), JCT-VC document, JCTVC-I0013, Geneva, CH, April 2012.

[13] ITU-T SG16 WP3 and ISO/IEC JTC1/SC29/WG11. JCT-VC AHG report: Lossless Coding (AHG11), JCT-VC document, JCTVC-J0011, Stockholm, SE, July 2012.

[14] ITU-T SG16 WP3 and ISO/IEC JTC1/SC29/WG11. CE11: Mode Dependent Coefficient Scanning, JCT-VC document, JCTVC-D393, Daegu, KR, Jan. 2011.

[15] ITU-T SG16 WP3 and ISO/IEC JTC1/SC29/WG11. CE11: Parallelization of HHI_TRANSFORM_CODING (Fixed Diagonal Scan), JCT-VC document, JCTVCF129, Torino, IT, July 2011.

[16] ITU-T SG16 WP3 and ISO/IEC JTC1/SC29/WG11. AHG22: A lossless coding solution for HEVC, JCT-VC document, JCTVC-G664, Geneva, CH, April 2012.

[17] ITU-T SG16 WP3 and ISO/IEC JTC1/SC29/WG11. Common HM test conditions and software reference configurations, JCT-VC document, JCTVC-I1100, Geneva, CH, April 2012.

[18] JCTVC HEVC Test Model (HM). http://hevc.kw.bbc.co.uk/trac/browser/tags/HM-7.0

Chapter 2

Compensation Methods for Video Coding

Ben-Shung Chow

Additional information is available at the end of the chapter

1. Introduction

The standard dynamic image compression is usually composed of motion compensation and a DCT transformation for the error image from the motion compensation. The DCT coefficients are also classified by the cases to be coded by Huffman compression. However, the DCT coding will be inefficient for the binary images due to its broad dynamic range. It is noted that the binary images are usually described properly by their shapes. In this sense, a novel idea of shape compensation is proposed to replace the DCT processing. A schematic diagram to present this idea is illustrated in Fig. 1.

More clearly, the binary dynamic images are compressed by the shape compensation following the motion compensation. Our binary images are coded by the motion vectors and the kinds of shape transformations. For this transformation, a morphological filter is selected to modify the shape of the objects in image. Morphological processing [1] is a type of operation, by which the spatial form or structure of objects within an image are modified in a nonlinear way. The computation cost of nonlinear processing for conventional numerical image processing is very expensive. However, the morphology image processing treats the image components as sets and deals with the changes of shapes very efficiently. Thus, the morphology processing has recently been applied successfully to the industry auto-inspection and medical image processing [2-3]. The efficiency of morphological image processing makes the shape compensation in the decoding procedure very simple.

2. Conventional compensation method: Motion compensation

It is the speech transmission conventionally to be the major application in the real time communication. Thus, the basic rate in ISDN (Integrated Services Digital Network) was 2B+D =

2*64+16 kbps in earlier days. Accordingly, there is no motive to propose video coding with fewer bit rates. As one example, video conference was developed under the ITU H.320 [4]. One exceptional research [5] works on the video coding to fit into the 20-40 kbps bandwidth range because this range can be stably provided in the 2.5 G wireless networks such as General Packet Radio Service (GPRS) and Code Division Multiple Access (CDMA) although the theoretical bandwidths of GPRS and CDMA 1X are 115 and 153.6 kbps respectively. In this mainstream, MPEG/H.26x [6] performs well in the bandwidth range about 64 kbps.

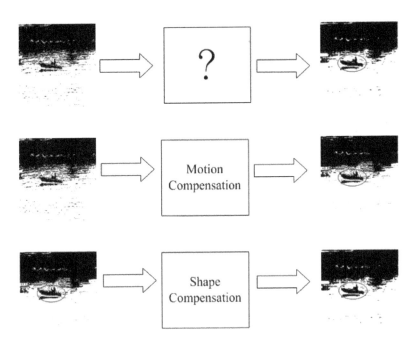

Figure 1. A schematic diagram to present the idea of shape compensation and comparison with motion compensation.

The MPEG digital video-coding techniques are statistical in nature. Video sequences usually contain statistical redundancies in both temporal and spatial directions. The basic statistical property upon which MPEG compression techniques rely is inter pixel correlation, including the assumption of simple, correlated motion between consecutive frames. Thus, it is assumed that the magnitude of a particular image pixel can be predicted from nearby pixels within the same frame (using intraframe coding techniques) or from pixels of a nearby frame (using interframe techniques). Intuitively, it is clear that in some circumstances, i.e., during scene changes of a video sequence, the temporal correlation between pixels in nearby frames is small or even vanishes. The video scene then assembles a collection of uncorrelated still images. In this case, intraframe coding techniques are appropriate to explore spatial correlation to achieve efficient data compression.

Motion in many video-conferencing scenes can be modeled to be primarily translational in nature. One popular procedure to estimate this type of motion is the block-matching technique [7]. Here the motion of a group of pixels (block) is represented by a single displacement vector, which is found by a matching technique. The so-called block motion-compensated coding schemes estimate the displacements of moving objects and only encode the block differences in moving areas between the current frame and the translated previous frame. Researchers have shown that this technique can increase coding efficiency significantly. A complete block motion-compensated coding system typically consists of three stages: (1) a motion detector which detects the moving blocks, (2) a displacement estimator which estimates the displacement vectors of moving blocks, and (3) a data compressor, which encodes the differences after motion compensation. Some terminology excerpted from GENERIC CODING OF MOVING PICTURES AND ASSOCIATED AUDIO, Recommendation H.262, ISO/IEC 13818-2 [8] are listed below for quick reference.

3. Terminology

Macroblock: The four 8-by-8 blocks of luminance data and the two (for 4:2:0 chrominance format), four (for 4:2:2 chrominance format) or eight (for 4:4:4 chrominance format) corresponding 8-by-8 blocks of chrominance data coming from a 16-by-16 section of the luminance component of the picture. Macroblock is sometimes used to refer to the sample data and sometimes to the coded representation of the sample values and other data elements defined in the macroblock header of the syntax defined in this part of this specification. The usage is clear from the context.

Motion compensation: The use of motion vectors to improve the efficiency of the prediction of sample values. The prediction uses motion vectors to provide offsets into the past and/or future reference frames or reference fields containing previously decoded sample values that are used to form the prediction error signal.

Motion estimation: The process of estimating motion vectors during the encoding process.

Motion vector: A two-dimensional vector used for motion compensation that provides an offset from the coordinate position in the current picture or field to the coordinates in a reference frame or reference field.

Non-intra coding: Coding of a macroblock or picture that uses information both from itself and from macroblocks and pictures occurring at other times.

- P-field picture: A field structure P-Picture.

- P-frame picture: A frame structure P-Picture.

- P-picture; predictive-coded picture : A picture that is coded using motion compensation.

With the above terminology, some illustrating examples and schematic diagrams are presented below to explain the details of motion compensation in MPEG.

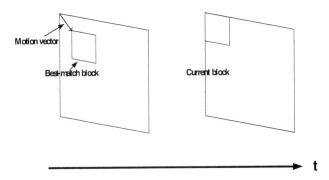

Figure 2. Illustration example for forward direction motion vector.

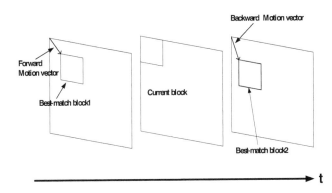

Figure 3. Illustration example for bi-direction motion vector.

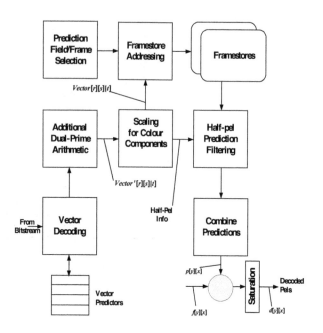

Figure 4. Flow chart for MPEG coding procedures.

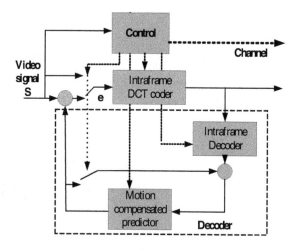

Figure 5. Schematic diagrams for MPEG coding procedures.

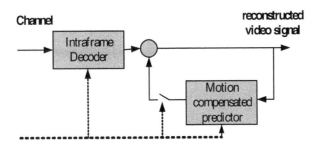

Figure 6. Schematic diagrams for MPEG decoding procedures.

Figure 7. Image examples to illustrate motion compensation (a) the reference image (b)the coding image (c) the motion compensated image (d) the error image between b and c.

4. Shape transform by mathematical morphology

Mathematical morphology refers to a branch of nonlinear image processing and analysis developed initially by Serra [1] that concentrates on the geometric structure within an image. The morphological approach is generally based upon the analysis of a two value image with some predetermined geometric shape known as a structuring element. The basic idea, arising out of stereology, is to probe an image with a structuring element and to quantify the manner in which the structuring element fits or does not fit within the image. The analysis of the geometric objects must be quantitative, because only such an analysis and description of geometric objects can provide a coherent mathematical framework for describing the spatial organization. The quantitative description of geometrical structures is the purpose of mathematical morphology.

The scope of morphological method is as wide as image processing itself. These include enhancement, segmentation, restoration, edge detection, texture analysis, particle analysis, feature generation, skeletonization, shape analysis, compression, component analysis, curve filling, and general thinning. There are many areas where morphological methods have been successfully applied, including robot vision, inspection, microscopy, medical imaging, remote sensing, biology, metallurgy, and automatic character reading.

The language of mathematical morphology is set theory. As such, morphologies offer a unified and powerful approach to numerous image processing problem. Sets in mathematical morphology represent the shapes of objects in an image. In binary images, the sets in question are members of 2-D integer space Z^2, where each element of a set is a tuple(2-D vector) whose coordinates are the (x,y) coordinates of image object pixel(foreground by convention) in the image.

In the following sections we illustrate several important concepts in mathematical morphology, and a detailed discussion can be found in [1].

4.1. Dilation and erosion

The simplest morphological transformation is dilation and erosion. In loose terms, these operations cause the swelling or the shrinking of areas when structuring element has a disklike shape. They are the base for most of the morphological operations discussed later.

Some basic definitions

Let A and B be sets in Z^2, with components $a=(a_1, a_2)$ and $b=(b_1, b_2)$, respectively. The translation of A by $x=(x_1, x_2)$, denoted, is defined as

$$(A)_x = \{c \mid c = a + x, \ for \ a \in A\} \tag{1}$$

The reflection of B, denoted , is defined as

$$\overset{\vee}{B} = \{x \mid x = -b, \ \text{for } a \in B\} \qquad (2)$$

The complement of set A is

$$A^c = \{x \mid x \notin A\} \qquad (3)$$

4.1.1. Dilation

With image A and a structuring element B as sets in Z^2, the dilation of A by B, denoted $A \oplus B$, is defined as

$$A \oplus B = \{y \mid y = a + b, \ a \in A, \ b \in B\} \qquad (4)$$

There are two equivalent formulations of dilation that deserve. First,

$$A \oplus B = \bigcup_{b \in B} (A)_b \qquad (5)$$

So that the dilation can be found by translating the input image by all points in the structuring element and then taking the union. Fig 2.1 illustrates the concept.

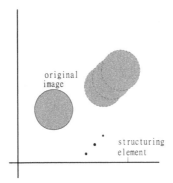

original
image

structuring
element

Figure 8. Dilation as a union of translates

Another formulation of dilation involves translates of the rotated structuring element that "hit"(intersect) the input image.

$$A \oplus B = \{x \mid (\overset{\vee}{B})_x \cap A \neq \varnothing\} \qquad (6)$$

Thus the dilation process consists of obtaining the reflection of B about its origin and then shifting this reflection by x. The dilation of A by B then is the set of all x displacements such that $\overset{\vee}{B}$ and A overlap by at least one nonzero element.

4.1.2. Erosion

For sets A and B in Z^2, the erosion of A by B, denoted $A \ominus B$, is defined as

$$A \ominus B = \{x \mid x + b \in A \text{ for every } b \in B\} \tag{7}$$

Equivalently, we may write

$$A \ominus B = \bigcap_{b \in B} (A)_{-b} \tag{8}$$

Here, the erosion is found by intersecting all translates of the input image by negatives of points in the structuring element. The method is illustrated in Fig 2.2.

Another definition of erosion is the following:

$$A \ominus B = \{x \mid (B)_x \subseteq A\} \tag{9}$$

Which, in words, says that the erosion of A by B is the set of all point x such that B, translate by x, is contained in A. If the origin lies inside the structuring element, then erosion has the effect of shrinking the input image. Geometrically, the disk B has been moved around inside of A and the positions of the origin has been marked to produce the eroded image. Formally, we can state the following property: if the origin is contained within the structuring element, then the eroded image is a subset of the input image.

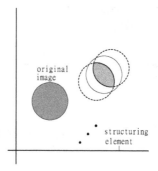

Figure 9. Erosion as an intersection of translates

Dilation and erosion are duals of each other with respect to set complementation and reflection. That is,

$$A \ominus B = (A^c \oplus \check{B})^c \tag{10}$$

$$A \oplus B = (A^c \ominus \check{B})^c \tag{11}$$

proof: Let $z \in (A^c \ominus B)^c$. Then $z \notin A^c \ominus B$. This happens if and only if there exists a $b \in B$ such that $z \notin A_b^c$. This also happens if and only if there exists a $b \in B$ such that $z \in A_b$, i.e. $z \in A \oplus B$.

If we think of a disk structuring element, then dilation fill in small (relative to the disk) holes and protrusions into image, whereas erosion eliminates small components and extrusions of the image into its complement. Here, we only discuss the implementation of dilation instead of erosion. Applying the duality property of dilation and erosion, we can easily employ both logical and geometric negation to implement erosion because of the different roles of the image and the structuring element in an expression employing these morphological operations.

5. Application of Matheron representation theorem

Matheron representation theorem with the notion of kernel and basis are the fundamental theory for morphological filter applied to video coding. However, the theory of representation of morphological filter is usually lengthy in textbooks [1]. We therefore have a brief introduction here.

The basic image operations for morphology processing are dilation and erosion. Erosion is the dual of dilation. They are totally built upon the Boolean operations: set union, intersection and complementation. The result of the dilation is the union of all translates of the original image. Every translation distance is determined by the coordinate of the corresponding black pixel in another image called the structuring element.

Definition 1: increasing

A mapping $\Psi : 2^{R*R} \rightarrow 2^{R*R}$ is increasing if whenever $A \subset B$, then $\Psi(A) \subset \Psi(B)$.

The definition of decreasing can be similarly defined.

Definition 2: translation invariant

A mapping Ψ is translation invariant if $\Psi(T(A)) = T(\Psi(A))$ for all $A \in 2R*R$, where T is the translation mapping.

Definition 3: kernel

The kernel of an increasing translation invariant mapping Ψ, denoted by Ker[Ψ], is important to the theory of morphological filters and is defined by the collection of all the images that will contain the origin pixel $(0, 0)$ mapped by that translation invariant mappingΨ.

The set of kernel can be further reduced to the basis defined below.

Definition 4: basis

A basis for the Kernel of an increasing translation invariant mapping is defined by satisfying the following two conditions:

1. No element of this basis is a proper subimage of any other element of this basis

2. For any element T belonging to the corresponding kernel, there exists an element T' of this basis such that T' is a subset T.

Theorem 1: Matheron Representation Theorem 1

Any increasing (decreasing) translation invariant morphological filter can be expressed as a union (intersection) of erosions (dilation) over sets of its kernel as follows

$\Psi(A) = \cup\, B \in Ker[\Psi]$ Erosion(A, B).

Theorem 2: Matheron Representation Theorem 2

$\Psi(A) = \cup\, B \in Bas[\Psi]$Erosion(A, B), where Bas[Ψ] is the basis of Ker[Ψ].

From Matheron representation theorem, every decreasing (increasing) translation invariant image mapping can be composed of a union (join) of erosion (dilation) operations. According to this theorem, the idea of kernel for the above mentioned increasing mapping is introduced by referring the set of the structuring elements of those erosions or dilations to characterize that mapping. Furthermore, to simplify the computation of the above mapping, the concept of the basis for kernel is further introduced, borrowing the idea of the basis from linear space, to reduce the number of the involved structuring elements.

As a summary, the morphological mapping is characterized by its kernel, and the kernel is characterized by its basis. Consequently, the proposed morphological transform (shape compensation) is coded by the kinds of basis or morphological filter.

6. Shape compensation: Selection of morphological filters

The concept of shape compensation is implemented on two image blocks: source block and target block. The source block is shape compensated (filtered) to look like the target block. The frames are divided into blocks of the size of 16*16. We need to select a filter for each source block. We first define the pattern of a cross form on the source block. In the proposed coding method, the source block is the motion compensated previous coded block and the target block is the current coding block.

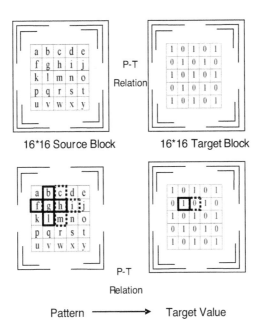

16*16 Source Block   16*16 Target Block

Pattern ⟶ Target Value

Figure 10. Pattern-Target relation illustration: pattern block and target values are scanned through the source block and the target block respectively; 3*1 mask is used in this illustrative example.

We then define the target pixel on the target block by the corresponding pixel with a same center location for the pattern on the source block. For each pattern, the filtered result is either consistent with the target pixel or not. The optimal filter is the filter causing the least inconsistent results. The optimal filter can be selected pattern by pattern. To reduce computation, the filter is selected group by group. The group is the pattern group classified by its kind of pattern. There are only 32 groups in the 14*14 patterns from the source block. The pattern group associated with the target value is called pattern-target relation or pattern-target occurrence table. One realization of this relation is shown in Table 1.

In practice, we first scan the source and target blocks to have this occurrence table. We next filter every group to have the pattern-filter relation table as in Table 2. It is noted that this table can be prepared in advance. One typical table composed of erosion filters is shown in Table 2. Finally, we build a pattern-filter conflict table from the pattern-target relation (pattern-target occurrence table) and the pattern-filter relation table. Using this table, the least inconsistent filter is obtained. One example of the pattern-filter conflict table deduced from Table 1 and Table 2 is shown in Table 3. A schematics diagram to introduce the relation between the pattern and target pixel is illustrated in Fig. 2. It is noted that the conflict count is produced in a single scan of the block pairs in the source and target image frames to save time.

Pattern-Target Relation					
Pattern Type	Target Value	Occurrence#	Pattern Type	Target Value	Occurrence#
00000	0	65	10000	0	0
	1	1		1	0
00001	0	1	10001	0	0
	1	0		1	0
00010	0	1	10010	0	0
	1	1		1	0
00011	0	2	10011	0	0
	1	0		1	1
00100	0	0	10100	0	0
	1	0		1	0
00101	0	0	10101	0	0
	1	0		1	0
00110	0	1	10110	0	0
	1	0		1	0
00111	0	0	10111	0	0
	1	1		1	1
01000	0	10	11000	0	0
	1	0		1	0
01001	0	2	11001	0	1
	1	1		1	0
01010	0	0	11010	0	0
	1	0		1	0
01011	0	0	11011	0	0
	1	0		1	0
01100	0	0	11100	0	1
	1	0		1	0
01101	0	3	11101	0	3
	1	1		1	6
01110	0	0	11110	0	0
	1	0		1	2
01111	0	0	11111	0	28
	1	1		1	62

Table 1. One example of pattern-target relation

Filter Pattern	Filter 00000	Filter 00001	Filter 00010	Filter 11111
Pattern Type	Filtered Value	Filtered Value	Filtered Value	Filtered Value
00000	0	0	0	0
00001	0	0	0	1
00010	0	0	0	1
00011	0	0	0	1
00100	0	0	0	0
00101	0	0	0	1
00110	0	0	0	1
00111	0	0	0	1
01000	0	0	0	0
01001	0	0	0	1
01010	0	0	0	1
01011	0	0	0	1
01100	0	0	0	0
01101	0	0	0	1
01110	0	0	0	1
01111	0	0	0	1
10000	0	0	0	0
10001	0	0	0	1
10010	0	0	0	1
10011	0	0	0	1
10100	0	0	0	0
10101	0	0	0	1
10110	0	0	0	1
10111	0	0	0	1
11000	0	0	0	0
11001	0	0	1	1
11010	0	0	0	1
11011	0	1	1	1
11100	0	0	0	0
11101	1	0	1	1
11110	1	1	1	1
11111	1	1	1	1

Table 2. One example of pattern-filter relation

Filter Pattern	Filter 00000	Filter 00001	Filter 00010	Filter 11111
Pattern Type	Occurrence #	Occurrence #	Occurrence #	Occurrence #
00000	1	1	1	1
00001	0	0	0	1
00010	1	1	1	1
00011	0	0	0	2
00100	0	0	0	0
00101	0	0	0	0
00110	0	0	0	1
00111	1	1	1	0
01000	0	0	0	0
01001	1	1	1	2
01010	0	0	0	0
01011	0	0	0	0
01100	0	0	0	0
01101	1	1	1	3
01110	0	0	0	0
01111	1	1	1	0
10000	0	0	0	0
10001	0	0	0	0
10010	0	0	0	0
10011	1	1	1	0
10100	0	0	0	0
10101	0	0	0	0
10110	0	0	0	0
10111	1	1	1	0
11000	0	0	0	0
11001	0	0	1	1
11010	0	0	0	0
11011	0	0	0	0
11100	0	0	0	0
11101	3	6	3	3
11110	0	0	0	0
11111	28	28	28	28
Total Conflict	39	42	40	43

Table 3. One example of pattern-filter conflict

As an illustrating example, two 16*16 block obtained from Fig. 14(a) and Fig. 13(b) in the same location are used for the data in Table 1, 2, and 3. In the source block from Fig. 14(a), there are 66 occurrences of pattern 00000, while 65 of which are aimed to be 0 and 1 is aimed to be 1 according to the target block in Fig. 13(b) as shown in the first square in Table 1. Next, there are 32 selected filaters, each of which are composed of two erosion masks. The first filter 00000, composed of the masks 11110 and 11101, will filter the pattern 00000 to be the value 0 as shown in the first square in Table 2. Thus, there is 1 occurrence of pattern 00000 that will not favor the action of filter 00000 since this filter will change it to the value 0 (as in Table 2) but 1 of this pattern is targeted to 1 (as in Table 1). Consequently, the occurrence of conflict between the pattern 00000 and the filter 00000 is 1 as shown in the first square in Table 3.

7. Experimental results

The video streams of the "boat" are tested in our experiment. The original streams are of the CIF format with the gray levels of 256. They are first to be reduced to the size of 256*256, then threshold to be bi-level 256*256 sequences. Binary image processing is thus applied to the bi-level sequences in the encoding stage, which includes the motion vectors search and the optimal morphological filters determination. The block would be refreshed if the motion compensated error is above the threshold. Correspondingly, there are two possibilities in the decoding process: block refreshing or shape compensation after motion compensation.

For the purpose of comparison, two coding schemes are arranged. The first one is the conventional coding by motion compensation only. The second is coding with motion compensation followed by shape compensation. The frame errors of the three coding methods for the entire boat streams are plotted in Fig. 11. For visual quality demonstration, the first frame of the streams is shown with the forms of grey-leveled 256*256 in Fig. 12(a) and the form of bi-leveled are shown in the Fig. 12(b). Finally, the image samples of the decoded streams from coding one and two are illustrated in the Fig. 13 and Fig. 14 with being magnified to see the detail in Fig. 15.

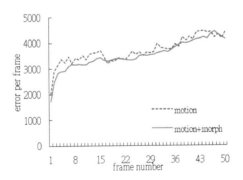

Figure 11. Error comparison to illustrate the error improvements by using the proposed shape compensation after motion compensation.

Figure 12. Frame 1 in the form of 256*256 (a) gray levels (b)bi-level for visual quality demonstration.

Figure 13. Frame 13 in the form of 256*256 (a) gray levels (b)bi-level.

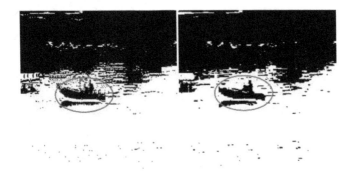

Figure 14. a) The conventional decoded (b) the decoded by motion and shape compensation.

Figure 15. a) The conventional decoded (b) the decoded by motion and shape compensation, magnified to see the detail.

8. Conclusions

Our coding procedures are simple: binary coding by motion compensation and shape compensation without using DCT coding. In the encoding stage, every motion compensated block has a shape compensation by a suitable morphological filter. This filter is selected on-line from a set of filters, which is selected off-line based on known statistics and experiences. The selection is by voting strategy. Decoding is simply a motion compensation followed by an efficient morphological filtering.

Visual quality for human is not concerned in this method as in the cases of telephony or conferences. In some situations such as the wild filed monitoring system, the decision function of security systems can be shifted to the concerned human if the video information can be provided inexpensively. For instance, the existence or the location of the intruder, which is the key information should be provided to the monitoring system. The low visual quality is tolerated with the convenient help of human decision-making as presented in this chapter.

Acknowledgements

This research is partially supported by the National Science Council of the Republic of China under the contract NSC 99-2625-M-009-004-MY3

Author details

Ben-Shung Chow

Address all correspondence to: bschow@ee.nsysu.edu.tw

Department of Electrical Engineering, National Sun Yat-Sen University, Lienhai Rd., Kaohsiung, Taiwan, R.O.C.

References

[1] J. Serra . Image Analysis and Mathematical Morphology. New York: Academic Press, 1983.

[2] J. W. Klingler, C. L. Vaughan, and L. T. Andrews, "Segmentation of echoboatdiographic images using mathematical morphology, " IEEE Trans. on Biomedical Engineering, vol.35, No.11, pp. 925-933, 1988.

[3] J. M. Higgins, D. T. Eddington, S. N. Bhatia, and L. Mahadevan1, "Statistical dynamics of flowing red blood cells by morphological image processing," PLoS Comput Biol., 5(2): e1000288. 2009.

[4] G. J. Sullivan, and T. Wieland, "Video Compression- From concept to the H.264/AVC standard," Proc IEEE, vol. 93, pp. 18-35, Jan. 2005.

[5] J. Li, K. Yu, T. He, Y. Lin, S. Li, and Q. Zhang, "Scalable portrait video for mobile video communication," IEEE Trans. Circuits Syst. Video Technol., vol. 13, no. 5, pp. 376–384, May 2003.

[6] B. G. Haskell, P. G. Howard, Y. A. LeCun, A. Pury, J. Ostermann, M. R. Civanlar, L. Rabiner, L. Bottu, and P. Haffner. "Image and video coding - emerging standards and beyond, " IEEE Trans. Circuits. Syst. Video Technol., vol. 8, no. 7, pp. 814-837, Nov. 1998.

[7] Jian Feng, Kwok-Tung Lo, Mehrpour, H., Karbowiak, A.E . Adaptive block matching motion estimation algorithm using bit-plane matching. Proceedings., 1995 International Conference on Image Processing, pp. 496 – 499.

[8] MPEG-2 Standard. ISO/IEC Document 13818-2. Generic Coding of Moving Pictures and Associated Audio Information, 1994.

Chapter 3

Multiple Descriptions Coinciding Lattice Vector Quantizer for H.264/AVC and Motion JPEG2000

Ehsan Akhtarkavan and M. F. M. Salleh

Additional information is available at the end of the chapter

1. Introduction

Recent advances in high-performance portable processing equipment, such as mobile processors, have enabled users to experience new-generation devices, including networked
gaming consuls, smart televisions and smart phones. Video coding, video compression and
video communication are essential parts of the aforementioned applications. However,
networking infrastructures do not offer unlimited bandwidth, and storage devices do not offer
unlimited capacities. Therefore, there is significant demand for reliable high-performance
video communication/compression protocols. Video compression refers to the process of
reducing the amount of video data used to represent digital videos; it is a combination of spatial
image compression and temporal motion compensation (Hanzo et al., 2007).

Multiple description (MD) coding has appeared to be an attractive technique to decrease the
impact of network failures and increase the robustness of multimedia communications (Goyal,
2001). The MD coding is especially useful for those applications in which retransmission is not
possible or is too expensive. Lattice vector quantization (LVQ) is a well-known lossy compression technique for data compression. LVQ is used for spatial compression and is less
computationally complex due to the regular structure of the lattice (Conway & Sloane, 1988).
MD image coding has been presented in several studied (Bai & Zhoa, 2007) (Akhtarkavan &
Salleh, 2010) (Akhtarkavan & Salleh, 2012).

In (Reibman et al., 2002), an MD video coder is presented that uses motion-compensated
predictions. This MD video coder utilizes MD transform coding and three separate prediction
paths at the encoder. Another MD video coding technique is introduced in (Biswas et al.,
2008). In this scheme, the 3D Set Partitioning in a hierarchical tree (3D-SPIHT) algorithm is
used to modify the traditional tree structure. Multiple description video coding based on LVQ
was presented in (Bai & Zhao, 2006). In that study, MDLVQ is combined with the wavelet

transform to produce a robust video coder. An error-resilient video coding scheme using the MD technique is proposed in (Chen, 2008) that employs MDLVQ with channel optimization (MDLVQ-CO). In that study, the central codebook is locally trained according to known channel erasure statistics, and two translated lattices are used for side codebooks to reduce distortion in the case of erasure.

In (Yongdong & Deng, 2003), MD video coding has been used to form an authentication scheme for Motion JPEG2000 (Fukuhara & Singer, 2002) streaming in a lossy network. In this study, the video frames are first transcoded into media fragments that are protected with integrity tokens and a digital signature. Then, the integrity tokens and signature are encoded into codewords using the forward error correction (FEC) for data loss resilience. Because of the use of MD video coding and sequence numbers, the scheme provides content integrity and defeats collage attacks.

In (Franchi et al., 2005), two MD video coding schemes are proposed, i.e., drift-compensation multiple description video coder (DC-MDVC) and an independent flow multiple description video coder (IF-MDVC). An interesting feature of DC-MDVC is the ability to use the actual reconstructed frame as the new reference frame for the side prediction loops instead of the original frame.

In (Zandoná et al., 2005), a second-order predictor is inserted in the encoder prediction loop. In (Campana, et al., 2008), a new MD video coding scheme for the H.264/AVC standard (Wiegand et al., 2003) is proposed based on multiple description scalar quantization. In that study, a splitting block is inserted in the standard H.264/AVC scheme after quantization. This block generates two descriptions by duplicating the control structures, picture parameter set, slice header, and information about the motion vectors. The MD coding video scheme presented in (Radulovic et al., 2010) splits the video information into several encoding threads, and redundant pictures are inserted to reduce the error drift packet loss that occurs. In (Zandoná et al., 2005), a novel RD model for H.264 video encoding in a packet loss environment is proposed. In that study, the end-to-end distortion is estimated by inserting a block-based distortion map to store the potential errors of the current frame that may propagate to the future frames. This scheme is intended for low-delay applications over lossy networks.

The IF-MDVC is designed for transmission in environments in which the packet loss rate is directly proportional to the packet size and thus having more descriptions with a smaller packet size at the same bit-rate is advantageous (Franchi et al., 2005). The MD coding scheme in (Radulovic et al., 2010) requires the channel conditions to allocate the coding rate to primary and redundant pictures, to minimize the total distortion experienced at the receiver. The study described in (Zhang et al., 2004) requires that the potential channel distortions of its reference frames be known a priori. The descriptions generated by the MD scheme presented in (Tillo et al., 2008) based on redundant H.264 pictures are not independent; thus the decoder cannot take advantage of all of the available information.

In this chapter a generic MD video coding based on the coinciding similar sublattices of the hexagonal lattice is presented. The coinciding similar sublattices are special sublattices because they have the same index; even though they are generated by different generator matrices

(Akhtarkavan & Salleh, 2012). The proposed multiple descriptions coinciding lattice vector quantization (MDCLVQ) video coding scheme forms a diversity system for MD video coding that can be exploited for any video coding standard such as H.264/AVC or Motion JPEG2000. Extensive simulations and the experimental results of applying the proposed MD coding scheme to several reference QCIF video sequences demonstrate that our MD coding algorithm outperforms state-of-the-art single- and two-description video coding schemes in terms of the compression ratio and transmission robustness. In addition, small differences between the peak signal to noise ratio (PSNR) of the side video sequences compared to the central decoder show significant capability to resist channel failures. Finally, the proposed MD video coding scheme provides acceptable fidelity criteria in terms of PSNR, which means that there is a negligible drop in the quality of the video and a significant increase in error resiliency and compression efficiency.

2. Background

2.1. Multiple-description coding

Multiple-description (MD) coding is a method to address network impairments when the re-transmission is expensive or impossible. According to Goyal (2001), MD coding can effectively address packet loss without the need for retransmission, thus it can meet the network requirements. In this scheme, a stream of input data is transformed into several different independent descriptions and sent over different channels of a diversity system. At the receiver if all the descriptions are received correctly, the original data will be reconstructed accurately. But, in case some of the descriptions fail to reach the destination, due to channel failure, the rest of the descriptions, which are fed via side decoders, are used to find an estimate of the original data. The performance of the MD system to reconstruct the original data can be of several levels of accuracy. A typical 2-channel MD coding scheme is shown in Fig. 1. Consider the simplest scheme in which two descriptions are the same. If either description is lost then the other would be useful. However, if both descriptions are available then one will be useless and hence the bandwidth has been wasted. In other word, receiving more descriptions must result in better reconstruction quality which can be offered by the MD coding (Goyal, 2001). According to information theoretic approach, the MD coding scheme may not require more bit rate (bandwidth) than the single description system. In the MD coding system, there is always a trade-off between the required bit rate and the distortion. Thus, in MD coding scheme, compression efficiency is sacrificed in order to gain error resiliency. Therefore, MD coding should be applied only if it does not require too extra bit rate or a wider bandwidth (Goyal, 2001).

2.2. Elementary of lattices

In mathematics (algebra), a lattice is defined as a partially ordered set (poset) in which any two elements have a unique supremum (the element's least upper bound or join) and an infimum (greatest lower bound or meet). In other words, a lattice is considered as a subset of points in the Euclidean space that share a common property. For example the lattice A_n is a subset of

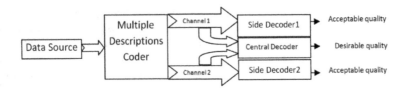

Figure 1. A general scheme of the MD coding scheme.

points with n+1 coordinates, such that the sum of these coordinates is zero. Therefore, the lattice A_n can be defined as:

$$A_n = \{(x_0, x_1, \ldots, x_n) \in Z^{n+1} : x_0 + x_1 + \ldots + x_n = 0\}$$ (1)

An n-dimensional lattice Λ in $\mathbf{R}^n$ is denoted by $\Lambda = \langle b_1, b_2, \ldots, b_n \rangle$. It means that Λ consists of all integer linear combinations of a basis vectors $\{b_1, b_2, \ldots, b_n\}$ in $\mathbf{R}^n$ (Heuer, 2008). The fundamental parallelotope of a lattice Λ is defined as (Conway & Sloane, 1988)

$$\theta_1 b_1 + \theta_2 b_2 + \ldots + \theta_n b_n \quad (0 \le \theta_i < 1)$$ (2)

The fundamental parallelotope is the building block of the lattice because if it is repeated many times, the whole space is filled in a way that there is only one lattice point in each parallelotope. The lattice points are generated using a generator matrix. The generator matrix of the lattice Λ with the basis vectors $b_1 = (b_{11}, b_{12}, \ldots, b_{1m})$, $b_2 = (b_{21}, b_{22}, \ldots, b_{2m})$, $\ldots$, $b_n = (b_{n1}, b_{n2}, \ldots, b_{nm})$ is given as (Conway & Sloane, 1988):

$$G = \begin{vmatrix} b_{11} & b_{12} & \cdots & b_{1m} \\ b_{21} & b_{22} & \cdots & b_{2m} \\ \vdots & \vdots & \ddots & \vdots \\ b_{n1} & b_{n2} & \cdots & b_{nm} \end{vmatrix}$$ (3)

The Gramm matrix of a lattice Λ is defined as $A = GG^t$, where G^t is the transposed matrix of G. The Gramm matrix determines the linear independence of the basis vectors, that is, they are linearly independent if and only if the determinant of the Gram matrix is non-zero. Two lattices are called equivalent if they have the same Gramm matrix or if the Gramm matrices are proportionate. There are many ways of choosing a basis and a fundamental parallelotope for a lattice Λ. But the volume of the fundamental region is uniquely determined by Λ, and the square of this volume is called the determinant of the lattice (Conway & Sloane, 1988). The determinant of a lattice Λ is also equal to the determinant of the Gramm matrix (Conway & Sloane, 1988):

$$det \ \Lambda = det \ A = (det \ G)^2 \tag{4}$$

Thus, the volume of the fundamental parallelotope of a lattice Λ is calculated as (Conway & Sloane, 1988)

$$vol = det \ G = \sqrt{det \ \Lambda} = \sqrt{det \ A} \tag{5}$$

The hexagonal lattice is a subset of the complex space C, and at unit scale it is generated by the basis vectors $\{1, \ \omega\} \subset C$, where $\omega = -1/2 + i\sqrt{3}/2$ (Vaishampayan et al., 2001). The hexagonal lattice is generated by

$$G_{2 \times 2} = \begin{pmatrix} Re(1) & Im(1) \\ Re(\omega) & Im(\omega) \end{pmatrix} = \begin{pmatrix} 1 & 0 \\ \frac{-1}{2} & \frac{\sqrt{3}}{2} \end{pmatrix} \tag{6}$$

and the Gramm matrix of $G_{2 \times 2}$ is calculated as (Conway & Sloane, 1988)

$$\mathbf{A}_{2 \times 2} = G_{2 \times 2} G_{2 \times 2}{}^t = \frac{1}{2} \begin{pmatrix} 2 & -1 \\ -1 & 2 \end{pmatrix} \tag{7}$$

and $det \ \Lambda_{2 \times 2} = det \ A_{2 \times 2} = \frac{3}{4}$. Thus, the volume (or area) of fundamental parallelotope of Λ will be calculated as $vol = \sqrt{det \ \Lambda_{2 \times 2}} = \frac{\sqrt{3}}{2}$. The hexagonal lattice is also generated by

$$G_{2 \times 3} = \begin{pmatrix} 1 & -1 & 0 \\ 0 & 1 & -1 \end{pmatrix} \tag{8}$$

and the Gramm matrix of $G_{2 \times 3}$ can be calculated as

$$A_{2 \times 3} = G_{2 \times 3} G_{2 \times 3}{}^t = \begin{pmatrix} 2 & -1 \\ -1 & 2 \end{pmatrix} = 2A_{2 \times 2} \tag{9}$$

According to $A_{2 \times 3} = 2A_{2 \times 2}$, the lattices generated by $G_{2 \times 2}$ and $G_{2 \times 3}$ are equivalent lattices. However, the determinant of $\Lambda_{2 \times 3}$ is 3 and the volume of fundamental parallelotope of $\Lambda_{2 \times 3}$ is $\sqrt{3}$. This is because $G_{2 \times 2}$ and $G_{2 \times 3}$ both describe the hexagonal lattice but in different coordinates and on different scales (Conway & Sloane, 1988). In an n-dimensional lattice Λ, the Voronoi region of a lattice point is defined as the union of all non-lattice points within R^n that are closer to this particular lattice point than any other lattice point. Thus, the Voronoi region of $\lambda \in \Lambda$ is defined as (Vaishampayan et al., 2001)

$$V(\lambda) \triangleq \{x \in R^n : \|x - \lambda\| \le \|x - \lambda'\| , \forall \lambda' \in \Lambda\} \tag{10}$$

As a consequence, all the points within $V(\lambda)$ must be quantized to λ. The Voronoi regions of the points in the A_2 are hexagons; therefore, it is called the hexagonal lattice. The Voronoi region of a sublattice point λ' is the set of all lattice points that are closer to λ' than any other sublattice points. Thus, the Voronoi region of $\lambda' \in \Lambda'$ is defined as

$$V(\lambda') \triangleq \{\lambda \in \Lambda : \|\lambda - \lambda'\| \le \|\lambda - \lambda''\| , \forall \lambda'' \in \Lambda'\} \tag{11}$$

Lattice vector quantization (LVQ) is a vector quantization technique that reduces the amount of computation for codebook generation since the lattices have regular structures. A finite set of points $y_1, \ldots, y_M$ in an n-dimensional Euclidean space, R^n, is called an Euclidean code (Conway & Sloane, 1982a). An n-dimensional quantizer is a mapping function $Q : R^n \to R^n$ that sends each point $x R^n$ into $Q(x)$ provided that $Q(x)$ is the nearest code point. The code points may be selected according to any type of relationship. If the code points are selected from a lattice, then the quantizer would be called a lattice vector quantizer. Fast quantizing algorithms are a family of lattice vector quantization algorithms presented in (Conway & Sloane, 1982b) for different root lattices. The quantization using A_n lattice points is a projection from n-dimensional space onto $\sum_{i=1}^{n+1} x_i = 0$, $x_i \in Z$ hyper plane. The fast quantizing algorithm first projects the n-dimensional input vector onto n+1 dimensional vectors on $\sum_{i=1}^{n+1} x_i = 0$, $x_i \in R$ hyper plane using a matrix multiplication (Conway & Sloane, 1982b). Then, using a manipulation the projected point is mapped onto a lattice point. In case of A_2 lattice, the input stream of data is vectorized into 2-dimensional vectors. Then, each input vector (i_1, i_2) is projected onto the 3-dimensional space, $(x_0, x_1, x_2) \in Z^3$ using the transformation matrix T given as (Conway & Sloane, 1982b)

$$\mathbf{T} = \begin{pmatrix} 1 & 0 & -1 \\ 1/\sqrt{3} & -2/\sqrt{3} & 1/\sqrt{3} \end{pmatrix} \tag{12}$$

If the expression $x_0 + x_1 + x_2 = 0$ does not hold, all the coordinates need to be rounded to the nearest integer points, while keeping the original values in another variable. The projected 3-dimensional vector is easily quantized (mapped) to the nearest lattice point by a simple manipulation. The sum of the differences between each coordinate of the original projected point to the nearest integer is calculated. If the sum of the differences is positive, then 1 is subtracted from the coordinate farthest from the integer. On the other hand, if the sum is negative, then 1 is added to the coordinate with the most difference. Thus, performing the computation-intensive nearest neighboring search algorithm is avoided. The two-dimensional version of the result point is calculated by right multiplying the quantized point by $\frac{1}{2}T^t$ (Conway & Sloane, 1982b).

2.3. Coinciding similar sublattices of A_2

Assume that Λ is an n-dimensional lattice with the generator matrix G. A sublattice $\Lambda' \subset \Lambda$ with generator matrix G' is said to be geometrically similar to Λ if and only if $G' = cUGB$, for nonzero scalar c, an integer matrix U with $\det U = \pm 1$, and a real orthogonal matrix B (with $BB^t = I$) (Conway & Sloane, 1988). The index N is defined as the ratio of the fundamental volume of the sublattice Λ' to the fundamental volume of the lattice Λ. Therefore, the value of N controls the coarse degree of the sublattice as well as the amount of redundancy in the MD coder (Vaishampayan et al., 2001).Thus, N is calculated by

$$N = \frac{vol'}{vol} = \sqrt{\frac{\det \Lambda'}{\det \Lambda}} = \frac{\det G'}{\det G} \tag{13}$$

Sublattice $\Lambda' \subset \Lambda$ is considered as a clean sublattice if all the points of the Λ reside only inside the Voronoi region of the sublattice points rather than on the boundary of the Voronoi region (Conway et al., 1999). It has been shown in (Bernstein et al., 1997) and (Vaishampayan et al., 2001) that, for the hexagonal lattice, Λ' is similar to Λ if N is of the form

$$N = \alpha^2 - \alpha\beta + \beta^2 \text{ for } \alpha, \ \beta \in \mathbf{Z} \tag{14}$$

In addition, N must be in the form of $N = \sum_{i=0}^{K} n_i$, where, n_i denotes the number of points at squared distance i from the origin. The sublattices of A_2 are clean, if and only if, α and β are relatively primes. It follows that A_2 has a clean similar sublattice of index N if and only if N is a product of primes congruent to 1 (mod 6) (Conway et al., 1999). The sequence of integers that generate clean sublattices of the hexagonal lattice are named A038590 by Sloane (Sloane, 2000). If these conditions are met then the basis vectors of the sublattice Λ' will be $u = \alpha + \beta\omega$ and $v = (\alpha + \beta\omega)\omega$. In other words, α and β are selected such that the value of N satisfies these conditions and hence a clean similar sublattice of the hexagonal is generated. Thus, the basis vectors are calculated as $u = \alpha + \beta\omega = \left(\alpha - \frac{\beta}{2}\right) + \frac{\beta\sqrt{3}}{2}i$ and $v = (\alpha + \beta\omega)\omega = \frac{-1}{2}(\alpha + \beta) + \frac{\sqrt{3}}{2}\left(\alpha - \beta\right)i$.   The   corresponding generator matrix will be

$$G_i' = \begin{pmatrix} Re(u) & Im(u) \\ Re(v) & Im(v) \end{pmatrix} \tag{15}$$

For example, with $\alpha = -3$ and $\beta = 2$, a clean similar sublattice of the hexagonal lattice with index $N = (-3)^2 - (-3)(2) + (2)^2 = 19$ is   generated.   The   basis   vectors   are   calculated   as $u = (-3) + (2)\omega = -4 + i\sqrt{3}$ and $v = \left(-4 + i\sqrt{3}\right)\omega = 0.5 - 2.5i\sqrt{3}$. Thus, the corresponding generator matrix will be calculated as

$$G_i' = \begin{pmatrix} Re(u) & Im(u) \\ Re(v) & Im(v) \end{pmatrix} = \begin{pmatrix} \alpha - \frac{\beta}{2} & \frac{\beta\sqrt{3}}{2} \\ \frac{-(\alpha+\beta)}{2} & \frac{\sqrt{3}(\alpha-\beta)}{2} \end{pmatrix} = \begin{pmatrix} -4 & \sqrt{3} \\ 0.5 & -2.5\sqrt{3} \end{pmatrix} \tag{16}$$

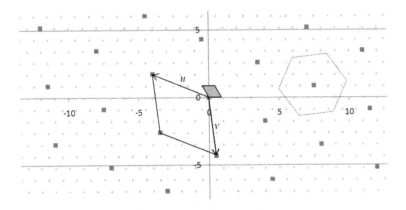

Figure 2. The geometrically similar sublattice of A_2 with index $N=19$ generated by Eq. (16).

It is also possible to calculate the index of the sublattice generated by G_i' using Eq. (13). The determinant of the generator of the hexagonal lattice at unit scale is $\sqrt{3}/2$. The determinant of G' is calculated as $det(G_i') = (-4) \times (-2.5\sqrt{3}) - (0.5) \times (\sqrt{3}) = 19\sqrt{3}/2$. Thus, the index will be $(19\sqrt{3}/2)/(\sqrt{3}/2) = 19$. The sublattice generated by G' is shown in Fig. 2 with blue squares and the hexagonal lattice points are shown with light blue triangles. The fundamental parallelotope of the hexagonal lattice and the similar sublattice generated by G' are shown with small and big parallelogram, respectively. The basis vectors, u and v, are also shown. The Voronoi region of the sublattice point $\lambda' = (7.5, \; 0.5\sqrt{3})$ is shown with a dashed hexagon.

It is seen in Fig. 2 that G' has generated a clean similar sublattice because there are no lattice points on the boundary of the Voronoi region of the sublattice points. The coinciding similar sublattices are defined as geometrically similar sublattices of a root lattice with the same index N but generated by different generator matrices. The commonly used values of N are 7, 13, 19, and 37. Therefore, α and β must be selected such that clean sublattices of the hexagonal lattice with a desired index is generated. In order to find the suitable values of α and β, all twofold combinations of integers [-10, -10] ... [+10, +10] have been examined and only the combinations that generate clean similar sublattices of the hexagonal lattice with index $N = 7$ are provided in Table 1.

The similar sublattices of the hexagonal with index $N=7$ corresponding to the generator matrices G_1' to G_{12}' provided in Table 1, are plotted in Fig. 3. The sublattice points corresponding to G_1' are shown with blue squares and the sublattice points corresponding to G_2' are shown with red circles. It can be observed that in the area that is shared between all the sublattices, only two distinct sublattices exist. In other words, the similar sublattices are coinciding with each other in a regular manner. Thus, these sublattices are called coinciding similar sublattices of the hexagonal lattice. In other words, the sublattices form two groups, the first group of sublattices coincide with G_1' and the second group coincide with G_2'. Each group consists of 6 sublattices which are coinciding with each other. Another apparent property of the coinciding sublattices, G_1' and G_2', is that they overlap with each other in a regular pattern, that is, they overlap with each other every N lattice points in every direction. These points are shown by big red circles with black border. The SuperVoronoi set of an overlapping point is the set of all lattice points that are closer to this point than any other overlapping point. The Super-Voronoi set of the overlapping points are shown with a blue hexagon. This symmetry is used in construction of the partitions. Partitions are used to define the new equivalence relation and the new shift-property that can be used to simplify the labeling function.

i	α	β	c	i	α	β	G_i'
1	-3	-2	$G_1'=\begin{pmatrix} -2.0 & -\sqrt{3} \\ 2.5 & -\sqrt{3}/2 \end{pmatrix}$	7	1	-2	$G_7'=\begin{pmatrix} 2.0 & -\sqrt{3} \\ 0.5 & 3\sqrt{3}/2 \end{pmatrix}$
2	-3	-1	$G_2'=\begin{pmatrix} -2.5 & -\sqrt{3}/2 \\ 2.0 & -\sqrt{3} \end{pmatrix}$	8	1	3	$G_8'=\begin{pmatrix} -0.5 & 3\sqrt{3}/2 \\ -2.0 & -\sqrt{3} \end{pmatrix}$
3	-2	-3	$G_3'=\begin{pmatrix} -0.5 & -3\sqrt{3}/2 \\ 2.5 & \sqrt{3}/2 \end{pmatrix}$	9	2	-1	$G_9'=\begin{pmatrix} 2.5 & -\sqrt{3}/2 \\ -0.5 & 3\sqrt{3}/2 \end{pmatrix}$
4	-2	1	$G_4'=\begin{pmatrix} -2.5 & \sqrt{3}/2 \\ 0.5 & -3\sqrt{3}/2 \end{pmatrix}$	10	2	3	$G_{10}'=\begin{pmatrix} 0.5 & 3\sqrt{3}/2 \\ -2.5 & -\sqrt{3}/2 \end{pmatrix}$
5	-1	-3	$G_5'=\begin{pmatrix} 0.5 & -3\sqrt{3}/2 \\ 2.0 & \sqrt{3} \end{pmatrix}$	11	3	1	$G_{11}'=\begin{pmatrix} 2.5 & \sqrt{3}/2 \\ -2.0 & \sqrt{3} \end{pmatrix}$
6	-1	2	$G_6'=\begin{pmatrix} -2.0 & \sqrt{3} \\ -0.5 & -3\sqrt{3}/2 \end{pmatrix}$	12	3	2	$G_{12}'=\begin{pmatrix} 2.0 & \sqrt{3} \\ -2.5 & \sqrt{3}/2 \end{pmatrix}$

Table 1. Different values of α and β for different values of $N=7$.

As shown in Table 1 there are 12 generator matrices corresponding to every indices $N=7$. The choice of the generator matrix changes the quantization process because the transformation matrix is calculated based on the generator matrix, that is, the choice of the generator matrix determines the transformation matrix used. The root lattice A_n has two different definitions. One is in n-dimensional space, that is, with $n \times n$ dimensions. Another group of generator matrices are with $n \times (n+1)$ dimensions. For example, A_2 lattice has a 3-dimensional generator $G_{2\times 3}$, in addition to the generators in 2-dimesional G_i' space. The transformation matrix is calculated using the relation

$$T_i = (G_i')^{-1} \times G_{2\times3} \tag{17}$$

By substituting G_i', $G_{2\times3}$, and T_i in Eq. (3-7), the corresponding transformation matrix will be

$$T_i = \frac{1}{\left(\alpha^2\sqrt{3} - \alpha\beta\sqrt{3} + \beta^2\sqrt{3}\right)} \begin{pmatrix} \sqrt{3}(\alpha - \beta) & -\alpha\sqrt{3} & \beta\sqrt{3} \\ (\alpha + \beta) & \alpha - 2\beta & -(2\alpha - \beta) \end{pmatrix} \tag{18}$$

For example, the transformation matrix corresponding to $\alpha = -3$ and $\beta = -2$ is calculated as

$$T_1 = \frac{1}{3.5\sqrt{3}} \begin{pmatrix} -0.5\sqrt{3} & 1.5\sqrt{3} & -\sqrt{3} \\ -2.5 & 0.5 & 2 \end{pmatrix} = \begin{pmatrix} -0.143 & 0.429 & -0.286 \\ -0.412 & 0.082 & 0.330 \end{pmatrix} \tag{19}$$

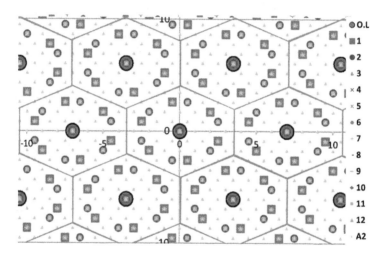

Figure 3. The coinciding similar sublattices of hexagonal lattice with index $N=7$ but in a limited range

3. MD video coding based on coinciding similar sublattices of A_2

MD coding has appeared to be an attractive scheme to be used for representing fault tolerant communication schemes and lattice vector quantization has been known for representing high compression performance with low computational needs. A multiple-description lattice vector quantizer encodes the vectorized source for transmission over a two-channel communication system.

In this section, multiple-description lattice vector quantization based on the coinciding similar sublattice of A_2 (hexagonal lattice) are presented. These schemes are called MDCLVQ-H.

264/AVC and MDCLVQ-Motion JPEG2000. The experimental results will be presented in section 4.

3.1. System overview

A video is a sequence of two dimensional images coming with certain timing details. Therefore, it is possible to consider a given video as a three-dimensional array in which the first two dimensions serve as spatial directions of the moving pictures, and the third dimension represents the time domain. In this way, a frame is defined as a set of all pixels that correspond to a single moment.

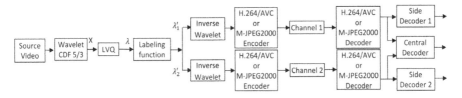

Figure 4. MDCLVQ video coding scheme applied to H.264/AVC and Motion JPEG2000.

In the proposed MD video coding schemes the input video is converted into two descriptions before being encoded by the standard video encoder. Then, the encoded descriptions are sent on the channels. If both descriptions reach the receiver, then a high quality video can be reconstructed by the central decoder. However, if only one description arrives, then a degraded video is reconstructed by the appropriate side decoder. The MDCLVQ is a generic scheme and it can be adopted for any video coding standard.

However, in this research it has been applied to H.264/AVC and Motion JPEG2000 only. Thus, two MD video coding schemes MDCLVQ-H.264/AVC and MDCLVQ-Motion JPEG2000 are defined, respectively. In other words, MDCLVQ-H.264/AVC uses the H.264/AVC video encoder while MDCLVQ-Motion JPEG2000 uses the Motion JPEG2000 video encoder. Therefore, both schemes are shown in a single schematic diagram in Fig. 4. The MDCLVQ video coding scheme is described in following subsections. In the proposed MDCLVQ scheme A_2 lattice points are used as the codebooks of the quantizer and the coinciding similar sublattice points are used as the labels. The schematic diagram of the MDCLVQ is illustrated in Fig. 6. The MDCLVQ scheme includes: the wavelet transformation module, the vectorization module, the LVQ module, the labeling function module, the arithmetic coder/decoder module, and the MD decoders. These modules are described in following subsections.

3.2. Wavelet decomposition module

It is possible to consider a video as a three dimensional array in which the first two dimensions serve as spatial directions of the moving pictures, and the third dimension represents the time domain. In this way, a frame is defined as a set of all pixels that correspond to a single moment. Every frame is decomposed into several wavelet coefficients (sub-bands), where the biorthogonal Cohen-Daubechies-Feauveau (CDF) 5/3 wavelet transforms (with lifting implementation) with 1 level of decomposition is used. Finally, the wavelet coefficients are streamed to the LVQ module.

3.3. Lattice vector quantizer module

In the LVQ module, the 2-D vectors, constructed in vectorization module are mapped to the nearest neighbouring lattice point using the fast quantizing algorithm. Lattice A_2 is used in the LVQ as the codebook. The details of the fast quantizing algorithm have been presented in section 2.2.

3.4. The coinciding labeling function

The proposed coinciding labeling function is composed of the hexagonal lattice Λ, coinciding sublattice number 1, Λ'_1 and coinciding sublattice number 2, Λ'_2. The first coinciding sublattice is generated by $\mathbf{G'_1}$; while the second coinciding sublattice is generated by $\mathbf{G'_2}$. The labeling function maps each lattice point into two coinciding sublattice points that form a label. The first coinciding sublattice point belongs to Λ'_1; while the second coinciding sublattice point belongs to Λ'_2. The two produced descriptions are encoded using a basic zero-order arithmetic codec prior being transmitted over the channels.

There are a lot of similarities between the terminologies of MDCLVQ-A_2 schemes and traditional MDLVQ schemes. The coinciding similar sublattices overlap with each other in a regular pattern, that is, they have overlapping points every N lattice point in every direction. These points comprise the set of overlapping point S_{ov}. It is defined as

$$S_{ov} \stackrel{\text{def}}{=} \left\{ \lambda : \lambda \in \left(\Lambda \cap \Lambda'_1 \cap \Lambda'_2 \right) \right\} \tag{20}$$

where, Λ is the lattice, Λ'_1 is the first coinciding similar sublattice, and Λ'_2 is the second coinciding similar sublattice. In other words, the overlapping points are the lattice points on where the two coinciding similar sublattices coincide with each other. The Voronoi region/set of a coinciding sublattice is defined in Eq. (13). The SuperVoronoi region/set of an overlapping sublattice point λ' is the set of all lattice and sublattice points that are closer to λ' than any other overlapping point. In other words, the SuperVoronoi region S_{sv} of λ' is defined as

$$S_{sv}(\lambda') \stackrel{\text{def}}{=} \left\{ \lambda \in \Lambda, \ \lambda' \in S_{ov} : \|\lambda - \lambda'\| \leq \|\lambda - \lambda''\|, \ \forall \lambda'' \in S_{ov} \right\} \tag{21}$$

where Λ is the lattice and S_{ov} is the set of overlapping points. The coinciding similar sublattices partition the space into SuperVoronoi regions. The coinciding similar sublattices of the hexagonal lattice with index $N = 7$ and the SuperVoronoi regions of the overlapping sublattice points are plotted in Fig. 3. The coinciding similar sublattice points are within the partitions.

Thus, the labels all reside within the same SuperVoronoi region as the labelled lattice points. Therefore, both vertices of the label will be as close as possible to the original lattice point and the side distortions will be low.

The labeling function maps every hexagonal lattice point λ to a label. In the MDCLVQ scheme, the label is considered as a directed edge $\vec{e} = \langle \lambda_1', \lambda_2' \rangle$ which consists of two coinciding sublattice points λ_1' and λ_2' selected from the coinciding similar sublattices Λ_1' and Λ_2' respectively. The set of labels corresponding to every overlapping point λ_{ov} is defined as:

$$\varepsilon(\lambda_{ov}) = \left\{ (v_1, v_2) : \left(\Lambda_1' \cap S_{sv}(\lambda_{ov}) \right) \times \left(\Lambda_2' \cap S_{sv}(\lambda_{ov}) \right) \right\}$$ (22)

In other words, $\varepsilon(\lambda_{ov})$ is the set of all possible labels within the SuperVoronoi set of the overlapping point λ_{ov}. The coinciding similar sublattices have inherent symmetries that can be used to define a new equivalence relation. In order to define the new equivalence relation, a modified version of the congruency relation is used. The traditional congruency relation $\equiv (mod\ k)$ accepts natural modulus; however, the modified version of the congruency accepts real modulus.

Let's assume that λ_x and λ_y denote the x-coordinate and y-coordinate of the lattice point λ, respectively. Although λ_x and λ_y may take on values from an unlimited range of real numbers, using $\equiv (mod\ k)$, the remainders only take on values from a finite set of real numbers. It has been observed that according to the congruency relation the remainders are repeated in a regular pattern. For example, in case of the coinciding similar sublattice with index N the remainders of $\lambda_x \equiv \left(mod\ \frac{N}{2} \right)$ take on values $\frac{0}{2}, \frac{1}{2}, \frac{2}{2}, \frac{3}{2} \dots \frac{N-1}{2}$ and the remainders of $\lambda_y \equiv \left(mod\ \frac{N\sqrt{3}}{2} \right)$ take on values $\frac{0}{2}, \frac{\sqrt{3}}{2}, \frac{2\sqrt{3}}{2}, \frac{3\sqrt{3}}{2} \dots \frac{(N-1)\sqrt{3}}{2}$. Thus, it is possible to define a new equivalence relation for the coinciding similar sublattice with index N. The equivalence relation enables the labeling function to find the SuperVoronoi sets of the sublattice points without using the computation intensive neighbourhood search. The new equivalence relation, denoted as $\equiv'$, is defined as:

$$\lambda' \equiv' \lambda'' \Leftrightarrow \lambda_x' \equiv \lambda_x'' \left(mod\ \frac{N}{2} \right) \wedge \lambda_y' \equiv \lambda_y'' \left(mod\ \frac{N\sqrt{3}}{2} \right)$$ (23)

Eq. (23) shows that the two points of the lattice, λ' and λ'', are equivalent, if and only if their x-coordinates are congruent modulo $N/2$ and their y-coordinates are congruent modulo $N\sqrt{3}/2$. Thus, the lattice points are divided into N^2 partitions. Each equivalence class is denoted by a twofold $[a,\ b]$ as the following:

$$[m_x,\ m_y] = \left[m_x = \lambda_x mod\ \frac{N}{2},\ m_y = \lambda_y mod\ \frac{N\sqrt{3}}{2} \right]$$ (24)

The proposed labeling procedure has three properties. First, it utilizes different sublattices rather than a single sublattice. Second, it utilizes a new rule of equivalence as well as a new partitioning scheme. Third, the coinciding labeling scheme utilizes a new shift property in order to simplify the labeling procedure. The new shift property is defined as:

$$\alpha(\tilde{\lambda}) = \alpha(\lambda) + \tilde{\lambda} - \lambda \text{ if } \tilde{\lambda} \equiv' \lambda, \ \lambda \in S_{sv}(O) \tag{25}$$

This finding shows that in order to label an arbitrary lattice point, $\tilde{\lambda}$, it is just enough to obtain its equivalent point within the SuperVoronoi set of the origin, and translate the label of the equivalent point by $\tilde{\lambda} - \lambda$. Thus, the problem of labeling all lattice points has been simplified to the problem of labeling only the lattice points within the SuperVoronoi set of the origin. These labels are obtained from the set of labels corresponding to the origin $\varepsilon(O)$.

The rule for assigning labels within $\varepsilon(O)$ to points within $S_{sv}(O)$ is the parallelogram law. According to the parallelogram law if a lattice point λ is labelled using $e = (\lambda_1', \lambda_2')$. Then, sum of the side distortions, $(\lambda - \lambda_1')^2 + (\lambda - \lambda_2')^2$ is equal to $\frac{1}{2}(\lambda_1' - \lambda_2')^2 + 2\left(\lambda - \frac{\lambda_1' + \lambda_2'}{2}\right)^2$, where $\frac{\lambda_1' + \lambda_2'}{2}$ is the midpoint of the label. Thus, in order to minimize the distortions, the algorithm chooses the shortest label that its mid point is as close as possible to the lattice point. The distance between the label and the lattice point is considered as the length of the line connecting the midpoint of the label to the lattice point. The labeling function is performed in the following nine steps;

1. Generate the coinciding similar sublattices Λ_1' and Λ_2'

2. Obtain the set of overlapping points S_{ov}

3. Obtain the SuperVoronoi set of the origin , $S_{sv}(O)$

4. Construct the partitions using the defined relation $\equiv'$

5. Obtain $\varepsilon(O)$, the set of labels corresponding to the origin

6. Assign every lattice point within $S_{sv}(O)$, to the shortest edges within $\varepsilon(O)$ that its midpoint is as close as possible to λ

7. For any point outside the SuperVoronoi set of the origin, $\tilde{\lambda} \notin S_{sv}(O)$, obtain its equivalent point within the SuperVoronoi set of the origin, $\lambda \in S_{sv}(O)$

8. Obtain the label of the equivalent point

9. Translate the label of the equivalent point by $\tilde{\lambda} - \lambda$

As the two sublattices can be used interchangeably in the labeling algorithm, there is no preference between the two descriptions. Thus, there is no need to use the alternative transmission technique. As for example, consider the hexagonal lattice with unit fundamental area and the coinciding similar sublattices with index $N = 7$ shown in Fig. 5. The first sublattice points are shown with circles and the second sublattice points are shown with squares. The sublattice points within $S_{sv}(O)$ are labeled with numbers. In Fig. 5, the lattice points outside the SuperVoronoi set of the origin are shown with triangles and the overlapping points are shown with circled-squares.

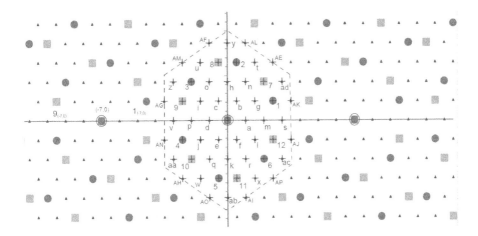

Figure 5. The labeling scheme for index $N=7$. The lattice, the first sublattice, and the second sublattice are shown with triangles, circles, and squares.

In general, for the sublattices of the hexagonal lattice with index N, there are $N^2 + N - 1$ points within the SuperVoronoi set of the origin. There are N^2 possible labels within $\varepsilon(O)$ that are obtained by the Cartesian product of $\Lambda_1' \cap S_{sv}(O)$ and $\Lambda_2' \cap S_{sv}(O)$. According to the new equivalence relation defined in Eq. (23), the partitions are constructed by dividing the x-coordinate of the lattice points modulo $N/2$ and the y-coordinate of the lattice points modulo $N\sqrt{3}/2$. Thus, the lattice points are divided into N^2 partitions. The partitions are divided into N^2 single-point partitions and $N - 1$ double-point partitions. In case of index $N=13$, there are 181 lattice points inside the SuperVoronoi set of the origin. These points are also partitioned into $N^2=169$ single-point partitions and 12 double-point partitions. In case of the coinciding sublattice with index $N=7$ there are 55 lattice points within the SuperVoronoi set of the origin that are shown with crosses in Fig. 5. The points within the SuperVoronoi sets of the origin are divided into 49 partitions, including 43 single-point partitions and 6 double-point partitions. The double-point partitions are shown with capital letters in Fig. 5. The same partitioning scheme is repeated for every overlapping point due to the inherent symmetry of the coinciding similar sublattices. The constructed partitions are listed in Table 2.

λ	(λ_x,λ_y)	$[m_x, m_y]$	λ	(λ_x,λ_y)	$[m_x, m_y]$	λ	(λ_x,λ_y)	$[m_x, m_y]$
a	(1,0)	[1,0]	n	(1,√3)	[1,√3]	AO-AE	(2.5,1.5√3)	[2.5,1.5√3]
b	(0.5,0.5√3)	[0.5,0.5√3]	o	(-1,√3)	[2.5, √3]	AP-AF	(-1,2√3)	[2.5,2√3]
c	(-0.5,0.5√3)	[3.0,0.5√3]	p	(-2,0)	[1.5,0]	AK-AG	(-3.5,0.5√3)	[0,0.5√3]
d	(-1,0)	[2.5,0]	q	(-1,-√3)	[2.5,2.5√3]	AL-AH	(-2.5,-1.5√3)	[1,2√3]
e	(-0.5,-0.5√3)	[3.0,3√3]	r	(1,-√3)	[1.0,2.5√3]	AM-AI	(1,-2√3)	[1,1.5√3]
f	(0.5,-0.5√3)	[0.5,3√3]	s	(3,0)	[3.0,0]	AN-AJ	(3.5,-0.5√3)	[0,3√3]
g	(1.5,0.5√3)	[1.5,0.5√3]	t	(1.5,1.5√3)	[1.5,1.5√3]	aa	(-3,-√3)	[0.5,2.5√3]
h	(0,√3)	[0, √3]	u	(-1.5,1.5√3)	[2.0,1.5√3]	ab	(0,-2√3)	[0.0,1.5√3]
i	(-1.5,0.5√3)	[2.0,0.5√3]	v	(-3,0)	[0.5,0]	ac	(3,-√3)	[3.0,2.5√3]
j	(-1.5,-0.5√3)	[2,3√3]	w	(-1.5,-1.5√3)	[2.0,2√3]	ad	(3,√3)	[3.0,√3]
k	(0,-√3)	[0.0,2.5√3]	x	(1.5,-1.5√3)	[1.5,2√3]	6	(2,-√3)	[2.0,2.5√3]
l	(1.5,-0.5√3)	[1.5,3√3]	y	(0,2√3)	[0.0,2√3]	7	(2,√3)	[2.0,√3]
m	(2,0)	[2.0,0]	z	(-3,√3)	[0.5, √3]	8	(-0.5,1.5√3)	[3.0,1.5√3]
0	(0,0)	[0,0]	3	(-2,√3)	[1.5, √3]	9	(-2.5,0.5√3)	[1,0.5√3]
1	(2.5,0.5√3)	[2.5,0.5√3]	4	(-2.5,-0.5√3)	[1.0,3√3]	11	(0.5,-1.5√3)	[0.5,2√3]
2	(0.5,1.5√3)	[0.5,1.5√3]	5	(-0.5,-1.5√3)	[3.0,2√3]	12	(2.5,-0.5√3)	[2.5,3√3]

Table 2. The SuperVoronoi set of the origin and their partitions for $N=7$.

The points inside the double-point partitions are located on the boundaries of the SuperVoronoi regions of the overlapping sublattice points. The points residing on the borders are always equidistant from the two adjacent overlapping points. Thus, it is possible to label them according to two overlapping points. However the labeling function must be injective. Therefore, a simple rule is invented to the labeling function in order to avoid confusion of having double-point partitions. The invented rule must be to label the equidistant points using either the first overlapping point or the second overlapping point. In the current labeling function these points are labelled using the overlapping point with smaller x-coordinate.

Consider the points AG and AK in Fig. 7 that form a double-point partition; since $x_{AG} \equiv x_{AK} \ (mod \ N/2)$ and $y_{AG} \equiv y_{AK} \ (mod \ N\sqrt{3}/2)$. According to the new rule, AK is labelled due $\lambda_{ov}=(0,0)$ and the label is $\langle 1_{(0, 0)}, 9_{(0, 0)} \rangle$. In contrast, AG is labelled due $\lambda_{ov}=(-7,0)$ and its label is $\langle 1_{(-7, 0)}, 9_{(-7, 0)} \rangle$. This rule is repeated for other double-point partitions. However, every single-point partition within the SuperVoronoi sets of the origin is labelled using the shortest edge within $\varepsilon(O)$ which its midpoint is as close as possible to the lattice point. The complete list of the labels is given in Table 3.

λ	e	λ	e	λ	e	λ	e	λ	e	λ	e	λ	e
O	<0,0"/>	f	<1,10"/>	l	<1,11"/>	r	<5,12"/>	y	<2,8"/>	6	<6,0"/>	AN-AJ	<4,12"/>
a	<2,11"/>	g	<2,12"/>	m	<6,7"/>	s	<1,12"/>	z	<3,9"/>	7	<0,7"/>	AO-AE	<5,7"/>
b	<3,12"/>	h	<3,7"/>	n	<1,8"/>	t	<2,7"/>	1	<1,0"/>	8	<0,8"/>	AL-AH	<2,10"/>
c	<4,7"/>	i	<4,8"/>	o	<2,9"/>	u	<3,8"/>	2	<2,0"/>	9	<0,9"/>	AM-AI	<3,11"/>
d	<5,8"/>	j	<5,9"/>	p	<3,10"/>	v	<4,9"/>	3	<3,0"/>	10	<0,10"/>	AP-AF	<6,8"/>
e	<6,9"/>	k	<6,10"/>	q	<4,11"/>	x	<6,11"/>	4	<4,0"/>	11	<0,11"/>	AK-AG	<1,9"/>
aa	<4,10"/>	ab	<5,11"/>	ac	<6,12"/>	ad	<1,7"/>	5	<5,0"/>	12	<0,12"/>		

Table 3. Points inside SuperVoronoi set of the origin and their labels.

3.5. Inverse wavelet transforms

In this step the side descriptions are inverse wavelet transformed and the two different video streams are produced. The inverse wavelet module uses the biorthogonal inverse lifting (CDF) 5/3 wavelet transform. The experimental results related to the application of MDCLVQ-A$_2$ to MD video coding are presented in section 4.

3.6. Video encoders/decoders

In the encoder modules, the input side video streams are encoded by H.264/AVC or Motion JPEG2000 encoders. In case the H.264/AVC is selected as the video encoding standard, then the JM reference encoder is used. On the other hand, the Motion JPEG 2000 is another choice of the video encoding module that is done using the software provided by OpenJPEG library. The bit streams are sent over the channels. In the receiver side, the bit streams are decoded using the corresponding decoders. The decoding in this step is almost lossless.

3.7. The decoders in the receiver side

There are two different decoding processes in this scheme. One is the lossy decoding that is done in the side decoders and central decoder. Another is the lossless decoding that is done in H.264/AVC (Motion JPEG2000) decoder. The latter is the reverse of the encoding process that is done in H.264/AVC (Motion JPEG2000) encoder and the former is the reverse of the labeling function.

The received video data streams are decoded by H.264/AVC (Motion JPEG2000) then sent to the central decoder and the side decoders. There are an 2^m - 1 of decoders in an m-channel MD coding schemes, that is, a central decoder and 2^m side decoders (Ostergaard, 2007). In the MDCLVQ, a two channel MD coding scheme is used. Thus, there are three decoders: the central decoder, side decoder 1, and side decoder 2. At the receiver, if both descriptions are received correctly, then the central decoder is used to map the labels back to the original lattice points. The side decoders are used to find an approximation of the original lattice point if only one single description is received.

The central decoder is the reverse of the labeling process described above. When the two descriptions are received correctly, they are sent to the central decoder to be mapped back to the corresponding lattice point. Assume that the received label is $e' = \langle \lambda_1', \lambda_2' \rangle$. In order to decode e' the following three steps are performed:

1. Obtain the equivalent label of e' within $\varepsilon(O)$. Denote it as $e'' = \langle \lambda_1'', \lambda_2'' \rangle$. Two labels are said to be equivalent if their vertices are equivalent points; i.e. $\lambda_1'' \equiv \lambda_1'$ and $\lambda_2'' \equiv \lambda_2'$.

2. Obtain the lattice point $\lambda \in S_{sv}(O)$ corresponding to the label e''.

3. Translate λ by $e'' - e'$ to find the original lattice point.

In this scheme, if only the description from channel i is received while the other channel is corrupted, then λ_i' is used in the side decoder i to find the approximate of the original lattice point using the following steps:

1. Obtain the equivalent sublattice point of λ_i' within $S_{sv}(O)$ and denote it as λ_e.

2. Obtain the subset of labels that use λ_e as one of their coordinates by:

$$\varepsilon_p(\lambda_e) = \left\{ \forall \langle e_1', e_2' \rangle \in \varepsilon(0), \, e_1' = \lambda_e \vee e_2' = \lambda_e \right\} \tag{26}$$

3. Obtain the midpoint of the lattice points within $S_{sv}(O)$ that their labels are members of $\varepsilon_p(\lambda_e)$. It is denoted as λ_m.

4. Obtain the approximate point λ by translating λ_m by $\lambda_i' - \lambda_e$.

In other words, the equivalent label for the corrupted data is one of the labels within $\varepsilon_p(\lambda_e)$. There is no way to determine the original label as well as the original lattice point. Thus, it is required to obtain the approximate point by finding the weighted midpoint of the lattice points corresponding to the labels residing within $\varepsilon_p(\lambda_e)$. In order to find the approximate point, the weighted midpoint is translated by $\lambda_i' - \lambda_e$, using the shift property.

As for example, if the received descriptions are given as $\lambda_1' = (9.5, \, 0.866)$ and $\lambda_2' = (9, \, 1.7321)$. Since 9.5 is congruent to 2.5 $(mod \, 7/2)$ and 0.866 is congruent to $0.5\sqrt{3} \, (mod \, 7\sqrt{3}/2)$. Therefore, λ_1' belongs to the partition $[2.5, \, 0.5\sqrt{3}]$. Similarly, it is possible to show that λ_2' belongs to the partition $[2, \, \sqrt{3}]$. Thus, the label $e' = \langle \lambda_1', \lambda_2' \rangle$ is equivalent to the label $e'' = \langle 1,7 \rangle$ according to Table 4. Both labels are shown with black arrows in Fig. 6. The necessary translation to shift e' to e'' would be $t = e' - e'' = (-7,0)$, according to the shift property. It is shown with a red arrow.

In the next step, the lattice point corresponding to e'' is obtained from Table 3, that is $\lambda d = (3, \, \sqrt{3})$. The necessary shift to translate λd to the original lattice point is also $t = (7,0)$.

Therefore, the original lattice point is (10, 1.734). The decoding procedure is depicted in Fig. 6. However, assume that one of the descriptions is lost and therefore only one description is received correctly. As the labeling function is balanced, it does not matter which label is received. In case $\lambda_1^{'}$ is received, it is processed by the side decoder 1 to find the approximate point. As showed before $\lambda_1^{'}$ belongs to the partition $\lfloor 2.5, \ 0.5\sqrt{3} \rfloor$ and its equivalent sublattice point that is residing within $S_{sv}(O)$ is given by $\tilde{\lambda}_e = 1$.

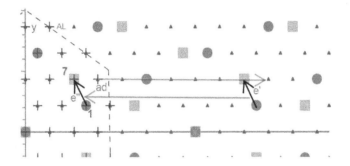

Figure 6. The decoding procedure performed by central decoder.

According to Table 4-2, the lost description may be within $\varepsilon_p(1) = \{0, \ 10,11,8, \ 12,7, \ 9\}$. Thus, the approximate equivalent point $\tilde{\lambda}_m$ will be the midpoint of the lattice points within $\{1, \ f, \ l, \ n, \ s, \ ad, \ AK - AG\}$. In order to find the approximate of the original point $\tilde{\lambda}_m$ is translated by $\lambda_1^{'} - \tilde{\lambda}_e$ which obtains as result the point (9.8235, 0.7121). On the other hand, if $\lambda_2^{'}$ is received then the side decoder 2 is used to process it. The coinciding sublattice points are used either as the first or the second vertex of the label. Therefore, at the receiver it is possible to determine the channel to which the received description belongs.

4. Experimental results for MDCLVQ-A₂ applied to video coding

In this section, the experimental results of the MDCLVQ-A_2 video coding schemes are presented. The proposed MDCLVQ-A_2 is applied to H.264/AVC and Motion JPEG2000 schemes. Section 4.1 presents the experimental results for MDCLVQ-H.264/AVC and the results for MDCLVQ-Motion JPEG2000 are presented in section 4.2.

4.1. MDCLVQ-H.264/AVC

The standard videos of "Akiyo", "Coastguard", "Carphone", and "Foreman" with the QCIF format (144×176 pixels) and 7.5 fps are chosen to evaluate the benefits of the proposed MDCLVQ-H.264/AVC scheme over the original single description scheme in terms of bit rate-efficiency and error-resiliency. The default settings of the original JM9.4 reference encoder are used for encoding the original videos and the side videos.

The MDCLVQ scheme is a multivariable system because it is controlled by three factors: the wavelet threshold, the fundamental area of the hexagonal lattice, and the index of the coinciding sub-lattices. The performance of the MD coding scheme is evaluated based on the average required bit rate and reconstruction fidelity in the decoders. The fundamental area of the lattice is changed by multiplication of a factor called *sigma* to transformation matrix. Increasing the fundamental area increases the required bandwidth (bit rate) for encoding the video and the reconstruction fidelity. On the other hand, increasing the index decreases the required bit rate. In these experiments the labeling function with index $N=7$ has been used constantly and the wavelet threshold is constantly zero. Then, the value for the bit rate is calculated at the end of every encoding runs. Therefore, the analyses provided below are based on values of *sigma*.

The fundamental area of the hexagonal lattice is changed by $sigma = 0.1, 0.2... 1$, while keeping the shape of the hexagonal lattice fixed. Thus, the quantization error is adapted and central distortion, side distortions and the associated bit rates are affected. The required bit rate for encoding both descriptions must be compared with the required bit rate for encoding the single description source. Suppose that a given video source requires R b/s to be encoded by a single encoder. On the other hand, if for the same video source, the first description of the MD coding scheme requires R_1 b/s and the second description requires R_2 b/s. The bit rate efficiency is defined as

$$R_{\text{eff}} = \frac{R - (R_1 + R_2)}{R} \tag{27}$$

The bit rate efficiency R_{eff} is defined so that the performance of the proposed MD coding scheme is compared with the original video encoder in terms of the required bit rate. Thus, if the MD video coding scheme can encode both side videos with total bit rate $(R_1+R_2) \leq R$ then the bit rate efficiency R_{eff} will be positive and the MD coding is outperforming the original encoder. However, if $(R_1+R_2) > R$ the the bit rate efficiency R_{eff} will be negative and it indicates that the compression efficiency has been sacrificed for gaining error resiliency ((Goyal, 2001). Therefore, the bit rates required by the proposed MDCLVQ-H.264/AVC scheme for encoding the two descriptions are provided in Table 4. The bit rates required to encode the standard videos by the JM9.4 reference encoder and the bit rates efficiencies calculated using the Eq. (27) are also provided in Table 4.

According to Table 4, the bit rate efficiencies of the proposed MDCLVQ-H.264/AVC scheme corresponding to *sigma*= 0.1 to 0.7 for all the videos are positive; therefore, error resiliency and compression efficiency are both obtained and with the *sigma* lower than 0.7. However, for *sigma* 0.8 to 1 the compression efficiency is not achieved. As an example, the MDCLVQ-H.264/AVC with *sigma* = 0.1, in average shows 0.89 bit rate efficiencies for all the videos, which is an improvement as compared with the original encoder. However, for the values of *sigma* from 0.8 to 1, the proposed scheme requires more bit rates than the original H.264/AVC encoder, therefore, the compression efficiency has been traded off for error resiliency. The error resiliency of the proposed MCLVQ-H.264/AVC scheme is due to its MD coding nature, that is, it can provide a degraded version of the source if only one of the channels works, while a better reconstruction quality is achieved when both channels work and both descriptions arrive at the destination.

Video	Sigma	0.1	0.2	0.3	0.4	0.5	0.6	0.7	0.8	0.9	1
Akiyo	R_1	0.55	0.57	0.63	0.88	1.77	2.13	2.34	3.08	4.00	5.17
	R_2	0.55	0.57	0.64	0.89	1.28	1.77	2.42	3.17	4.16	5.45
	Total	1.10	1.14	1.27	1.77	3.05	3.90	4.76	6.25	8.16	10.62
	R	5.00	5.00	5.00	5.00	5.00	5.00	5.00	5.00	5.00	5.00
	R_{eff}	0.78	0.77	0.75	0.65	0.39	0.22	0.05	-0.25	-0.63	-1.12
Coastguard	R_1	0.56	0.67	1.40	2.92	5.02	10.48	13.54	20.51	29.41	40.01
	R_2	0.55	0.68	1.40	2.90	5.14	8.73	14.33	21.86	31.42	42.49
	Total	1.11	1.35	2.80	5.82	10.16	19.21	27.87	42.37	60.83	82.50
	R	38.55	38.55	38.55	38.55	38.55	38.55	38.55	38.55	38.55	38.55
	R_{eff}	0.97	0.96	0.93	0.85	0.74	0.50	0.28	-0.10	-0.58	-1.14
Carphone	R_1	0.56	0.75	1.62	3.25	5.41	9.31	12.74	17.94	24.21	31.39
	R_2	0.55	0.76	1.61	3.30	5.49	8.65	13.08	18.46	25.00	32.27
	Total	1.11	1.51	3.23	6.55	10.90	17.96	25.82	36.40	49.21	63.66
	R	30.66	30.66	30.66	30.66	30.66	30.66	30.66	30.66	30.66	30.66
	R_{eff}	0.96	0.95	0.89	0.79	0.64	0.41	0.16	-0.19	-0.61	-1.08
Foreman	R_1	0.56	1.03	2.22	3.87	6.04	10.65	12.04	15.90	20.67	26.09
	R_2	0.56	1.05	2.24	3.95	6.12	8.88	12.29	16.50	21.37	27.19
	Total	1.12	2.08	4.46	7.82	12.16	19.53	24.33	32.40	42.04	53.28
	R	25.39	25.39	25.39	25.39	25.39	25.39	25.39	25.39	25.39	25.39
	R_{eff}	0.96	0.92	0.82	0.69	0.52	0.23	0.04	-0.28	-0.66	-1.10

Table 4. Average bit rates (kb/s) for MDCLVQ-H.264/AVC. The corresponding bit rate efficiencies are also provided.

Although the bit rate efficiency is important for MD video coding, the quality of the reconstructed videos in the central and side decoders are also important. In other words, compression efficiency is not acceptable if it comes with significant drop in the quality of the video. A common measure to evaluate the quality of the video encoding is to compare the reconstructed video with the original video through the average peak signal to noise ratio (PSNR) of the luminance (Y) components. In the following results, the PSNR is measured for the luminance component.

The performance of the MDCLVQ-H.264/AVC scheme in terms of the required bit rate and the reconstruction fidelity is controlled by the fundamental area of the hexagonal lattice. The fundamental area of the hexagonal lattice is changed by *sigma*. Therefore, in Table 5 the average PSNR values of the reconstructed videos in the central decoder as well as the side decoders for the "Akiyo", "Coastguard", "Carphone", and "Foreman" video sequences are provided in Table 5 for different values of the *sigma*.

Video\sigma	0.1	0.2	0.3	0.4	0.5	0.6	0.7	0.8	0.9	1
Akiyo Side 1	16.32	21.92	25.12	28.12	30.69	32.84	34.79	36.37	37.73	37.48
Akiyo Side 2	13.62	22.42	25.24	28.12	30.70	32.88	34.89	36.35	37.61	38.28
Akiyo Central	17.42	22.62	25.65	28.60	31.38	33.81	35.69	37.27	38.70	38.19
Coastguard Side 1	15.03	19.06	22.32	24.86	27.36	29.40	31.53	33.18	34.47	35.22
Coastguard Side 2	13.64	19.23	22.32	24.92	27.40	29.63	31.59	33.17	34.34	35.00
Coastguard Central	16.29	19.47	22.22	25.33	27.97	30.40	32.53	34.32	35.65	36.26
Carphone Side 1	15.39	19.40	23.47	26.36	29.09	31.48	33.68	35.35	36.76	37.68
Carphone Side 2	13.51	19.83	23.46	26.42	29.19	31.58	33.72	35.35	36.68	37.50
Carphone Central	15.47	20.11	23.98	26.90	29.80	32.41	34.70	36.50	37.98	38.78
Foreman Side 1	14.46	19.09	23.41	25.97	28.70	30.94	33.08	34.82	36.15	36.96
Foreman Side 2	12.67	19.31	23.30	26.02	28.71	31.04	33.08	34.80	36.05	36.82
Foreman Central	14.58	19.67	23.82	26.46	29.38	31.97	34.07	35.96	37.35	38.05
Miss America Side 1	16.53	23.58	28.07	31.57	34.39	36.75	38.72	39.98	40.72	41.15
Miss America Side 2	15.42	23.65	28.00	31.68	34.19	36.74	38.60	39.97	40.63	40.97
Miss America Central	17.18	23.97	29.02	32.18	35.21	37.69	39.60	40.88	41.56	41.74

Table 5. The average PSNR (dB) of the central and the side decoders for the selected video sequences encoded by the MDCLVQ-H.264/AVC.

As shown in Table 5, the qualities of the reconstructed videos are directly proportional to the value of *sigma*. In other words, the PSNR of the central decoder and the PSNR of the side decoders improve as the *sigma* is increased. On the other hand, according to Table 4, the bit rate efficiencies decrease as the *sigma* is increased. Then, the quality of the reconstructed video is reversely related to the bit rate efficiency. Thus, as the value of *sigma* increases the compression efficiency is traded off for better reconstruction quality. As for example, the MDCLVQ-H.264/AVC shows the best reconstruction quality for the "Foreman" video when the *sigma* is 1; $PSNR = 36.96$ in the side 1 decoder, $PSNR = 36.82$ in the side 2 decoder, and $PSNR = 38.05$ in the central decoder. However the MDCLVQ-H.264/AVC shows the best bit rate efficiency $\left(R_{eff} = 0.96\right)$ for the "Foreman" video when the *sigma* is 0.1.

In addition, according to Table 5 the PSNR values for the central decoder and the side decoders are not significantly improved as *sigma* is increased from 0.7 to 1. This implies that the best performance of the MDCLVQ-H.264/AVC in terms of the bit rate efficiency and reconstruction quality for the "Foreman" video is seen with *sigma* = 0.7. As an example, for the "Foreman" video with *sigma* = 0.7 and with almost the same bit rate as the original encoder $(R_{eff} = 0.04)$ the MDCLVQ-H.264/AVC provides *PSNR = 34.07 dB* in the central decoder, *PSNR = 33.08 dB* in the side 1 decoder, and *PSNR = 33.08 dB* in the side 2 decoder.

According to Table 5, the reconstruction performance of the proposed MDCLVQ-H.264/AVC scheme in terms of the central PSNR and side PSNR do not significantly increase while the *sigma* is increased from 0.7 to 1. In order to demonstrate the visual quality of the reconstructed videos, the first frames of the central videos of "Foreman" sequence that have been encoded by the MDCLVQ-H.264/AVC with *sigma* = 0.1 to 1 are provided in Fig. 7.

According to Fig. 7, the quality of the reconstructed videos of the "Foreman" increase as the value of *sigma* is increased. The reconstruction qualities for the "Foreman" videos corresponding to *sigma* values lower than 0.3 are very low (PSNR = 14.58, PSNR = 19.67dB, and PSNR = 23.82dB) while the reconstruction quality of the videos corresponding to *sigma* higher than 0.4 are acceptable. For example the reconstructed video corresponding to *sigma* = 0.7 has central PSNR = 34.07dB.

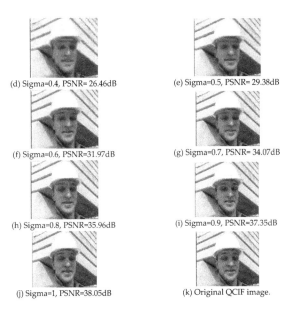

(d) Sigma=0.4, PSNR= 26.46dB

(e) Sigma=0.5, PSNR= 29.38dB

(f) Sigma=0.6, PSNR=31.97dB

(g) Sigma=0.7, PSNR= 34.07dB

(h) Sigma=0.8, PSNR=35.96dB

(i) Sigma=0.9, PSNR=37.35dB

(j) Sigma=1, PSNR=38.05dB

(k) Original QCIF image.

Figure 7. The 1ˢᵗ frames of the QCIF "Foreman" sequence reconstructed by the central decoder corresponding to *sigma* = 0.1 to 1.

However the difference between the PSNR corresponding to *sigma* = 0.7 and *sigma* = 1 is negligible. In other words, the extra bit rate that is required for higher values of *sigma* is not worth of the gained reconstruction fidelity, thus the best performance of the MDCLVQ-H. 264/AVC for the "Foreman" video is achieved with *sigma* = 0.7. In other words, using *sigma* = 0.7 the proposed scheme can offer acceptable side and central reconstruction qualities as well as error resiliency without requiring extra bit rate.

4.2. MDCLVQ-motion JPEG2000

The proposed MDCLVQ-Motion JPEG2000 scheme generates two descriptions of the input video that are encoded by the OpenJPEG software to motion jpeg files. In this subsection, the volume of the motion jpeg files generated by encoding the MD sequences are compared with size of the motion jpeg file of the original single description scheme and the encoding efficiencies are calculated similar to bit rate efficiency in Eq. (27). Suppose that volume of the motion jpeg file of a given video source is V (kB). On the other hand, if for the same video source the first description of the MD coding scheme generates a motion jpeg file with V_1 (kB) and the second description generates a motion jpeg V_2 (kB). Then, the compresssion efficiency is defined as

$$C_{eff} = \frac{V - (V_1 + V_2)}{V} \tag{28}$$

The compresssion efficiency C_{eff} is defined so that the performance of the proposed MD coding scheme is compared with the original video encoder in terms of the encoding efficiency. Thus, if the MD video coding scheme can encode both side videos with total volume of $(V_1+V_2) \leq V$ then the compression efficiency C_{eff} will be positive and the MD coding is outperforming the original encoder. However, if $(V_1+V_2) > V$, then the compresssion efficiency C_{eff} will be negative and it indicates that the compression efficiency has been traded off for gaining error resiliency

In these experiments, standard video sequences of "Akiyo", "Coastguard", "Carphone", and "Foreman" with the QCIF format (144×176 pixels) are used to evaluate the performance of the proposed MDCLVQ-Motion JPEG2000 encoding scheme. As stated in section 4.1, the performance of the MDCLVQ-A$_2$ and consequently the performance of the MDCLVQ-Motion JPEG2000 scheme in terms of the compression efficiency and reconstruction fidelity are controlled by the fundamental area of the hexagonal lattice. The fundamental area of the lattice is changed by multiplying the *sigma* to the generator matrix (transformation matrix). The compression efficiencies for the MDCLVQ-Motion JPEG2000 are provided in Table 6. According to Table 6, the volume of the motion jpeg files generated by the MDCLVQ-Motion JPEG2000 scheme increase as the *sigma* is increased. Thus, as the *sigma* increases the encoding efficiency is decreased.

This is similar to the results for the MDCLVQ-H.264/AVC because the encoding (compression) efficiency is due to the coarse degree of the quantization which is controlled by the *sigma*. In general, the compression efficiencies in Table 4 are lower than corresponding values in Table 5 because H.264/AVC standard has higher encoding (compression) efficiency than Motion JPEG2000.

Although the compression efficiency is important for MD video coding, the quality of the reconstructed videos in the central and side decoders are also important. In other words, compression efficiency is not acceptable if it comes with significant drop in the quality of the video. The performance of the MDCLVQ-Motion JPEG2000 scheme in terms of the compression efficiency and the reconstruction quality is affected by the value of the *sigma*. The average PSNR values of the reconstructed videos in the central decoder as well as the side decoders for the "Akiyo", "Coastguard", "Carphone", and "Foreman" video sequences are provided in Table 7.

Video	Sigma	0.1	0.2	0.3	0.4	0.5	0.6	0.7	0.8	0.9	1
Akiyo	V_1	932	1855	2544	3024	3594	4080	4340	4738	5061	5378
	V_2	895	1876	2546	3134	3717	4114	4463	4840	5136	5446
	Total	1827	3731	5090	6158	7311	8194	8803	9578	10197	10824
	V	4536	4536	4536	4536	4536	4536	4536	4536	4536	4536
	V_{eff}	0.60	0.18	-0.12	-0.36	-0.61	-0.81	-0.94	-1.11	-1.25	-1.39
Coastguard	V_1	1367	2352	3161	3667	4234	4851	5138	5541	5912	6230
	V_2	1245	2364	3159	3786	4368	4838	5298	5688	6049	6358
	Total	2612	4716	6320	7453	8602	9689	10436	11229	11961	12588
	V	5797	5797	5797	5797	5797	5797	5797	5797	5797	5797
	V_{eff}	0.55	0.19	-0.09	-0.29	-0.48	-0.67	-0.80	-0.94	-1.06	-1.17
Carphone	V_1	1279	2541	3637	4269	4999	5660	6079	6613	7055	7460
	V_2	1193	2538	3630	4381	5136	5695	6206	6707	7143	7518
	Total	2472	5079	7267	8650	10135	11355	12285	13320	14198	14978
	V	6699	6699	6699	6699	6699	6699	6699	6699	6699	6699
	V_{eff}	0.63	0.24	-0.08	-0.29	-0.51	-0.70	-0.83	-0.99	-1.12	-1.24
Foreman	V_1	1080	2240	3044	3513	4067	4645	4922	5346	5699	6012
	V_2	1030	2243	3017	3630	4193	4639	5055	5441	5795	6094
	Total	2110	4483	6061	7143	8260	9284	9977	10787	11494	12106
	V	5475	5475	5475	5475	5475	5475	5475	5475	5475	5475
	V_{eff}	0.61	0.18	-0.11	-0.30	-0.51	-0.70	-0.82	-0.97	-1.10	-1.21
Miss America	V1	368	851	1191	1403	1683	1910	2058	2261	2422	2570
	V2	360	852	1179	1463	1755	1939	2106	2288	2456	2594
	Total	728	1703	2370	2866	3438	3849	4164	4549	4878	5164
	V	1308	1308	1308	1308	1308	1308	1308	1308	1308	1308
	V_{eff}	0.44	-0.30	-0.81	-1.19	-1.63	-1.94	-2.18	-2.48	-2.73	-2.95

Table 6. Volume of the motion jpeg files (kB) and the encoding efficiency of the MDCLVQ-Motion JPEG2000.

The PSNR values of the central decoder and the side decoders of the MDCLVQ-Motion JPEG2000 provided in Table 7 are higher than the corresponding values of the MDCLVQ-H. 264/AVC provided in Table 5. This is because of better reconstruction quality of the Motion JPEG2000 as compared with the H.264/AVC. However, the general pattern is the same and all the PSNR values increase as the *sigma* is increased because reconstruction fidelity is affected by the performance of the MDCLVQ-A_2. On the other hand, the compression efficiencies of MDCLVQ-H.264/AVC are in general better than MDCLVQ-Motion JPEG2000 because of higher compression efficiency of the H.264/AVC.

The proposed MD coding schemes require low computational capabilities, due to the inherent symmetries of the coinciding similar sublattices of the hexagonal lattice. The labeling function and the partitioning scheme presented in section 3.4 are not computation intensive processes. The partitions are generated using the simple proposed two-fold real congruency relation. The proposed shift property simplifies the problem of labeling the entire lattice space to the problem of labeling the SuperVoronoi region of the origin. The SuperVoronoi region of the origin with index N includes N^2+N-1 lattice points and N^2 sublattice points. Thus, the labeling function is simplified to a table look up with N^2+N-1 entries. In addition, the proposed labeling function, the partitioning scheme, and the shift property are scalable and as a consequence using the *sigma* the performance of the entire scheme is adjustable, as shown in section 4.

Video*sigma*		0.1	0.2	0.3	0.4	0.5	0.6	0.7	0.8	0.9	1
Akiyo	Side 1	15.95	25.51	29.45	32.75	34.00	33.99	35.56	36.07	36.36	39.94
	Side 2	13.68	25.38	29.22	32.34	33.25	34.44	35.08	35.68	36.10	36.29
	Central	18.89	29.33	33.13	35.55	36.36	36.55	37.11	37.32	37.45	42.38
Coast-guard	Side 1	14.90	22.85	27.53	31.21	33.22	37.47	38.45	38.45	39.41	40.38
	Side 2	12.99	23.25	27.62	30.50	32.64	34.54	35.52	36.73	37.80	38.85
	Central	18.70	27.80	32.60	35.60	38.25	37.81	39.93	40.72	41.36	42.03
Carphone	Side 1	16.27	24.76	29.89	33.44	35.68	35.62	38.96	39.90	41.04	41.94
	Side 2	12.83	25.00	29.69	32.75	34.64	36.44	37.66	38.81	39.93	40.98
	Central	18.27	28.65	34.55	37.92	41.05	41.12	43.36	44.11	45.06	46.15
Foreman	Side 1	16.81	24.40	28.75	32.54	34.86	34.16	38.32	39.40	40.50	41.50
	Side 2	11.27	24.69	28.85	31.81	33.63	35.57	36.72	38.01	39.17	40.19
	Central	16.19	28.86	33.69	36.99	39.75	39.45	41.96	42.85	43.74	44.64
Miss America	Side 1	16.34	26.07	31.36	33.82	35.52	35.95	37.60	38.08	38.59	38.95
	Side 2	15.84	26.07	30.98	33.53	34.83	36.16	36.92	37.64	38.14	38.68
	Central	19.84	29.42	35.13	37.61	39.09	39.44	39.87	40.10	40.28	40.57

Table 7. The average PSNR (dB) of the central and the side decoders for the selected video sequences encoded by the MDCLVQ-Motion JPEG2000.

5. Conclusion

The main objective of this research is to design and implement a generic MD video coding scheme that can be adopted by different kinds of video coding standards. In other words, the proposed scheme does not rely on specific characteristics of the video coding standard being used and does not make any assumption about the state of the channel or probability distribution of errors. In this way, the proposed scheme is different from the MD video coding schemes presented in (Yongdong & Deng, 2003), (Franchi et al., 2005) (Zandoná et al., 2005). Thus, it can effectively increase the performance of the encoding system in terms of compression efficiency and reliability, regardless of the encoding scheme being used. In addition, the proposed scheme does not require significant hardware or software changes; therefore, it can be adopted for available hardware and software designs. Although running parallel H.264/AVC or Motion JPEG2000 encoders requires more computational resources than the original encoder, the total computation time of the MD encoders is less than that of the original because the entropies of the side videos are significantly decreased by the MDCLVQ, and thus, the time required by of the arithmetic coding is decreased.

6. Future research

As for future direction, it would be interesting to develop the MD client-server video encoding and decoding that are able to stream the real time videos on networks. The developed encoder module can be run on the server side and the decoder module is on the client side. The future MD client-server video codec must be adaptive or able to make the best use of the available bandwidth to meet its requirements. In other words, the user must be able to increase or decrease the quality of reconstruction with regard to the available bandwidth. Finally, it is suggested that the MDCLVQ schemes to be integrated with the H.264/AVC or Motion JPEG 2000 video encoding standards in a way that the built-in quantization and encoding procedures are replaced by the MD scheme in order to increase the performance of the MD coding. Thus the performances of the MD video coding schemes are optimized.

Author details

Ehsan Akhtarkavan and M. F. M. Salleh

Universiti Sains Malaysia, Malaysia

References

[1] Akhtarkavan, E.; Salleh, M. F. M. (2012). "Multiple descriptions coinciding lattice vector quantizer for wavelet image coding," *IEEE Transactions on Image Processing*, Vol. 21. No. 2, pp. 653 - 661, ISSN: 1057-7149.

[2]   Akhtarkavan, E.; Salleh M. F. M. (2010). "Multiple description lattice vector quantiza-
      tion using multiple A4 quantizers," IEICE Electronics Express, Vol. 7, No. 17, pp.
      1233-1239, ISSN: 1349-2543.

[3]   Bai, H.; and Zhao, Y. (2006). "Multiple description video coding based on lattice vector
      quantization," IEEE International Conference on Innovative Computing, Information and
      Control (ICICIC 2006), Vol. 2, pp. 241-244.

[4]   Bai, H.; and Zhoa, Y. (2007). "Optimized multiple description lattice vector quantiza-
      tion for wavelet image coding," IEEE Trans. on Circuits and Systems for Video Technology,
      Vol. 17, pp. 912 – 917, ISSN: 1051-8215.

[5]   Bernstein, M.; et al. (1997). "On sublattices of the hexagonal lattice," Discrete Matha-
      matics, Vol. 170, No. 1-3, pp. 29-39.

[6]   Biswas, M,; et al., (2008). "Multiple description wavelet video coding employing a new
      tree structure," IEEE Transactions on Circuits and Systems for Video Technology, Vol. 18,
      No. 10, pp. 1361-1368, ISSN: 1051-8215.

[7]   Campana, O.; et al., (2008). "An H.264/AVC video coder based on a multiple description
      scalar quantizer," IEEE Transactions on Circuits and Systems for Video Technology, Vol. 18,
      No. 2, pp. 268-72, ISSN: 1051-8215.

[8]   Chen, Q. (2008). "Error-resilient video coding using multiple description lattice vector
      quantization with channel optimization," IEEE Congress on Image and Signal Processing
      (CISP 08), Vol. 1, p. 539-42.

[9]   Conway, J. H.; Sloane, N. J. A. (1982a). "Voronoi regions of lattices, second moments
      of polytopes and quantization," IEEE Transactions on Information Theory, Vol. 28, No. 2,
      pp. 211-226, ISSN: 0018-9448.

[10] Conway, J. H; Sloane, N. J. A. (1982b). "Fast quantizing and decoding and algorithms
      for lattice quantizers and codes," IEEE Transactions on Information Theory, Vol. 28, No.
      2, pp. 227-232, ISSN: 0018-9448.

[11] Conway, J. H.; Sloane, N. J. A. (1988). Sphere Packings, Lattices, and Groups, Springer-
      Verlag, ISBN-10: 0387985859, New York.

[12] Conway, J. H.; et al. (1999). "On the existence of similar sublattices," Canadian Journal
      Math., Vol. 51, pp. 1300-1306.

[13] Sloane, N. J. A. (2000). "Sequences A002476/M4344, A092572, A092573, A092574, and
      A092575," The on-line encyclopedia of integer sequences, Available from: https://
      oeis.org/A038590.

[14] Franchi, N.; et al., (2005). "Multiple description video coding for scalable and robust
      transmission over IP," IEEE Transactions on Circuits and Systems for Video Technology,
      Vol. 15, No. 3, pp. 321-34, ISSN: 1051-8215.

[15] Fukuhara, T.; and Singer, D. (2002). "Motion JPEG2000 Version 2, MJP2 derived from
      ISO Media File Format," ISO/IEC JTC1/SC29/WG1 N2718.

[16] Goyal, V. K. (2001). "Multiple description coding: Compression meets the network," *IEEE Signal Processing Magazine*, Vol. 18, No. 5, pp. 74-93, ISSN: 1053-5888.

[17] Hanzo, L.; Cherriman, P.; and Streit, J. (2007). *Video compression and communications: from basics to H.261, H.263, H.264, and MPEG4 for DVB and HSDPA-style adaptive turbo-transceivers*, Wiley & Sons, ISBN-10: 0470518499, Chichester, West Sussex.

[18] Heuer, M. (2008). "Similar sublattices and coincidence rotations of the root lattice A4 and its dual," *10th International Conference on Aperiodic Crystals (ICQ10); Zeitschrift für Kristallographie*, p. 817-821, ISSN: 0044-2968.

[19] Ostergaard, J. (2007). "Multiple-description lattice vector quantization," PhD Thesis, Delft University of Technology, Netherlands.

[20] Radulovic, I.; et al., (2010). "Multiple description video coding with H.264/AVC redundant pictures," *IEEE Transactions on Circuits and Systems for Video Technology*, Vol. 20, No. 1, pp.144-148, ISSN: 1051-8215.

[21] Reibman, A. R.; et al., (2002). "Multiple-description video coding using motion-compensated temporal prediction," *IEEE Transactions on Circuits and Systems for Video Technology*, Vol. 12, No. 3, pp. 193 – 204, ISSN: 1051-8215.

[22] Tillo, T.; et al. (2008). "Redundant slice optimal allocation for H.264 multiple description coding," *IEEE Transactions on Circuits and Systems for Video Technology*, Vol. 18, No. 1, pp. 59-70, ISSN: 1051-8215.

[23] Vaishampayan, et al. (2001). "Multiple description vector quantization with lattice codebooks: Design and analysis," *IEEE Transactions on Information Theory*, Vol. 47, No. 5, pp. 1718-1734, ISSN: 0018-9448.

[24] Wiegand, T. S.; et al., (2003). "Overview of the H.264/AVC video coding standard," IEEE Transactions on Circuits and Systems for Video Technology, Vol. 13, No. 7, pp. 560-576, ISSN: 1051-8215.

[25] Yongdong, W.; Deng, R. H. (2003). "Content-aware authentication of motion JPEG2000 stream in lossy networks," *IEEE Transactions on Consumer Electronics*, Vol. 49, No. 4, pp. 792 – 801, ISSN: 0098-3063.

[26] Zandoná, N.; et al., (2005). "Motion compensated multiple description video coding for the H.264/AVC standard," *Internatiol Conference on Multimedia, Image Processing Computer Vision (IADAT-micv2005)*, Madrid, Spain.

[27] Zhang, Y.; et al., (2004). "Error resilience video coding in H.264 encoder with potential distortion tracking," *IEEE International Conference on Image Processing (ICIP2004)*, Vol. 1, pp. 163–166.

Chapter 4

Region of Interest Coding for Aerial Video Sequences Using Landscape Models

Holger Meuel, Julia Schmidt, Marco Munderloh and
Jörn Ostermann

Additional information is available at the end of the chapter

1. Introduction

Video coding standards traditionally work in a block-based manner wherein every block basically receives the same treatment. For certain kinds of videos, such as movies for television, this might indeed be the sensible thing to do.

Depending on the use-case, though, it often is helpful to treat different areas of the image with different coding parameter sets or techniques even. In applications with focus on moving objects for example, a better resolution in the identified *Regions of Interest* (ROI) might help subsequent processing steps within a larger system. Existing video coding standards, such as MPEG-1,2,4 video or the ITU-T H.26x standards, only provide basic support for ROI coding. In e. g. MPEG-4 *Video Object Planes* (VOPs) and the separate encoding of these planes is included [1]. Unfortunately these features aren't used to the extent possible, even though several real-life applications could be enhanced by such systems. Surveillance and videoconferencing tasks for example can benefit from a special ROI coding approach, wherein objects are automatically selected by e. g. motion (surveillance), color [2] (videoconferencing), shape or have been selected manually beforehand. Those regions are then coded with a higher quality than the rest of the picture. Especially for narrow-band transmission channels as used e. g. in aerial surveillance, it is important to keep the amount of data to be transmitted for the conduct of the task at hand to a minimum. In ROI coding it is one possibility to reduce this amount of data by degrading the quality of the parts of the image that are not as useful to the application.

Instead of decreasing the image quality by coarser quantization, it is also possible to code non-ROI regions in skip-mode. In the case of a static camera this leads to loss of changes and local motion in those areas. In the case of a moving camera, the lost motion information might be predicted and compensated, when only linear global movement is taken into account.

In general it is desirable to reconstruct high overall image quality at low data rates. For aerial video sequences, which often show predominantly static scenarios and only little changes in regions with moving objects, this can be done by allowing certain assumptions. One assumption to reduce data rates is the planarity of the landscape recorded. This simplification enables projecting the entire scene into one plane and rendering it as one big image when using *Global Motion Estimation/Compensation* (GME/GMC) at encoder side. At decoder side this opens the possibility of reconstructing the current image through outtakes of this so-called mosaic.

In existing GME/GMC approaches for aerial surveillance, GME is based on a projective transform [3]. To estimate the global motion of a scene, features have to be detected e.g. with a *Harris Corner Detector* [4] first. These features will be tracked from frame to frame e.g. with a KLT feature tracker to estimate their movements [5]. Finally, from all trajectories the global motion can be estimated based on an affine or projective transform. When transmitting the global motion parameters as additional side information, GMC can be applied at decoder side. With implementations employing GMC, data can be reduced dramatically for the example of aerial surveillance. However, to reconstruct moving objects at the decoder, additional data about those has to be transmitted. Consequently the achievable data rate reduction strongly depends on the number of moving objects in a scene. For scenes consisting of a static background and some moving objects, overall bit rate reductions of about 50 % can be easily achieved.

The true surface of most scenes however isn't flat at all. This leads to mapping errors during the GMC process due to the use of a projective transform. The effect will be more obvious for applications with low recording altitudes and scenes containing areas with large height differences, such as mountains or buildings. For aerial surveillance this leads to falsely detected moving objects and unnecessarily transmitted data when a difference-image-based moving object detector is used. For those cases a model that consists of several small planes, as it is realized through a mesh-based approach, takes into account the aforementioned differences. It prevents partial misregistration due to insufficient GMC of image content by better adapting to perceived local motion. The basic idea is that several feature points of an aerial video sequence are visible over consecutive frames and can therefore be tracked and triangulated into a mesh. All triangles of the mesh are motion compensated by using the motion vectors acquired during the tracking process. For motion compensation, only piecewise planarity is assumed, which is correct for small mesh patches.

In scenarios where interesting regions are identified by motion, the mesh approach yields several additional advantages and the rate of objects that are falsly classified as moving can be reduced by up to 90 % when compared to planar landscape model-based approaches [6].

This chapter gives a more real-life scenario oriented insight about the usage of different techniques for content adaptive video coding. The emphasis will lie on ROI coding and decoding for aerial sequences with a detailed view on:

- Assumption of planar earth surface: Projective transform-based global motion compensation and detection of moving objects

- Approximation of the earth surface using a mesh: Mesh-based global motion compensation and detection of moving objects

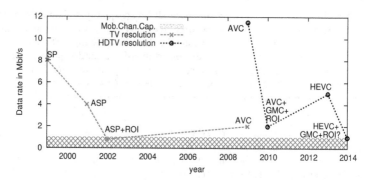

Figure 1. Data rates of different video codecs with and without *Region of Interest* (ROI) coding for aerial video sequences (*SP: MPEG-4 Simple Profile, ASP: MPEG-4 Advanced Simple Profile, AVC: Advanced Video Coding (MPEG-4 part 10/H.264), HEVC: High Efficiency Video Coding*).

1.1. Limits of standard-based coding

In its long tradition back to H.261 [7] from 1988, standardized digital video coding has reached amazing coding efficiency. *Advanced Video Coding* (AVC) is able to compress PCM (Pulse Code Modulation) coded data with a data rate of 166 Mbit/s for SDTV sequences (PAL resolution as used for DVB: 768 × 576 pel) to about 2–4 Mbit/s at a fairly high subjective quality. HDTV video with 1920 × 1080 pel can be compressed to about 10–20 Mbit/s depending on the video content. The latest standard, High Efficiency Video Coding (HEVC), needs only half the bitrate.

If mobile channels like WCDMA/UMTS and LTE are used for transmission, channel capacity is limited to a few Mbit/s. Especially when looking towards upcoming scenarios such as video transmission from *Unmanned Aerial Vehicles* (UAVs), there definitely is a need for a higher level of compression than offered by standardized coding techniques at the moment. Municipal agencies have recently started utilizing such UAVs for environmental and disaster area monitoring, so this use-case is especially important to work on. It has to be noted that in real-life scenarios other basic requirements, besides from what is known from television signal transmission, have to be met. While in the latter application the overall video quality has to be satisfying, in disaster area monitoring scenarios it is of highest priority to encode static infrastructure (background) and moving objects in highest quality, to be able to capture the scene adequately and react in an appropriate manner using all the knowledge about the situation at hand. However, with simple bit redistribution schemes, the quality of one part of the video image can only be increased at the cost of other image parts. The principle of *sprite coding* (see Section 3.2) was introduced with MPEG-4 to encode a static background separated from moving objects, so that the needed transmissions could be reduced to a minimum. GMC is a part of this technique, which is why it has to be mentioned here. In Figure 1 the encoding capabilities of recent video coding standards such as *MPEG-4 Simple Profile* (SP), *MPEG-4 Advanced Simple Profile* (ASP), AVC and HEVC are compared to versions with additional ROI coding for aerial landscape video sequences to give an impression of the amount of bitrate needed for transmission. Regions of interest in this case are moving objects and newly emerging areas in the picture hailing from the movement of the camera and the UAV, respectively. Since the amount of data of aerial video sequences really benefits from GMC, but MPEG-4 sprite coding was not inherited to AVC due to its insufficient coding performance for regular TV movies, an adaption of the concept for the current AVC codec is useful. To get an idea about where to integrate adaptations for Region of Interest coding, a basic understanding of hybrid video coders is necessary.

2. Hybrid video coding

Hybrid video coding was first introduced with H.261 in 1988 [7]. Since then, technical progress led to many improved versions of hybrid video coders, which were standardized later on as MPEG-1 [8], MPEG-2 [9], AVC [10] as well as its latest successor HEVC [11].

A basic block diagram of a hybrid video coder can be found in Figure 2. It basically consists of three main stages: first a motion estimation followed by a motion compensated (MC) prediction step is performed. Afterwards the prediction error is transformed and quantized, e. g. with a DCT-based integer transform, to decorrelate the spatial signal. Finally, entropy coding is the last important step in modern encoders. All processing is done in a block-wise manner, which means that all pixels are grouped into larger units and consequently treated as one. A group of such blocks (i. e. 16×16 pel for AVC) is commonly known as *macroblock*.

Two different types of video frames have to be distinguished, so called *intra frames* and *inter frames*. The former can be decoded independently from any other frame, while inter frames use temporal correlations between consecutive frames to predict the image content. In the following only inter frames will be further discussed, for most data reduction techniques use the correlations within those.

The purpose of the aforementioned motion estimation/compensation process is to estimate the position of the current block in an earlier coded (reference) picture and only encode a motion vector representing its displacement along with the transformed and quantized error of the motion prediction, the so called residual. Motion estimation is employed block-wise by comparing the current block to a list of reference blocks and calculating the difference. The best match is then assigned in a Rate-Distortion-Optimization process. For complexity reasons an often used measure for this comparison is *Sum of Absolute Differences* (SAD), albeit the logarithmic measure *Peak Signal-to-Noise Ratio* (PSNR) is commonly employed for quality evaluation of coded video sequences compared to their uncompressed original. Even though block-wise motion compensated prediction is very efficient in general

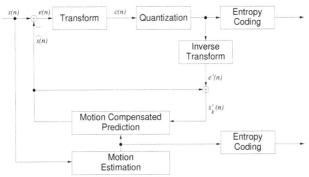

Figure 2. Simplified block diagram of a hybrid video coder.

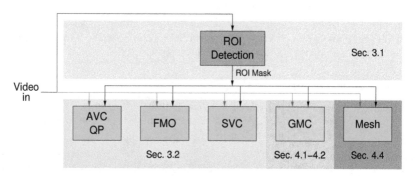

Figure 3. Schematic overview of ROI coding possibilities.

purpose coding, special scenarios can benefit from tailored solutions. In a number of real life use-cases, a differentiation of the scene in fore- and background can improve coding efficiency. Therefore, the background can be seen as a static scene (sprite image) which has to be reconstructed at decoder side. Afterwards, any moving objects can be mapped into the static background at appropriate positions. Systematic mapping errors caused by an inaccurate model assumption can emerge at block boundaries. For different moving objects with different directions contained in one macroblock, systematic problems occur, too. As a technique to code fore- and background separately, *sprite coding*, which will be explained in detail in Section 3.2, already existed in MPEG-4 and needed an adaption to AVC. By implementing this, benefits from the GMC-based coding concept from MPEG-4 sprite coding could be combined with the improved coding performance of AVC. Before being able to code fore- and background however, working solutions to separate the scene into these object layers have to be introduced.

3. Concept of ROI coding

A lot of research has been done in the field of segment- and object-based coding [12, 13]. Seeing that certain objects are indeed regions of interests, object-based coding can be considered ROI coding, which promises to grant more efficient coding of aerial video sequences (especially when employing landscape models). Therefore an overview of existing ROI coding techniques is a good starting point to introduce this concept, before additional assumptions for landscape model-based coding of aerial video sequences are presented.

The basic idea of *Region of Interest* (ROI) coding is to improve the quality of certain parts of the video. Therefore it first has to be clear, what the important or interesting regions of the image are, so that a fitting discriminatory factor to detect them can be determined. Afterwards, it has to be decided on how the ROI is treated in contrast to the rest of the image. The following sections are hence split according to these main issues:

1. How are ROIs detected?

2. How are ROIs encoded?

Figure 3 gives a schematic overview of the workflow including the different possibilities on how to encode ROIs with references to the appropriate sections of this chapter.

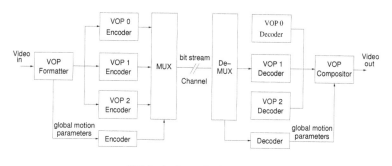

VOP 0:   background sprite
VOP 1:   object plane 1
VOP 2:   object plane 2

Figure 4. Simplified sprite-based MPEG4 coding.

3.1. ROI detection

The detection of ROIs can be arbitrarily realized, starting by the definition of fixed image positions (e. g. the center of the image) or skin color detection for teleconferencing systems [2, 14] to more sophisticated methods, which include several preprocessing steps, as described in the context of screen content coding [15], or the employment of a human attention model, even. A neural network-based approach is employed in [16] to determine foreground and background blocks. In [17] the *Sarnoff Visual Discrimination Model* is introduced to detect the *Just Noticeable Difference* (JND) by taking into account several parameters such as the distance from the observer to the image plane, the eccentricity of the image in the observer's visual field and the eye's point spread function. For coding aerial sequences regions of interest are often moving objects, such as cars and people. Generally, an easy way to find motion in pictures is to subtract the current from the preceding frame. If the background is relatively static, only the moving objects of the frame are left after this step. If an additional threshold or filter is added to decide whether the changed region is just noise or an actual object, the detection becomes even more accurate. The movement of the camera also causes newly emerging areas within a video sequence, which is another ROI in aerial video coding.

The suitable ROI detection method to *determine* a ROI depends on the application scenario.

3.2. ROI encoding

Different parts of one image may move into different directions, whereas motion vectors of objects with the same movement basically point in similar directions. These objects can be summarized as one *object plane*, in video coding referred to as *Video Object Plane* (VOP), as in MPEG-4 part 2 [18, 19]. VOPs can be of arbitrary shape and quality, thus different VOPs may be used for coding different ROIs (and the image background) independent of each other.

To efficiently encode composed scenes containing one background and one or more foreground planes, the concept of sprites was introduced [20], see Figure 4. The sprite represents the background either statically or dynamically. A static background sprite is a (off-line) preprocessed mosaic image, assembled from the background images of the whole

Figure 5. Example for ROI coding (white line emphasizes the *sharp* region).

sequence, which is generated at encoder side. It is transmitted as the first frame of a sequence and handled as a VOP. At decoder side, the background of the current frame is reconstructed from the sprite image. Global motion parameters are employed to determine the section to use from the sprite image. Afterwards, any other VOPs – containing foreground objects – can be mapped into the current frame. Basically, dynamic sprites are very similar, but they are able to change over time. The dynamic sprite is estimated during the encoding process utilizing global motion compensation (GMC). The current background image is composed out of an image generated from the warped sprite and the prediction error [21]. Any foreground objects are subsequently mapped into the image as it is done for static sprites. A detailed view into global motion estimation techniques will be given in Section 4.1.

Due to the mostly static landscapes in aerial video sequences, sprite coding can be quite useful. Thus, an adaption of sprite coding to AVC is of interest. To understand, how sprite-based-like coding can be introduced into a block-based coder, a closer look at certain AVC features is needed:

In AVC the basic independently decodeable part of one image is called *slice*. It consists of a group of macroblocks. The concept of *Flexible Macroblock Ordering* (FMO) initially was introduced into AVC for error resilience. The idea of FMOs is to order macroblocks in well defined different slices. Yet it also can be employed for ROI coding of different parts of the video image, since different slices can be coded in different qualities. Instead of setting the *Quantization Parameter* (QP) per slice, an alternative would be the direct QP variation on macroblock level according to the importance of an image region (low QP for important regions, higher QP for the rest). Since every QP change has to be signaled, this method is expensive in terms of bitrate [15]. A similarly simple, yet effective approach is to discard all residual data for non-ROI areas [22]. A basic assumption of this approach is, that the motion vectors have to match the real motion. Bitrate saved for residual data can be redistributed to improve ROI's quality. Recent developments also investigate the ROI coding with scalability features as e. g. proposed in [23].

All these approaches, which can be realized by a standard AVC coder, are based on the redistribution of bits: to encode ROIs in higher quality than in general video coding, more

(a) Complete frame 176 from *Stefan*.   (b)   Segmented   (c) Block raster for
                                                foreground.   coding.

Figure 6. Example of object segmentation for test sequence *Stefan* [24].

of the overall available bits are needed. These bits are saved at the cost of regions of lower importance whereby those are degraded in quality. An example of such a method is shown in Figure 5. A solution to overcome this issue for aerial video sequences is presented in Section 4.2.

Figure 6 illustrates the principle of *sprite coding*. Figure 6(a) shows one example frame from the test sequence *Stefan*, the *Region of Interest* segmentation was determined with the approach described in [24]. Therein a gradient-based approach with pixel-wise accuracy, which relies on an eight parameter perspective motion model to register two images, is employed. The error between the current image and the adjacent motion-compensated reference image is then calculated to produce a coarse segmentation of the frame. After binarization and morphological filtering, any moved (foreground) object remains in the error image (Figure 6(b)). Based on this detection method some details or even parts of any ROI can get lost. For instance, in Figure 6(b) parts of the hair and legs are missing. For encoding, this segmentation is expanded to fit the macroblock structure (Figure 6(c)). [3] uses similar techniques but considers low-complexity constraints for landscape-based aerial video sequence coding, which results directly in a block-based structure. The complete coding system is explained in detail in Section 4.2.

4. Video coding of aerial sequences using landscape models

This chapter focuses on video coding methods suitable for the coding of aerial sequences. Therefore the idea of ROI coding is extended by employing landscape models, which can save additional bit rate when compared to general video coding. Also one weakness of other existing ROI coding approaches, which is to improve certain areas while degrading other image parts in quality, will be overcome – basically by reassigning some more bits to *important regions* than to *non-important* ones.

A landscape model can be employed and used at en- and decoder side to estimate the movement of certain image parts. If the model is employed at both sides of the coding chain, only data not known from previous frames has to be transmitted. Image parts at the borders (*New Areas*) emerge in every frame and thus cannot be estimated from previous data. Moving objects like cars also cannot be covered by a landscape model due to their erratic movements. Handling these image parts as ROI is beneficial since existing ROI coding techniques can be applied and extended.

A generic block diagram for landscape model-based coding is depicted in Figure 7: a landscape model is applied to the video input stream, first. Although different landscape models will be discussed later on, further processing steps basically stay the same. Landscape extraction commonly begins with an estimation of the perceived global motion of the background of a scene. Details will be given in Section 4.1. The parameters of the landscape model necessary for decoding, have to be transmitted as side-information. In the case of a planar landscape model (GMC-based approach) no additional landscape model information beside the GMC mapping parameters are needed.

Simultaneously working *Region of Interest Detectors* are used for extracting different ROIs, such as *New Areas* (ROI-NA) or *Moving Objects* (ROI-MO), which will be prioritized in the following encoding. These two ROI detectors are specially tailored for aerial sequence coding and are included in the block diagram, but in principle any ROI detector, e. g. shape-based detectors for special buildings, can be added.

Before everything else, the benefits of general landscape model-based coding are introduced and the concept of model-based coding is depicted. The estimation of the perceived background motion is one essential part of it, hence a detailed explanation will be given first. Afterwards, a closer look into a practical coding system employing a GMC-based approach is taken, including detection of ROI, encoding and corresponding decoding. Finally, different landscape models are introduced and their special advantages and disadvantages are discussed.

4.1. Basic principles of background motion estimation

To estimate the global motion in a frame of a video sequence, it is necessary to know about the movement of the camera, which is fixed at an airplane or UAV. Given the accuracy limitations of GPS and drift problems of INS, features within the video sequence have to be used to get information about the motion [25].

At the common speed and flight height of an UAV, most of the content of one frame is available in the previous frame as well. This is illustrated in Figure 8.

To align two frames, there are several well-known possibilities to find significant features within each frame, e. g. feature-based approaches like SIFT [26] or corner detectors such as the *Harris Corner Detector* [4]. The latter was used in [3] and will be described in detail in the following.

The Harris Corner Detector is employed to detect corners within a frames. This detector is based on a two-dimensional gradient method which uses the luminance (gray values) within the picture. Features are defined as corners with high gradients in horizontal and vertical direction.

Afterwards, a correspondence analysis is performed, employing the KLT (Kanade-Lucas-Tomasi) feature tracker [5, 27]. Based on a local optical flow method the position of all features from frame $k - 1$ can be aligned with those in the consecutive frame k.

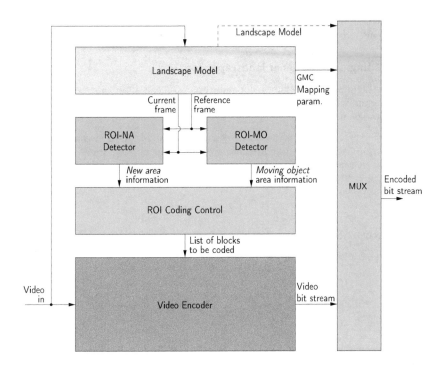

Figure 7. Block diagram of landscape model-based coding (dashed lines: optional, depending on the use-case). ROI-NA is a *Region of Interest detector for New Areas* (newly emerging areas within the picture, for example at the edge of one frame), whereas ROI-MO is a *Region of Interest detector for Moving Objects*, such as cars etc.

Figure 8. Detection of new areas by global motion compensation (GMC).

Block-matching as described in [28] would be an alternative, wherein the blocks of one frame are searched within the next one and their positions are used to align the frames. Seeing that in aerial video material lots of blocks look similar speaks against using this approach, though.

4.2. Video coding using a planar landscape model

Since from big flight heights the movement at the ground seems approximately translational, using a homography leads to a simple landscape model for the decoder, i. e. the landscape is assumed to be planar.

First, a matching process of corners in two consecutive frames is performed as explained in Section 4.1. With the assumption of a planar ground, it is possible to transform one entire frame into another using 8 parameters (perspective or projective transform parameters), Equation (1).

$$a_k = (a_{1,k}, a_{2,k}, \ldots, a_{8,k})^T \tag{1}$$

The projection describes for every pel x and y in frame $k-1$ a matching pel $\vec{p} = (x, y)$ in the succeeding frame k with the mapping parameter set $\vec{a_k}$.

$$F(\vec{p}, \vec{a_k}) = \frac{a_{1,k} \cdot x + a_{2,k} \cdot y + a_{3,k}}{a_{7,k} \cdot x + a_{8,k} \cdot y + 1}, \frac{a_{4,k} \cdot x + a_{5,k} \cdot y + a_{6,k}}{a_{7,k} \cdot x + a_{8,k} \cdot y + 1} \tag{2}$$

The parameters a_3 and a_6 stand for a translational movement in direction of x and y, whereas parameters a_1, a_2, a_4 and a_5 describe shearing and rotation.

The point-correspondences are used to register two consecutive frames and thus estimate the global motion of the camera. Therefore, an overdetermined linear equation system is set up for an estimation of the 8 parameters of the projective transform. By minimizing the *Mean Squared Error* (MSE), *Random Sample Consensus* (RANSAC) [29] estimates the resulting projection parameters, which are then used to align two frames and are employed for global motion compensation.

Since with GMC only shifting of the background can be described, additional efforts for coding of the areas not contained in the first frame have to be made. To cope with these image parts, a *New Area ROI* detector (ROI-NA) is employed. Like this an adaption of MPEG-4 sprite coding can be introduced into AVC as explained in [24]. [3] presented a similar approach especially fitting for landscape model-based coding, taking into account the computational possibilities on board of UAVs. Whereas the former approach was designed as a general video coder, the latter utilizes the planarity assumption of aerial landscape video sequences for further data rate reduction employing a GMC-based coding (without transmission of an additional prediction error). This coding scheme will be summarized shortly in the following. Drawbacks as well as their possible solutions are discussed in Section 4.4.

The block diagram of the coding scheme equals Figure 7 when replacing the block *Landscape Model* with *Global Motion Estimation & Compensation*. In this case background representation is similar to MPEG-4 dynamic sprites but employs improved AVC coding instead of MPEG-4.

As mentioned above, the camera movement is estimated with global motion estimation in the beginning. This estitmate is then used for detecting areas at border of the current frame s_k, which were not already part of the previous frame s_{k-1}. They are considered to be a *new area* and marked as ROI. The decoder only needs information about the global motion to warp the content of the previous frame to the current position. The *new area* is padded to the appropriate position at decoder side and thus, a mosaic is generated (Section 4.2.1) from which the complete current frame can be cut-out. This global motion compensated approach not only prevents the retransmission of redundant image parts but also freezes the noise so that data rate can be saved. On the downside moving objects like cars are also frozen at the position of their first occurrence in the video sequence. To solve this a *Moving Object detector* is employed (ROI-MO): a difference picture between two frames is derived in order to detect moving objects and uncovered background. To reduce false detections because of noise, the average of a 3×3 block is calculated and values below a predefined threshold t_1 are considered to be noise. If a region is larger than a predefined minimum m, a moving object is registered and the corresponding macroblock is additionally marked as ROI for further processing. Any desired other detectors could be added to work in parallel, e. g. shape-based ROI detectors for industrial buildings or image-based ROI detectors for hospitals or the like.

The *ROI Coding Control* combines all macroblocks containing any ROI and forwards the information to a video encoder, i. e. an AVC encoder. Thus, any macroblock (of size 16×16 pel) containing at least one ROI is considered to be encoded in high quality, whereas other macroblocks are encoded in skip mode, i. e. not encoded at all.

4.2.1. Decoding and Visualization of a ROI Controlled Bitstream

Since AVC does not support global motion compensation which is employed to transform the background image to the appropriate position, a GMC capable AVC decoder, here referred to as *ROI decoder*, has to be used.

A block diagram of this ROI decoder is depicted in Figure 9.

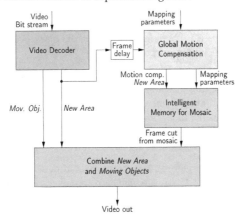

Figure 9. ROI decoder for combining GMC background with additional moving objects [3].

It basically shows that a video or a mosaic is created from the ROI-NA encoded data and afterwards ROI-MO blocks are inserted into the resulting video sequence or the mosaic at appropriate positions, respectively. This method is comparable to MPEG-4 sprite decoding and inserting other *objects*, e.g. from other VOPs. It is necessary to transmit the mapping parameters as side-information to the receiver in order to apply a GMC at the decoder. This can be done without modification of the standardized bit-stream when encapsulating the mapping parameters as SEI (*Supplemental Enhancement Information*) in the data stream. Information about the position of moving objects containing macroblocks has to be transmitted also.

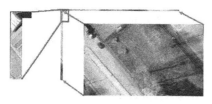
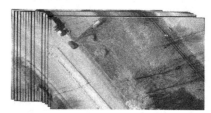

(a) Generation of the decoded video sequence out of *new area*.

(b) Principle of creating a mosaic. Black lines between frames are for illustration purpose.

Figure 10. Principle of decoding a ROI coded video sequence (sequence from 500 m flight height).

To reconstruct the initially intra coded frame from the background sprite, here referred to as mosaic, *new area* macroblocks are registered employing the transmitted mapping parameters to their final position in the mosaic. Like this the mosaic is growing with every new area stripe. Figure 10(a) shows the principle of stitching stripes of ROI-NA together. Figure 10(b) gives a closer look at the growing-process of the mosaic: it shows some succeeding stripes of new area which are stitched to the reference frame. The black marker lines between the single frames only serve illustration purposes.

The receiver can generate a decoded video sequence from the created mosaic. Therefore, the position of the current frame in the mosaic back to the last reference frame has to be derived using global motion parameters. Using the global coordinates of the current background frame as well as the binary mask for the current frame indicating the positions of macroblocks with moving objects (and the uncovered background as well), an entire frame with high-resolution background and moving objects can be reconstructed.

A complete mosaic is shown in Figure 11, with the level of details shown in magnification. The mosaic has a size of 21104 × 4500 pel, which corresponds to about 30 seconds of flight in a flight height of 350 m.

A decoded frame from the ROI decoder is shown in Figure 12, whereas white lines emphasize ROI [3].

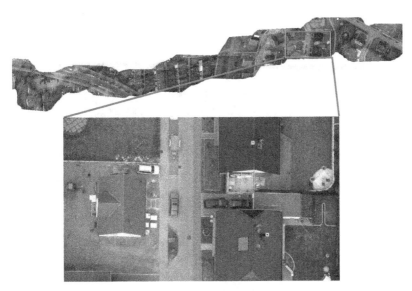

Figure 11. Mosaic and magnification (sequence from 350 m flight height).

Figure 12. Output frame from the ROI coding system, white lines emphasize ROI.

4.2.2. Limits of Global Motion Compensation-based Techniques

The previous approach works quite well for planar landscapes, where the coder is able to project one frame into another by use of global motion compensation. However, as the real landscape often can't be approximated by the assumption of a planar ground, several model violations can occur in aerial video sequences. Especially if recorded from a lower altitude, where the perceived diverging speeds of different image areas become obvious, the simplifications made do not hold true. An illustration of such a case can be found in Figure 13: while global motion compensation can handle most of the similar housings

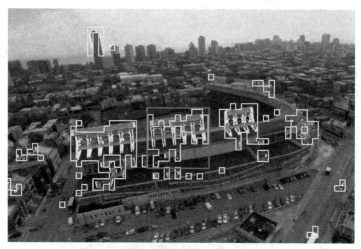

(a) Example frame including correctly classified moving objects and wrongly classified static structures.

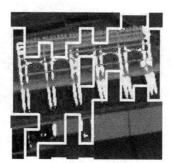

(b) Magnification of one static structure detected as moving.

Figure 13. Limits of translatory block matching. Yellow: motion candidates, white rectangles: areas found to contain moving objects. Test sequence *Chicago*.

correctly, the high structures of the stadium in the foreground are closer to the camera and seem therefore to be moving faster when compared to their surroundings (Figure 13(b)). Their approximated motion doesn't fit the global estimate and as a consequence the structures are classified as moving objects.

Since the corresponding macroblocks are handled as ROI, many false positive macroblocks have to be encoded and transmitted, leading to an increased data rate. To keep the needed bandwidth constant when faced with the worst case scenario in which all parts of the scene were recognized as ROIs, the overall quality of the image would have to be degraded. To avoid false detections and keep the transmitted data to a minimum while preserving details, other ways to model the surface of the scene had to be explored.

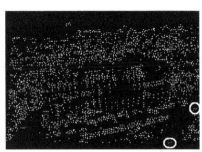

(a) Selected features (green crosses) and their trajectories (yellow lines).

(b) Green regions are considered background, while other colors are candidates for moving objects.

Figure 14. Feature selection, tracking (left) and clustering results (right).

4.3. Video coding using piecewise approximation of the Earth surface by planes

The global motion approach which uses only a single plane to approximate the earth surface leads to mistakes as described in Section 4.2.2. Several objects in aerial video sequences, houses for example, however, can be described as piecewise planar and therefore an approximation using more than just one plane seems natural.

One way to realize this is by computation of oriented tangential planes for a number of significant points as described in [30] and using those planes as a local linear approximation of the surface. Another method is introduced by [31], where the production of a piecewise planar model from a continuous aerial video stream is done in three stages: First half-planes are computed, afterwards lines are grouped and completed based on those planes, followed by a plane delineation and verification process which concludes the model building process. In both cases motion would be estimated and compensated for each of the computed planes separately in the same way described for the single-plane approach. A more purpose-built approach is described by [32], in which planar surfaces are first detected and segmented within a point cloud to seek out buildings from an aerial sequence. Using this step as a priori information could help to compensate the perceived motion of the different image parts, when motion is estimated for all of those found surfaces instead of just the assumed base plane.

4.4. Video coding using a mesh-based approach

When approximating a more complex surface structure, a sophisticated piecewise approach with whole planes often ignores smaller faces and becomes computationally difficult. In the case of UAVs, this can easily lead to problems, as there is only so much computational capacity available on-board. An alternative is using the points and correspondences already available through the corner detector and tracking mechanism introduced earlier for recognizing the moving objects. In Figure 14(a) an example for selected features is shown by the green crosses. The yellow lines mark the trajectories on which those features have moved over time.

The tracked features lead to a motion vector field which has to be cleared of outliers that were caused by false tracking. This is done by testing the motion vectors against a motion model and remove vectors that are not supported by it. Typically the model is a projective transform which is then treated by RANSAC for a global solution. In the case of a mesh-based motion estimation however, there is no global solution without a full 3D model available, which means another approach has to be chosen here. In [33] a region growing approach based on vector field smoothness is described: the spatial distance (Equation (3)) and displacement difference (Equation (4)) of adjacent motion vectors are compared to an adaptive threshold.

$$\|\vec{r}_k(x,y) - \vec{n}_k(x,y)\| < t_{d1} \tag{3}$$

$$\|\vec{d}_{\vec{r}_k}(x,y) - \vec{d}_{\vec{n}_k}(x,y)\| < t_{d2} \tag{4}$$

$\vec{r}_k(x,y)$ describes the position of the classified motion vector nearest to the yet unclassified motion vector $\vec{n}_k(x,y)$ in frame k, while $\vec{d}_{\vec{r}_k}$ and $\vec{d}_{\vec{n}_k}$ are displacement vectors of the associated motion vectors pointing to their position in the preceding frame. Through this representation the movement of a region is only described by the motion vectors at its boundaries. In contrast to this, block-based methods use the motion vector from the center of the block as a representation. If they are smaller than the threshold, the vectors are clustered into one object, otherwise they remain unclassified. In case none of the unclassified motion vectors fulfills the requirements mentioned, a new object is created. Large regions, in which the same motion vector prevails, are treated as background, smaller regions are considered to be potentially moving objects. Objects containing less than a certain threshold are considered outliers and are consequently removed. In Figure 14(b) the results of the process are given.

At this point, only the motion of the selected feature points is known. With the help of these features in combination with the information about their movement, the displacement of each pel (x_{t_k}, y_{t_k}) of the image can be interpolated. The found feature points form a point cloud, which can be transformed into a mesh through a triangulation algorithm ([6]). Delaunay Triangulation, as described in [34], is one example to complete this task. This method basically tries to connect the points of a plane in such a manner, that no other point within the circumcircle of a triangle exists and the minimum angle of all triangles gets maximal at the same time. The mesh derived for the stadium example can be found in Figure 15.

The planar assumption is then used on all of the resulting patches, which is an accurate estimation if the patches are small. By defining this, it is now possible to model each patch by an affine transform, whose parameters A_{t_k}, B_{t_k}, C_{t_k}, D_{t_k}, E_{t_k} and F_{t_k} can be calculated using the feature points that span the triangle t_k in the current frame k, as well as their position $(x_{t_{k-1}}, y_{t_{k-1}})$ in the preceding one $(k-1)$. Each position of a pel within a triangle can be connected to its eqivalent coordinate in the old frame via

$$\begin{pmatrix} x_{t_{k-1}} \\ y_{t_{k-1}} \end{pmatrix} = \mathbf{T_{t_k}} \cdot \begin{pmatrix} x_{t_k} \\ y_{t_k} \end{pmatrix} + \mathbf{b_{t_k}} \tag{5}$$

wherein

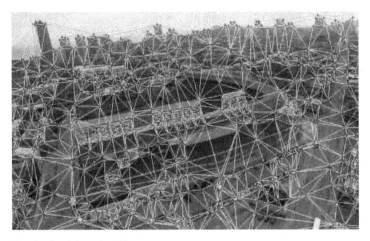

Figure 15. Triangulated mesh from selected features.

$$\mathbf{T_{t_k}} = \begin{bmatrix} A_{t_k} & B_{t_k} \\ C_{t_k} & D_{t_k} \end{bmatrix} \tag{6}$$

and

$$\mathbf{b_{t_k}} = \begin{pmatrix} E_{t_k} \\ F_{t_k} \end{pmatrix}. \tag{7}$$

To get the integer position pixel values, a final interpolation has to be performed. One example to get the needed accuracy is the usage of a two-stage filter as proposed in [6], where half-pel positions are calculated using a six tab Wiener filter and quarter-pel positions through bilinear filtering. Moving objects within the scene can be found by comparing the resulting motion compensated frame with the preceding one by e.g. sum of squared differences (SSD) and a subsequent low-pass filtering. Motion candidates are then determined by thresholding. When examining the result of the moving object detection hailing from the mesh-based method (Figure 16(a)) in contrast with the results from the earlier introduced single-plane approach (Figure 13), it becomes apparent that the number of falsely detected moving objects has reduced quite a lot. Only smaller regions of the high structures are still misclassified, the moving cars, which doesn't fit the model, however are correctly recognized. Overall the mesh-based approach leads to about 90 % less false positive detections.

Some moving objects however show only little motion from one frame to the next. If their surface is relatively uniform, as it is the case with car roofs for example, a comparison between adjacent frames would only show pieces of the object moving. This is because only changing parts of the image can be recognized by differencing. If a uniform area is moved though, chances are, that the new position overlaps with the old one, so that the difference in these parts equals zero. As a consequence, truly changing areas can be

(a) Mesh-based method.   (b) Mesh-based method combined with mosaic approach.

Figure 16. Result of moving object detection. Yellow: motion candidates, white rectangles: areas found to contain moving objects.

rather small, so that a filter threshold to get rid of false motion has to be quite low to not loose them. If more candidates in valid regions would be available, this threshold could be raised so that falsely detected moving regions could be discarded while the real moving objects are kept. By combining the mosaicking technique described in Section 4.2.1 with the mesh-based approach, this can be achieved. First a motion compensated reference picture from the preceding N frames is created by tracking the features and mapping them into the coordinate system of the current frame. With temporal distance as a weighting factor for the pixel values, the emerging image has the perspective of the current frame, only created from the previous frames. Moving object areas, which were already identified via differencing for preceding images or the aforementioned clustering step, are skipped during the mapping process, so that those areas are removed from the resulting reference image. If now the difference between the reference picture and the current image is calculated, the number of motion candidates increases, so that a higher noise filtering threshold can be used. This in turn leads to less misclassified regions and therefore less data that has to be transmitted. The result can be seen in Figure 16(b).

An option yet to be explored for coding purposes is the usage of a full 3D model instead of the comparatively simple mesh just described. To get the mesh as it is to the decoder side, a transmission of such a model would be necessary anyway, so its advantages could as well be used. 3D reconstruction from image sequences via depth estimation as described in [35] for example could be an alternative way to get such a model. Otherwise the mesh would be used as a base and turned into a 3D model by mapping texture from the video sequence onto it. Eventhough computationally expensive, the availability of such a model could provide several advantages, such as a better recognition of moving objects and a better understanding of the area for the following processing steps in a more elaborate system, wherein the coding and transmission of image sequences is only one step.

5. Results

In this section improvements in terms of coding efficiency for aerial video sequences employing the methods introduced in Section 4 will be evaluated.

Therefore, the coding efficiency of the AVC implementation *x264* [36] is compared to an encoder optimization which suppresses all residual data for non-ROI blocks, first. This

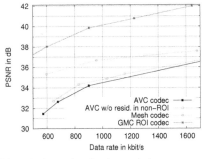

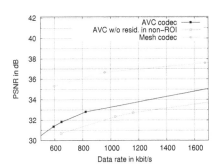

(a) RD plot for AVC-based systems, only for ROI areas. Mesh-based coder for comparison.

(b) RD plot for comparison of mesh coding system with AVC for the **entire frame**.

Figure 17. *Rate-distortion* (RD) diagrams for ROI-based coding systems and mesh coding system, each compared with AVC for very low bit rates.

(a) Reconstructed image from the mosaic.

(b) Detail of the original image.

(c) Detail of the GMC-based reconstr. image.

Figure 18. Mapping errors due to perspective distortions in the GMC-based coding system.

is expected to provide improved ROI quality at cost of non-ROI quality (Section 3.2). Additionally, the GMC-based approach is included in the comparison, which encodes all non-ROI in skip mode. Thus, apart from signalization, the entire data rate can be used to encode the ROIs (Section 4.2). Both encoders are controlled by the external *ROI Coding Control* (cf. Figure 7).

Bitstreams were created and decoded either with a standard video player or, for the GMC-based implementation, with a special *ROI decoder* (cf. Section 4.2.1). For quality comparison, the widely used image difference measure *Peak-Signal-to-Noise Ratio* (PSNR) can not be used for entire frames, because the output of the GMC-based ROI decoder is not pel-wise the same as the input – especially at object borders. To overcome this issue and to give a realistic performance analysis, only the PSNR of those macroblocks containing a ROI is considered for different coding systems (Figure 17(a)). Mapping errors caused by the projective transform of non-planar frames into a mosaic occur. Thus, any object not matching the planarity assumption causes shifted edges as depicted in Figure 18. The GMC-based approach however, was designed to buy a reduction of data rate for the price of such errors which are considered to be not as grave as they do only occur in small partitions of the frame. This can be seen in Figure 18(a).

For ROI, the encoder without residual coding performs slightly better for very low bit rates (≤ 1500 kbit/s) than the (unmodified) AVC coder, as was expected. Since the residual isn't coded anymore, block artifacts become larger. They also serve as a base for motion vector derivation, which leads to an inhomogeneous motion vector field that is expensive to code with the AVC differential encoding. Thus, only little additional gain can be gathered by discarding residual data for non-ROI. The GMC-based approach outperforms both opponents by far in terms of PSNR at any bit rate, since significantly more bits are available to encode a very small image area (compared to the entire frame).

Informal subjective tests support these findings and demonstrate the achievable quality. The resulting image quality after ROI coding and decoding is shown once for a magnification of non-ROI (Figure 19) and once for ROI areas (Figure 20), respectively. For this comparison all coders were operated with the same parameters, except for the *Quality Parameter* (QP), which was adjusted for each coder to match an overall bit rate of about 1000 kbit/s.

Starting with the results of non-ROI (Figure 19), a magnified outtake of the original frame is shown as it was recorded by a camcorder mounted to a motorized glider in Figure 19(a). A magnified outtake of the coding result of the unmodified AVC coder is printed in Figure 19(b). The loss of details is obvious as can be seen e. g. in the tree and with the man holes on the right (light green/dark blue markers). Essentially, the modified AVC codec with disabled residual coding in non-ROIs delivers similar image degradations as the previous codec. But since no residual information was employed, additional block errors occur e. g. at the street light (Figure 19(c), red arrow). The *ROI controlled* GMC-based codec from Section 4.2) is able to provide the highest level of details for the entire frame (Figure 19(d)).

For ROI (Figure 20), the results look quite similar. Figure 20(a) again is the reference, representing the recorded quality. In contrast to the results for non-ROI, the standard AVC performs worst, because the available bitrate has to be spread over the entire frame (Figure 20(b)) leading to heavy loss of details (e. g. markers at the road, dark red ellipses), whereas the modified AVC codec (without residual coding for non-ROI) is able to preserve slightly more details at a relatively bad overall quality (Figure 20(c)). The *ROI controlled*

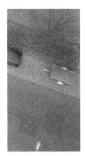

| (a) Original. | (b) AVC. | (c) AVC w/o residual coding for non-ROI. | (d) GMC-based ROI coding with *ROI Control*. |

Figure 19. Quality visualization of **non-ROI areas** (outtakes) coded with 1000 kbit/s with different coders:
(a) Original
(b) AVC encoded and decoded
(c) Modified AVC: coding of non-ROI blocks without residual
(d) GMC-based ROI coding using *ROI Control* from Section 4.2

| (a) Original. | (b) AVC. | (c) AVC w/o residual coding for non-ROI. | (d) GMC-based ROI coding with *ROI Control*. |

Figure 20. Quality visualization of **ROI areas**, here outtakes of *new area*, coded with 1000 kbit/s with different coders:
(a) Original
(b) AVC encoded and decoded
(c) Modified AVC: coding of non-ROI blocks without residual
(d) GMC-based ROI coding using *ROI Control* from Section 4.2

GMC	Mesh
One plane assumption	Multiple plane assumption
Mosaic creation of *planar* landscapes only	Mosaic containing 3D structures can be derived
Adapts to *global* motion	Adapts to *local* motion
Coarse MO-classification results	Refined classification results of MO
Very robust	Sensitive to unremoved outliers
Easy computation	More complex computation

Table 1. Differences between GMC-based and mesh-based approach.

GMC-based codec (Section 4.2) also performs best, since it is able to provide full spatial resolution over the entire frame (Figure 20(d), light green ellipses). For aerial video sequences in full HDTV resolution, with a GMC-based ROI coder, a bit rate of 0.8–2.5 Mbit/s at 1000 kbit/s (depending on the sequence) can be reached, which is much less than the bit rate needed for detail preserving regular AVC video coding.

In Section 4.4 mesh-based coding was presented as an alternative to the GMC approach. The main differences between those two are summarized in Table 1.

To make use of the mesh-based concept, motion vectors as well as residual data have to be transmitted from the encoder to the decoder. Seeing as the decoder already knows the preceding image when decoding the current one, a transmission of the feature points isn't necessary. Finding the mesh grid points at the decoder can be achieved by the same steps used at encoder-side, which were described in Section 4.1.

[37] showed, that for a QP of 30 nearly 20 % of the data rate of a video is needed for the coding of motion vectors. For mesh-based coding only a fourth of the data rate necessary for the transmission of motion information in AVC is needed. This is because only motion vectors for the grid points of the mesh have to be taken into account in contrast to sending motion vectors for every block. Another advantage is the omission of modes and the fact, that the signaling of how the image is divided for coding isn't necessary anymore. The residual is thought to be equally big for both methods.

In Figure 17(b) a comparison between mesh and AVC coding is performed. It has to be noted that in this plot the PSNR for the *entire frame* was used, in contrast to using the "quality" of ROIs only in Figure 17(a). It is obvious that the mesh is able to achieve a better overall PSNR at any bitrate when compared with the AVC coder. Though the bitrate of the GMC-based approach is still below this of the mesh for the same PSNR, the reconstructed mesh image doesn't show perspective distortions anymore. Overall, compared to AVC, a reduction of data by about 10 % when using the mesh-based approach seems realistic, taking into account the findings of [37].

6. Conclusion

In this chapter, an improvement of coding efficiency for standardized video coding is shown for user scenarios, in which a discrimination between *Regions of Interest* and background is reasonable. Aerial video sequences, as captured e. g. by an airplane or an *Unmanned Aerial*

Vehicle (UAV), were used as an example for cases, where smart usage of encoder control and optimization techniques can help to reduce data rate significantly.

Two properties of these video sequences were exploited: firstly, in common airborne video sequences most of the content of one frame was already present in one of the previous frames. But only the parts *not* previously known are regions of interest and are called *new area*. Secondly, a flat surface of the scene can often be assumed. Thus, a projective transform is sufficient to warp the background of the previous frame to the one of the current frame. To make use of both of those properties, AVC was extended by a *global motion compensation* to represent the background movement in the scene similar to *MPEG-4 sprite coding*.

This GMC-based approach, however, has two consequences: on the one hand noise remains frozen, on the other hand, moving objects contained in the recorded sequence are also frozen at the position of their first occurrence. To overcome this issue, a (difference-image-based) detector for *moving objects* is employed for this type of ROI. In the GMC-based coding scheme, only image parts containing new areas and/or moving objects are encoded, whereas remaining parts of the image are coded in skip mode. To enable appropriate reconstruction at decoder side, a special *ROI decoder* is necessary. The decoder basically creates a mosaic in a buffer, while the video sequence is generated by cutting single frames out of it. Finally, moving objects are pasted in the resulting video sequence. Additionally, a high-resolution mosaic is available to get an overview of the entire scene. At the cost of small perspective degradations in the decoded video, an overall subjectively very good quality can be reached, whereas a bitrate reduction from 8–15 Mbit/s to 0.8–2.5 Mbit/s can be realized.

For low flight heights or high structures on the ground (high buildings, trees etc.), many static background-elements are misclassified as moving objects because they violate the model-assumption of planarity. Hence, the data rate increases as more erroneous moving objects have to be transmitted.

To overcome this issue, employing a mesh can further improve the coding efficiency by creating small patches fitting local perspective distortions. In this approach, feature points are detected and a mesh is triangulated between them. Motion estimation is done for all of these patches and not just globally as it was done in GMC. Thus, perspective distortions can be avoided. Another bonus of the mesh-based approach is a lower misclassification rate of static objects as moving ones, which is quite helpful if those are considered to be ROIs. In the worst case, the coding efficiency for the GMC-based approach as well as for the mesh-based one is equal to this of AVC.

Summarizing, it can be noted that *Region of Interest* coding is able to reduce the data rate by 80–90 % without encumbering the surveillance task for particular application scenarios, as it is shown in this chapter using the example of aerial video coding based on landscape models.

Author details

Holger Meuel, Julia Schmidt,
Marco Munderloh and Jörn Ostermann

Institut für Informationsverarbeitung, Leibniz Universität Hannover, Germany

References

[1] Fernando Pereira and Touradj Ebrahimi. *The MPEG-4 Book*. Prentice Hall International, 2002.

[2] Mei-Juan Chen, Ming-Chieh Chi, Ching-Ting Hsu, and Jeng-Wei Chen. Roi video coding based on h.263+ with robust skin-color detection technique. In *Consumer Electronics, 2003. ICCE. 2003 IEEE International Conference on*, pages 44 – 45, june 2003.

[3] H. Meuel, M. Munderloh, and J. Ostermann. Low bit rate roi based video coding for hdtv aerial surveillance video sequences. In *Computer Vision and Pattern Recognition Workshops (CVPRW), 2011 IEEE Computer Society Conference on*, pages 13 –20, june 2011.

[4] C. Harris and M. Stephens. A Combined Corner and Edge Detection. In *Proceedings of The Fourth Alvey Vision Conference*, pages 147–151, 1988.

[5] Jianbo Shi and Carlo Tomasi. Good Features to Track. In *IEEE Conference on Computer Vision and Pattern Recognition (CVPR'94)*, Seattle, June 1994.

[6] M. Munderloh, H. Meuel, and J. Ostermann. Mesh-based global motion compensation for robust mosaicking and detection of moving objects in aerial surveillance. In *Computer Vision and Pattern Recognition Workshops (CVPRW), 2011 IEEE Computer Society Conference on*, pages 1 –6, june 2011.

[7] ITU-T. *Recommendation ITU-T H.261: Video codec for audiovisual services at p x 64 kbit/s*. Geneva, Switzerland, November 1988.

[8] ISO/IEC. *ISO/IEC 11172-2 (MPEG-1 Part 2): Information technology - Coding of moving pictures and associated audio for digital storage media at up to about 1.5 Mbit/s - Part 2: Video*. August 1993.

[9] ISO/IEC and ITU-T. *Recommendation ITU-T H.263 and ISO/IEC 13818-2 (MPEG-2 Part 2): Information technology - Generic coding of moving pictures and associated audio information: Video*. March 1995.

[10] ISO/IEC and ITU-T. *Recommendation ITU-T H.264 and ISO/IEC 14496-10 (MPEG-4 Part 10): Advanced Video Coding (AVC) - 3rd Edition*. Geneva, Switzerland, July 2004.

[11] Benjamin Bross, Woo-Jin Han, Jens-Rainer Ohm, Gary J. Sullivan, and Thomas Wiegand. High efficiency video coding (HEVC) text specification draft 6. In *JCT-VC Document JCTVC-H1003*, 8th Meeting: San José, CA, USA, February 2012.

[12] A. Kaup. Object-based texture coding of moving video in MPEG-4. *Circuits and Systems for Video Technology, IEEE Transactions on*, 9(1):5 –15, Feb 1999.

[13] Michael Hötter and Jörn Ostermann. Analysis-synthesis coding based on the model of planar, rigid, moving objects. *1st International Workshop on 64 kbits/Coding of Moving Video, Hannover*, Jun 1988.

[14] J.-C. Terrillon, M. David, and S. Akamatsu. Automatic detection of human faces in natural scene images by use of a skin color model and of invariant moments.

In *Automatic Face and Gesture Recognition, 1998. Proceedings. Third IEEE International Conference on*, pages 112 –117, apr 1998.

[15] H. Meuel, J. Schmidt, M. Munderloh, and J. Ostermann. Analysis of coding tools and improvement of text readability for screen content. In *Proceedings of Picture Coding Symposium*, May 2012a.

[16] N. Doulamis, A. Doulamis, D. Kalogeras, and S. Kollias. Low bit-rate coding of image sequences using adaptive regions of interest. *Circuits and Systems for Video Technology, IEEE Transactions on*, 8(8):928 –934, Dec 1998.

[17] J Lubin. *A visual discrimination model for imaging system design and evaluation*, pages 245–283. World Scientific Publishing Company, 1995.

[18] ISO/IEC. *ISO/IEC 14496:2000-2: Information technology - Coding of Audio-Visual Objects - Part 2: Visual*. December 2000.

[19] T. Sikora. The MPEG-4 video standard verification model. *Circuits and Systems for Video Technology, IEEE Transactions on*, 7(1):19 –31, feb 1997.

[20] J.Y. Wang and E.H. Adelson. Representing moving images with layers. In *IEEE Trans. Image Processing*, volume 3, pages 625–638, 1994.

[21] M. Van Der Schaar, D.S. Turaga, and T. Stockhammer. *MPEG-4 Beyond Conventional Video Coding: Object Coding, Resilience, and Scalability*. Synthesis lectures on image, video, and multimedia processing. Morgan & Claypool Publishers, 2006.

[22] Joern Ostermann. Feedback loop for coder control in a block-based hybrid coder with a mesh-based motion compensation. *ICASSP 97, München, Deutschland*, pages 2673–2676, Apr 1997.

[23] D. Grois, E. Kaminsky, and O. Hadar. Roi adaptive scalable video coding for limited bandwidth wireless networks. In *Wireless Days (WD), 2010 IFIP*, pages 1 –5, oct. 2010.

[24] M. Kunter, A. Krutz, M. Drose, M. Frater, and T. Sikora. Object-based multiple sprite coding of unsegmented videos using h.264/avc. In *Image Processing, 2007. ICIP 2007. IEEE International Conference on*, volume 1, pages I –65 –I –68, 16 2007-oct. 19 2007.

[25] S. Yahyanejad, D. Wischounig-Strucl, M. Quaritsch, and B. Rinner. Incremental mosaicking of images from autonomous, small-scale uavs. In *Advanced Video and Signal Based Surveillance (AVSS), 2010 Seventh IEEE International Conference on*, pages 329 –336, Sept. 2010.

[26] David G. Lowe. Distinctive image features from scale-invariant keypoints. *International Journal of Computer Vision*, 60(2):91–110, 2004.

[27] Carlo Tomasi and Takeo Kanade. Detection and Tracking of Point Features. Technical Report CMU-CS-91-132, Carnegie Mellon University, April 1991.

[28] T. Saito and T. Komatsu. Extending block-matching algorithms for estimating multiple image motions. In *Image Processing, 1994. Proceedings. ICIP-94., IEEE International Conference*, volume 1, pages 735 –739 vol.1, nov 1994.

[29] Martin A. Fischler and Robert C. Bolles. Random sample consensus: a paradigm for model fitting with applications to image analysis and automated cartography. *Commun. ACM*, 24(6):381–395, June 1981.

[30] Hugues Hoppe, Tony DeRose, Tom Duchamp, John McDonald, and Werner Stuetzle. Surface reconstruction from unorganized points. In *ACM SIGGRAPH 1992 Proceedings*, pages 71–78, 1992.

[31] C. Baillard and A. Zisserman. Automatic reconstruction of piecewise planar models from multiple views. In *Computer Vision and Pattern Recognition, 1999. IEEE Computer Society Conference on*, volume 2, 1999.

[32] M. Peternell and T. Steiner. Reconstruction of piecewise planar objects from point clouds. *Computer-Aided Design*, 36:333–342, 2004.

[33] M. Munderloh, S. Klomp, and J. Ostermann. Mesh-based decoder-side motion estimation. In *Proceedings of IEEE International Conference on Image Processing*, pages 2049–2052, September 2010.

[34] Mark de Berg, Otfried Cheong, Marc van Kreveld, and Mark Overmars. *Computational Geometry: Algorithms and Applications*. Springer-Verlag, 2008.

[35] M. Pollefeys, R. Koch, M. Vergauwen, and L. Van Gool. Metric 3d surface reconstruction from uncalibrated image sequences. In *Proceedings SMILE Workshop (post-ECCV'98)*, pages 138–153. Springer-Verlag, 1998.

[36] VideoLAN Organization. http://www.videolan.org/developers/x264.html, 2011.

[37] S. Klomp, M. Munderloh, and J. Ostermann. Decoder-side motion estimation assuming temporally or spatially constant motion. *ISRN Signal Processing*, 2011(0), apr 2011.

Video Coding for Transmission

Chapter 5

Optimal Bit-Allocation for Wavelet Scalable Video Coding with User Preference

Guan-Ju Peng and Wen-Liang Hwang

Additional information is available at the end of the chapter

1. Introduction

In this chapter, we introduce the concept and the details of the wavelet-based scalable video coding. The content of this chapter includes the following topics:

- *Fundamentals of Wavelet-Based Scalable Video Coding :* The purpose and the general concept of scalable video coding will be introduced in this section. We also give a brief comparison between the major two scalable video coding methods, which are the wavelet-based scalable video coding and H.264/SVC. In addition, we introduce the structure of wavelet-based scalable video coding in this section. A wavelet scalable video encoder consists of two steps. The first step is to decompose each GOP (group of pictures) into multiple subbands, and the second one is to perform entropy coding, which is usually implemented by (embedded zero block coding) [1]. We are going to discuss why and how these two steps achieve video compression and provide universal scalability in a theoretical style.

- *The Objective Function of Scalable Video Coding :* The objective of the scalable video coding will be discussed in this section. In the the discussion, the essential elements that affects the performance of scalable video coding will be considered. These essential elements are the status of network transmission, subscribers' preferences, and the video quality in terms of the conventional Peak-to-Noise-Ratio (*PSNR*). And then according to the discussion, an objective function that considers these elements simultaneously is established for the optimization of the scalable video coder.

- *The Rate Allocation of Wavelet-Based Scalable Video Coding :* Since the entropy coding procedure needs to know the number of bits allocated (which is usually referred to as "*rate*") to each subband, the encoder should decides the rates of the subbands before the entropy coding applied to the subbands. In this section, we are going to introduce how to perform rate allocation that optimize the SVC coder with respect to the proposed objective function and compare its performance with those of the existing rate allocation methods. We will also discuss several issues related to the performance of the rate allocation, such as the concept of rate-distortion curve and the inequivalent energy between the pixel and transform domains caused by non-orthogonal filters.

- *Implementation Issues and Experimental Results :* We will discuss the computational complexity of the proposed rate allocation method and raises several points that can efficiently reduce the computational time. The experimental results that compare the proposed methods and the existing methods will also be given in the section.

- *Conclusion and Future Work :* A conclusive discussion will be given in this section. The discussion will list the contribution of the works mentioned in this chapter and point out some possible issues for the future research.

2. Fundamentals of wavelet-based Scalable Video Coding

Scalable video coding (SVC) encodes a video into a single bitstream comprised of several subset bitstreams. A subset bitstream represents a lower resolution of the video in the spatial, temporal, or quality resolution [2, 3]. SVC is a natural solution to compress the video for a video broadcasting system because the bit-stream generated by the SVC can be divided and separately decoded to support different resolutions. Compared to H.264/SVC [4], which is recently developed based on the prevailing conventional close-loop codec H.264/AVC, the multi-resolution property of 3-D wavelet representation based on motion-compensated temporal filtering (MCTF) is a more natural solution to the scalability issue in video coding [5–8]. However, to compete with the great success of scalable coding methods based on H.264, the MCTF-based 3-D wavelet video codec must be constantly improved.

2.1. The structure of the wavelet scalable video coding

In a MCTF-EZBC wavelet video coding scheme, the video frames are first decomposed into multiple wavelet subbands by spatial and temporal wavelet transforms, then the quantization and entropy coding are sequentially applied to the wavelet subbands. According to the order of the spatial and the temporal decompositions, the wavelet coding schemes can be categorized into two categories : 2D+T (spatial filtering first) and T+2D (temporal filtering first). However, no matter 2D+T or T+2D scheme is applied, the spatial and the temporal filterings can be described independently.

The purpose of spatial filtering is separating low and high frequency coefficients from a video frame. The spatial filtering usually consists of multiple sequential 2D wavelet decompositions. In a 2D wavelet decomposition, the input signal, which is represented by a N by N two dimensional matrix, is decomposed into four $N/2$ by $N/2$ two dimensional matrices, which are denoted by LL, HL, LH, and HH. For these subbands, the previous letter means that the subband contains the low (L) or high (H) frequency coefficients after the horizontal 1D wavelet transform and the following letter means the subband contains the low (L) or high (H) frequency coefficients after the vertical 1D wavelet transform. After the decomposition, subband LL is sequentially taken as the input of the next level spatial decomposition.

If we let $\mathcal{H}_{k,0}$ and $\mathcal{H}_{k,1}$ denote the analyzing matrices in the k-th spatial decomposition, the corresponding wavelet subbands can be computed as

$$\begin{bmatrix} F_{k0} & F_{k1} \\ F_{k2} & F_{k3} \end{bmatrix} = \begin{bmatrix} \mathcal{H}_{k0} \\ \mathcal{H}_{k1} \end{bmatrix} F_{(k-1)0} \begin{bmatrix} \mathcal{H}_{k0}^T & \mathcal{H}_{k1}^T \end{bmatrix} \tag{1}$$

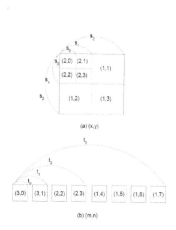

(a) (x,y)

(b) (m,n)

Figure 1. An example of indexing the spatial and temporal decomposed subbands. The above figure shows the indices of the spatially decomposed subbands, in which the subband indexed by (x, y) represents the subband is the y-th after the x-th spatial decomposition. The below figure shows the indices of the temporally decomposed subbands, in which the subband indexed by (m, n) represents the subband is the n-th after the m-th spatial decomposition. Accordingly, any subband obtained by the MCTF can be indexed by (xy, mn).

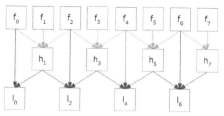

Figure 2. An example of the lifting structure used in the temporal decomposition. The subbands h, which contain high frequency coefficients, are first obtained after the prediction stage. Then the subbands l, which contain the low frequency coefficients, are obtained after the update stage.

where F_{k0}, F_{k1}, F_{k2}, and F_{k3} correspond to the LL, HL, LH, HH subbands, respectively. If there is another spatial decomposition applied to the frame, the subband F_{k0} is further decomposed by the $k + 1$-th analyzing matrices $\mathcal{H}_{k+1,0}$ and $\mathcal{H}_{k+1,1}$. According to this definition, the subband F_{00} is the frame before any spatial decomposition and any wavelet subband after the spatial filtering can be indexed by xy, which represent the subband is the y-th subband after the x-th spatial decomposition. In Figure 1(a), the example shows the wavelet subbands with the indices after performing the spatial filtering consisting of two spatial decompositions.

To reconstruct $F_{(k-1)0}$ from the wavelet subbands F_{k0}, F_{k1}, F_{k2}, and F_{k3}, the synthetic matrices $\mathcal{G}_{k0}$ and $\mathcal{G}_{k1}$ are used in the synthetic procedure, which can be represented by several matrix operations as

$$F_{(k-1)0} = \begin{bmatrix} \mathcal{G}_{k0} & \mathcal{G}_{k1} \end{bmatrix} \begin{bmatrix} F_{k0} & F_{k1} \\ F_{k2} & F_{k3} \end{bmatrix} \begin{bmatrix} \mathcal{G}_{k0}^T \\ \mathcal{G}_{k1}^T \end{bmatrix}. \tag{2}$$

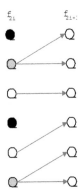

Figure 3. An example of MCTF motion estimation. The types of connectivity pixels in the example are single-connected, multiple-connected, and unconnected pixels. The corresponding prediction (P) and update (U) matrices are given in Eq.(5), where $P^{2i,2i+1}[x,y] = 1$ indicates that the x-th pixel in frame f_{2i+1} is predicted by the y-th pixel in frame f_{2i}. Note that $U^{2i+1,2i}(x,y) = 1$ means the x-th pixel in frame f_{2i} is updated by the y-th pixel in frame f_{2i+1}.

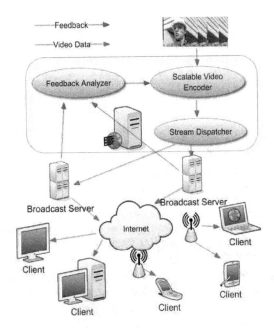

Figure 4. A video broadcasting system usually contains a video source, a scalable video coder, broadcasting servers, the network, and subscribers. Users' information can be delivered to the servers via feedback links.

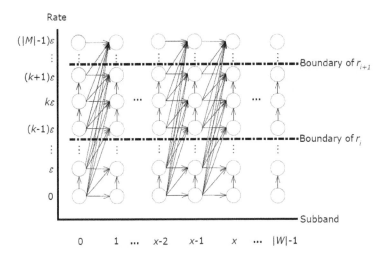

Figure 5. The construction of the DP graph. The x-axis indicates the subbands and the y-axis indicates the rate. For an arc, we calculate the number of bits assigned to the subband associated with the sink node of the arc, and derive the weighted distortion of the subband. For any node on a path, we can calculate the number of bits assigned to the subband corresponding to the node as well as its weighted distortion. The node (x, k) maps to subband $seq^{-1}(x)$ and to quality resolution $q(k) = r_{i+1}$. Note that all the nodes indexed by $(., k-1)$, $(., k)$, and $(., k+1)$ belong to quality resolution r_{i+1}.

Compared to the spatial filtering, which takes a frame as its input, the temporal filtering takes multiple frames (T+2D) or the subands with the same spatial indices (2D+T) as its input. The temporal filtering consists of multiple temporal decompositions. However, unlike the spatial filtering, which only needs several 2-D wavelet transforms during the procedure, the temporal filtering needs multiple 1-D wavelet transforms and motion estimation/compensation to specify the input coefficients of each wavelet transform. So the temporal filtering is more complicated compared to the spatial filtering.

Usually, a temporal decomposition is implemented by the lifting structure, which consists of the predicting stage and the updating stage. As depicted in Figure 2, the H-frames (denoted by h) are firstly obtained after the predicting stage, then the L-frames (denoted by l) are obtained after the updating stage. The lifting structure can be described by the matrix operations, in which a frame is represented by a one dimensional matrix f. If each input frame of the temporal filtering has the size N by N and can be represented by a N by N two dimensional matrix F, the one dimensional matrix f has the size N^2 and can be mapped from F by letting $f[i * N + j] = F[i, j]$.

The motion vectors are computed before the predicting and updating stages. We use the $P_m^{x,y}$, which is a two dimensional N^2 by N^2 matrix, to denote the motion vectors obtained by predicting the y-th frame from the x-th frame in the m-th temporal decomposition. Then the predicting stage of the m-th temporal decomposition can be written as

$$h_m^{2i+1} = f_{m-1}^{2i+1} - (\mathcal{H}_m[2i]P_m^{2i,2i+1}f_{m-1}^{2i} + \mathcal{H}_m[2i+2]P_m^{2i+2,2i+1}f_{m-1}^{2i+2}), \tag{3}$$

where $\mathcal{H}_m$ is the corresponding coefficient of the wavelet filter. Since the index m represents the m-th lifting stage, the term f^i_{m-1} represents the i-th frame which is obtained after the $(m-1)$-th lifting stage. If the 5-3 wavelet transform is used, the value of $\mathcal{H}_m$ in the predicting stage is -0.5.

In the updating stage, the inverse motion vector matrix $U^{y,x}_m$, which has the same size as $P^{x,y}_m$ and can be calculated from the matrix $P^{x,y}_m$ [9], is used to compute the decomposed L-frame as

$$l^{2i}_m = f^{2i}_{m-1} + (\mathcal{H}_m[2i+1]U^{2i+1,2i}_m h^{2i+1}_m + \mathcal{H}_m[2i-1]U^{2i-1,2i}_m h^{2i-1}_m), \tag{4}$$

where $\mathcal{H}_m$ is the corresponding coefficient of the wavelet filter. If the 5-3 wavelet transform is used, the value of $\mathcal{H}_m$ in the updating stage is 1.

To understand how to represent the motion vectors with a matrix, an example is given in Figure 3. And these two matrices are constructed as follows:

$$P^{2i,2i+1} = \begin{bmatrix} 0 & 1 & 0 & 0 & 0 & 0 \\ 0 & 1 & 0 & 0 & 0 & 0 \\ 0 & 0 & 1 & 0 & 0 & 0 \\ 0 & 0 & 0 & 0 & 1 & 0 \\ 0 & 0 & 0 & 0 & 0 & 1 \\ 0 & 0 & 0 & 0 & 0 & 1 \end{bmatrix}, \quad U^{2i+1,2i} = \begin{bmatrix} 0 & 0 & 0 & 0 & 0 & 0 \\ 1 & 0 & 0 & 0 & 0 & 0 \\ 0 & 0 & 1 & 0 & 0 & 0 \\ 0 & 0 & 0 & 0 & 0 & 0 \\ 0 & 0 & 0 & 1 & 0 & 0 \\ 0 & 0 & 0 & 0 & 1 & 0 \end{bmatrix}. \tag{5}$$

After the m-th temporal decomposition, if another temporal decomposition is needed for the temporal filtering, the L-frames generated by the current temporal decomposition are taken as its input. So we let f^i_m, which is the i-th frame of the $(m+1)$-th temporal decomposition, as l^{2i}_m, which is the output $2i$-th frame of the m-th temporal decomposition. Although the H-frames do not participate in the $(m+1)$-th temporal decomposition, we still arrange the indices to them by letting $f^{i+S}_m = h^{2i+1}_m$, in which S is the number of the input frames in the $(m+1)$-th temporal decomposition. So any frames obtained by the temporal filtering can be indexed by mn, which represents it is the n-th subband after the m-th temporal decomposition.

Usually, the temporal decompositions are sequentially performed until the output has only one L-frame. Since the decomposed frame can be synthesized, only the frames which can not be synthesized are necessary to reconstruct all the frames. In Figure 1(b), an example, in which the size of the group of pictures (GOP) is 8, shows the indices of the frames that can not be synthesized from the decomposed frames.

To recover the original frames, the synthesis is applied to the decomposed frames. The frame which is decomposed last is synthesized first, and vice versa. In the procedure of the synthesis, the inverse updating is firstly performed as

$$f^{2i}_{m-1} = l^{2i}_m - (\mathcal{G}_m[2j+1]U^{2j+1,2i}_m h^{2j+1}_m + \mathcal{G}_m[2j-1]U^{2j-1,2i}_m h^{2j-1}_m), \tag{6}$$

where $\mathcal{G}_m$ is the coefficient of the wavelet transform used in the inverse updating stage. If the temporal 5-3 tap filter is used, the value of $\mathcal{G}_m$ is -1 in the inverse updating stage. After the inverse updating stage, the inverse predicting stage is performed as

$$f_{m-1}^{2i+1} = h_m^{2i+1} + (\mathcal{G}_m[2j]P_m^{2j,2i+1}f_{m-1}^{2j} + \mathcal{G}_m[2j+2]P_m^{2j+2,2i+1}f_{m-1}^{2j+2}). \tag{7}$$

If the temporal 5-3 filter is used, the value of $\mathcal{G}_m$ is 0.5 in the inverse updating stage. For some wavelet filters, such as $9-7$ filter, a temporal decomposition needs multiple level lifting structure, and can be easily extended by cascading multiple one level lifting structures.

After the spatial and temporal filterings, the quantization and entropy coding are applied to these wavelet subbands. The coefficients of these subbands may be quantized by scalar or vector quantization, then the quantized coefficients are coded without loss by the entropy coder. The method is common in the still image compression standard, such as JPEG 2000 [10]. In the decoding process, the quantized coefficients are obtained by decoding the received bitstream, then the subbands are rescaled according to the quantization step used in the encoder. The advantage of separating the quantization and the entropy coding is that the quality of the reconstructed video can be predicted according to the quantization step.

The quantization and the entropy coding can also be combined with the bitplane coding method, such as the EZBC entropy coder [1]. In these methods, the rates allocated to the subbands are calculated first, then the entropy coder encodes the subbands with these rates. The advantage of the scheme is the rates of the subbands can be any non-negative integers and the performance of the bit-allocation can be improved accordingly.

3. The objective function of Scalable Video Coding

Many researchers employ a weighting coefficient to represent the relative importance of a resolution. For example, Ramchandran, Ortega, and Vetterli [11] model the distortion as the summation of the weighted mean-square-errors (MSE) on different resolutions, and propose a bit-allocation algorithm based on the exhaustive search technique. Schwarz and Wiegrand [12] adopt a similar approach by weighting the MSEs of the base layer and the enhancement layer, and demonstrate the effect of employing different weightings on each layer on the overall coding performance. The above works do not explain the meaning of the weights or how to derive them. Because the peak-signal-to-noise ratio (PSNR) is most commonly used as a quality measurement of a coding system, instead of weighting the MSE of a resolution, we weight the PSNR as a measurement of relative importance of the resolution to the overall coding performance.

3.1. Design the objective function of Scalable Video Coding

A good coding performance metric for SVC should consider the subscriber's preference for different resolutions. For example, if we want to produce bitstreams in two scenarios: one where all the subscribers prefer the QCIF display and the other where all the subscribers prefer the CIF display, then the optimal bitstreams for the two scenarios should be different. In the first scenario, the optimal bit-allocation can only be obtained by allocating all the bits to the subbands that support the QCIF display. Obviously, this allocation cannot be optimal for the second scenario in which the optimal bit-allocation must encode more spatial subbands to support a higher spatial resolution display with the CIF format.

A general video broadcasting system consists of a video source, a scalable video coder, broadcasting servers, the network, and subscribers, as shown in Figure 4. The scalable coder encodes a source video so that the network's bandwidth requirement can be met and the subscriber's demand can be satisfied. The satisfaction of the subscriber's demand can be quantified to measure the system's performance. In [3], the performance of SVC is measured as follows:

$$Q_{all} = \sum_{i \in N} Q_i, \tag{8}$$

where N denotes the set of subscribers, and Q_i denotes the satisfaction of subscriber i's demand by SVC, which is usually measured by the $PSNR$. However, we found that the $PSNR$ is not sufficient to satisfy the demand of a subscriber because he/she may prefer higher frame rates or spatial resolutions than the $PSNR$. Thus, we introduce the preference factor $\psi \in [0,1]$ for each subscriber and combine it with the $PSNR$ to obtain the following performance measurement:

$$Q_{all} = \sum_{i \in N} \psi_i PSNR_i. \tag{9}$$

If we let S, T, and R denote the sets of spatial, temporal, and quality resolutions respectively, then a resolution in SVC can be represented by (s,t,r), where $s \in S$, $t \in T$, and $r \in R$. Denote subscriber i's preference for the resolution (s,t,r) as $\psi_{i,(s,t,r)}$, and let the $PSNR$ of the resolution be $PSNR_{(s,t,r)}$. Then, Equation (9) can be re-written as follows:

$$Q_{all} = \sum_{s \in S, t \in T, r \in R} PSNR_{(s,t,r)} \sum_{i \in N} \psi_{i,(s,t,r)}. \tag{10}$$

The performance measurement can be normalized based on the subscriber's preference so that we obtain

$$
\begin{aligned}
Q_{average} &= \frac{Q_{all}}{\sum_{s \in S, t \in T, t \in R} \sum_{i \in N} \psi_{i,(s,t,r)}} \\
&= \sum_{s \in S, t \in T, r \in R} PSNR_{(s,t,r)} \left(\frac{\sum_{i \in N} \psi_{i,(s,t,r)}}{\sum_{s \in S, t \in T, t \in R} \sum_{i \in N} \psi_{i,(s,t,r)}} \right) \\
&= \sum_{s \in S, t \in T, r \in R} PSNR_{(s,t,r)} \mu_{(s,t,r)}. \tag{11}
\end{aligned}
$$

Because $\mu_{(s,t,r)}$ considers the preferences of all subscribers for the resolution (s,t,r), it can be regarded as the preference of the system to the resolution. Moreover, from the definition of $\mu_{(s,t,r)}$, we have $\mu_{(s,t,r)} \geq 0$ and

$$\sum_{s \in S, t \in T, r \in R} \mu_{(s,t,r)} = 1. \tag{12}$$

The $PSNR_{(s,t,r)}$ can be calculated as follows:

$$PSNR_{(s,t,r)} = 10log_{10}\frac{255^2}{\bar{D}_{(s,t,r)}},\tag{13}$$

where $\bar{D}_{(s,t,r)}$ denotes the average mean square error (MSE) of the frames in resolution (s,t,r). If we substitute Equation (13) into Equation (11) and use Equation (12), we have

$$Q_{average} = 10\log_{10}255^2 \sum_{s\in S, t\in T, r\in R} \mu_{(s,t,r)} - \sum_{s\in S, t\in T, r\in R} \mu_{(s,t,r)} \log_{10} \bar{D}_{(s,t,r)}$$

$$= 10\log_{10}255^2 - log_{10}\left(\prod_{s\in S, t\in T, r\in R} \bar{D}_{(s,t,r)}^{\mu_{(s,t,r)}}\right).\tag{14}$$

It is obvious that maximizing the average performance $Q_{average}$ is equivalent to minimizing the geometric mean of the distortion

$$\prod_{s\in S, t\in T, r\in R} \bar{D}_{(s,t,r)}^{\mu_{(s,t,r)}}.\tag{15}$$

Note that, in SVC, each temporal resolution involves a different number of frames. If a scalable coder adopts the dyadic temporal structure, which assumes that the number of frames in temporal resolution t is 2^t, then the overall distortion of the resolution (s,t,r) in a GOP is

$$D_{(s,t,r)}^{GOP} = 2^t\bar{D}_{(s,t,r)}.\tag{16}$$

3.2. Subband Weighting

The weighting factor indicates how much a unit quantization power in the subband contributes to the overall distortion in the reconstructed GOP. That is, for the subband indexed by z, its weighting $\gamma(z)$ is given to satisfy

$$D_{(s,t,r)}^{GOP} = \sum_{z\in W(s,t)} \gamma(z) \times D_z\tag{17}$$

where $D_{(s,t,r)}^{GOP}$ is the variance of the distortion in the pixel domain, D_z is the variance of subband's distortion in the wavelet domain, and $W(s,t)$ is the set including the subbands necessary to reconstruct the resolution (s,t,r). The weighting factor $\gamma(z)$ can be computed by

$$\gamma(z) = \alpha(z) \times \beta(z)\tag{18}$$

where $\alpha(z)$ is the spatial weighting factor and $\beta(z)$ is the temporal weighting factor.

The spatial weighting factors can be directly computed according to the error propagation model mentioned in [13]. However, to compute the temporal weighting factors, the effect of the motion compensation must also be considered, and the approach is mentioned in [14]. Since the computational complexity is extremely high, a fast algorithm is proposed in [15] to increase the computing speed.

3.3. Formulation of the rate-distortion function

In this sub-section, we formulate the rate-distortion function of a wavelet-based scalable video coder. We use non-negative integers to index the spatial and temporal resolutions. The lowest resolution is indexed by 0, and a higher resolution is indexed by a larger number. Let $\mathbf{p}$ and $\mathbf{q}$ denote the number of spatial and temporal decompositions respectively; then, the spatial resolution index s and temporal resolution index t are in the ranges $\{0, 1, \cdots, \mathbf{p}\}$ and $\{0, 1, \cdots, \mathbf{q}\}$ respectively. Note that we use (xy, mn) to denote the spatial-temporal subband, which is the y-th spatial subband after the x-th spatial decomposition and the n-th temporal subband after the m-th temporal decomposition. Thus, if we let $W_{s,t}$ denote the set of subbands used to reconstruct the video of spatial resolution s and temporal resolution t, then, $W_{s,t}$ is comprised of

$$\{(xy, mn) | x = \mathbf{p} - s + 1, ..., \mathbf{p}; y = 1, 2, 3; m = \mathbf{q} - t + 1, ..., \mathbf{q}; n = 2^{\mathbf{q}-m}, ..., 2^{\mathbf{q}-m+1} - 1\} \cup$$
$$\{(\mathbf{p}0, mn) | m = \mathbf{q} - t + 1, \cdots, \mathbf{q}; n = 2^{\mathbf{q}-m}, \cdots, 2^{\mathbf{q}-m+1} - 1\} \cup$$
$$\{(xy, \mathbf{q}0) | x = \mathbf{p} - s + 1, ..., \mathbf{p}, y = 1, 2, 3\} \cup \{(\mathbf{p}0, \mathbf{q}0)\}.(19)$$

Figure 1 shows an example of two spatial and three temporal resolutions.

We also assume that all the subscribers receive the same bitstream containing the quality resolution r; therefore, a subscriber to resolution (s, t, r) can decode the substream corresponding to the subbands that support the spatial resolution s and the temporal resolution t. For each quality resolution r, let $\beta_r[(xy, mn)]$ represent the number of bits assigned to subband (xy, mn) for the quality resolution. This assumption simplifies our bit-allocation analysis significantly because we only need to consider the distribution of the bits for the quality resolutions. Obviously, we have

$$\beta_{r+1}[(xy, mn)] \geq \beta_r[(xy, mn)] \tag{20}$$

for each subband (xy, mn). Let b_r denote the maximum number of bits for all the subbands of quality resolution r in a GOP, and let W be the set of all subbands; then, the bit constraint for the quality resolution r can be written as

$$b_r = \sum_{z \in W} \beta_r[z], \tag{21}$$

where z ranges over all subbands in W. Recall that the average distortion of all the subbands of the frames in the resolution (s, t, r) is represented by $\bar{D}^w_{(s,t,r)}$. We introduce a new notation

$\Theta(s,t,\beta_r)$ for $\bar{D}^w_{(s,t,r)}$ to explicitly represent the average distortion in the wavelet domain as a function of B_r. According to Equation (17), we have

$$\Theta(s,t,\beta_r) = \frac{1}{2^t} \sum_{z \in W_{s,t}} w_z^{s,t} \bar{D}_z^w(\beta_r[z])],\tag{22}$$

where $\bar{D}_z^w(\beta_r[z])$ indicates the average distortion of subband z encoded with $\beta_r[z]$ bits. Substituting the subbands support for the resolution (s,t,r), defined in Equation (19), for $W_{s,t}$ in Equation (22), we obtain

$$
\begin{aligned}
\Theta(s,t,\beta_r) = \frac{1}{2^t} \Big(& \sum_{m=q-t+1}^{q} \sum_{n=2^{q-m}}^{2^{q-m+1}-1} \sum_{x=p-s+1}^{p} \sum_{y=1}^{3} w_{(xy,mn)}^{s,t} \bar{D}_{(xy,mn)}^w (\beta_r[(xy,mn)]) \\
& + \sum_{m=q-t+1}^{q} \sum_{n=2^{q-m}}^{2^{q-m+1}-1} w_{(p0,mn)}^{s,t} \bar{D}_{(p0,mn)}^w (\beta_r[(p0,mn)]) \\
& + \sum_{x=p-s+1}^{p} \sum_{y=1,2,3} w_{(xy,q0)}^{s,t} \bar{D}_{(xy,q0)}^w (\beta_r[(xy,q0)]) \\
& + w_{(p0,q0)}^{s,t} \bar{D}_{(p0,q0)}^w (\beta_r[(p0,q0)]) \Big).
\end{aligned}
\tag{23}
$$

Let $\mathbf{v}$ be the number of quality resolutions indexed from $0 \cdots, \mathbf{v}-1$, and let $\{\beta_0, \cdots, \beta_{\mathbf{v}-1}\}$ be the bit-allocation profile. We can represent Equation (15) explicitly as $\mathcal{D}(\beta_0, \cdots, \beta_{\mathbf{v}-1})$ to indicate the dependence of the average distortion of a GOP on the bit-allocation profile. Then, we obtain

$$\mathcal{D}(\beta_0, \cdots, \beta_{\mathbf{v}-1}) = \prod_{r=0}^{\mathbf{v}-1} \prod_{s=0}^{p-1} \prod_{t=0}^{q-1} \bar{D}_{(s,t,r)}^{\mu_{(s,t,r)}}\tag{24}$$

$$= \prod_{r=0}^{\mathbf{v}-1} \prod_{s=0}^{p-1} \prod_{t=0}^{q-1} \Theta(s,t,\beta_r)^{\mu_{(s,t,r)}}\tag{25}$$

$$= \prod_{r=0}^{\mathbf{v}-1} \mathcal{D}_r(\beta_r),\tag{26}$$

where $\mathcal{D}_r(\beta_r)$ is the average distortion of quality resolution r when the subscriber's preference factor $\mu_{(s,t,r)}$ is considered in weighting $\Theta(s,t,\beta_r)$.

The rate-distortion problem (P) can now be formulated as finding the bit-allocation profile $\{\beta_0, \cdots, \beta_{\mathbf{v}-1}\}$ that satisfies the constraints in Equations (20) and (21) and minimizes the distortion function specified in Equation (26):

$$\min \mathcal{D}(\beta_0, \beta_1, \cdots, \beta_{\mathbf{v}-1})\tag{27}$$

$$\text{subject to } \sum_{z \in W} \beta_i(z) = b_i, \text{ for } i = 0, \cdots, \mathbf{v}-1,$$

$$\text{and } \beta_{i-1}(z) \le \beta_i(z) \text{ for } i = 1, \cdots, \mathbf{v}-1,$$

4. The rate allocation of wavelet-based Scalable Video Coding

The optimal bit-allocation problem (P) can be solved by solving a sequence of bit-allocation sub-problems (P_r), with quality resolution $r = 0, \cdots, \mathbf{v} - 1$. The sub-problem (P_r) is defined as follows:

$$\min \mathcal{D}(\beta_0, \beta_1, \cdots, \beta_{r-1}, \beta_r, \beta_r, \cdots, \beta_r) \tag{28}$$
$$\text{subject to } \sum_{z \in W} \beta_i(z) = b_i, \text{ for } i = 0, \cdots, r,$$
$$\text{and } \beta_{i-1}(z) \leq \beta_i(z) \text{ for } i = 1, \cdots, r,$$

where W is the set of all subbands, and $\{b_i\}$ is a given non-decreasing sequence that corresponds to the bit constraints. The problem (P_r) allocates bits from the quality resolution 1 to r; hence, all the subscriptions for a quality resolution $> r$ will use the bit-allocation result of the quality resolution r. Thus, we have $\beta_i = \beta_r$ for $i = r + 1, \cdots, \mathbf{v} - 1$ in Equation (28). The optimal bit-allocation problem (P) can be solved by solving (P_0), followed by (P_1) based on the solution of (P_0), and so on up to solving $(P_{\mathbf{v}-1})$. In the following subsections, we propose two methods to solve (P_r). The first finds the upper bound of (P_r) by a Lagrangian-based approach, and the second finds the exact solution by using the less efficient dynamic programming approach.

4.1. Lagrangian-based solution

The bit-allocation problem is usually analyzed by the Lagrangian multiplier method. By assuming that $\prod_{i=a}^{b} f_i = 1$ for any function f_i with $b > a$, the objective of (P_r) can be re-written as

$$\mathcal{D}(\beta_0, ..., \beta_{r-1}, \beta_r, ..., \beta_r)$$
$$= \prod_{s=0}^{\mathbf{p}-1} \prod_{t=0}^{\mathbf{q}-1} \left\{ \prod_{k=0}^{r-1} \Theta(s, t, \beta_k)^{\mu_{(s,t,k)}} \prod_{k=r}^{\mathbf{v}-1} \Theta(s, t, \beta_r)^{\mu_{(s,t,k)}} \right\}. \tag{29}$$

Because $\sum_{s \in \mathbf{S}, t \in \mathbf{T}, r \in \mathbf{R}} \mu_{(s,t,r)} = 1$ (See Equation (12)), by applying the generalized geometric mean - arithmetic mean inequality to Equation (29), we can obtain its upper bound as follows:

$$\mathcal{D}(\beta_0, ..., \beta_{r-1}, \beta_r, ..., \beta_r) \leq C + \sum_{s=0}^{\mathbf{p}-1} \sum_{t=0}^{\mathbf{q}-1} \sum_{k=r}^{\mathbf{v}-1} \mu_{(s,t,k)} \Theta(s, t, \beta_r), \tag{30}$$

where the constant $C = \sum_{s=0}^{\mathbf{p}-1} \sum_{t=0}^{\mathbf{q}-1} \sum_{k=0}^{r-1} \mu_{(s,t,k)} \Theta(s, t, \beta_k)$. Note that the constant C is computed from the bit-allocation results from resolution 0 to resolution $r - 1$.

Now we can find the solution for the problem (P_r^+), which is the upper bound of the problem (P_r). The problem (P_r^+) is defined as

$$\min_{\beta_r} \Omega_r(\beta_r) = \sum_{s=0}^{\mathbf{p}-1} \sum_{t=0}^{\mathbf{q}-1} \sum_{k=r}^{\mathbf{v}-1} \mu_{(s,t,k)} \Theta(s, t, \beta_r) \tag{31}$$
$$\text{subject to } \sum_{z \in W} \beta_r(z) = b_r.$$

After substituting Equation (22) into Equation (31) for $\Theta(s, t, \beta_r)$ and re-arranging the terms, we have

$$\Omega_r(\beta_r) = \sum_{z \in W} \rho_z^r \bar{D}_z(\beta_r[z]), \qquad (32)$$

where z is a subband, W is the set of all subbands, and ρ is the final weighting factor. Note that ρ is computed from the preference weighting μ and the spatial-temporal weighting $w^{s,t}$.

Now, replacing $\Omega_r(\beta_r)$ in Equation (31) with Equation (32), the problem (P_r^+) can be solved optimally by using the Lagrangian approach with the Lagrangian function:

$$L(\lambda, \beta_r) = \sum_{z \in W} \rho_z^r \bar{D}_z(\beta_r[z]) - \lambda(b_r - \sum_{z \in W} \beta_r[z]). \qquad (33)$$

A necessary condition for optimal bit-allocation can be satisfied by taking the partial derivative with respect to λ and β_r and setting the results to zero. Thus, the optimal bit-allocation vector β_r^* for the quality resolution r must satisfy

$$\frac{\partial L(\lambda, \beta_r)}{\partial \beta_r[z]} = \rho_z^r \frac{\partial \bar{D}_z(\beta_r[z])}{\partial \beta_r[z]} + \lambda = 0, \qquad (34)$$

and

$$\frac{\partial L(\lambda, \beta_r)}{\partial \beta_r[z]} = b_r - \sum_{z \in W} \beta_r[r] = 0. \qquad (35)$$

The two necessary conditions require that 1) the optimal bit-allocation β_r^* must exist when the rate-distortion functions of all the subbands have the same weighted slope; and 2) at that particular slope, the total number of bits of all the subbands is b_r.

It is straightforward to show that if $\bar{D}_z(\beta_r[z])$ is convex for any z, then $\sum_{z \in W} \rho_z^r \bar{D}_z(\beta_r[z])$ with $\rho_z^r \geq 0$ is a convex function; therefore, the necessary condition is also the sufficient condition for β_r^*. We can use a similar approach to that in [16] to derive an efficient algorithm to find the optimal bit-allocation vector. Thus, we modify the distortion function $\bar{D}_z(\beta_r[z])$ to make it a convex function. We initialize $\beta_r[z] = 0$ for all subbands, and divide b_r into $\lceil b_r/\delta \rceil$ segments with δ bits for each segment. In each stage of our algorithm, we calculate $\bar{D}_z(\beta[z] + \delta)$ and select the subband z' that has the largest weighted absolute slope:

$$\arg\max_{z \in W} \rho_z^r \frac{|\bar{D}_z(\beta[z] + \delta) - \bar{D}_z(\beta[z])|}{\delta}. \qquad (36)$$

Then, we only modify the bit-allocation vector of the component that corresponds to the subband z' by letting

$$\beta_r[z'] \leftarrow \begin{cases} \beta_r[z'] + \delta, & \text{if } \sum_{z \in W} \beta_r[z] \leq b_r - \delta, \\ \beta_r[z'] + (b_r - \sum_{z \in W} \beta_r[z]), & \text{otherwise .} \end{cases} \qquad (37)$$

We repeat the above process several times until the constraint is achieved.

4.2. Optimal solution based on dynamic programming

Although the proposed Lagrangian-based method is efficient and theoretically sound, it optimizes the upper bound of the true objective function. In this section, we propose another optimal bit-allocation method based on dynamic programming (DP). Although the proposed method uses more memory and requires more computation time than the Lagrangian-based method, it can find the optimal bit-allocation for the true objective function.

To solve the bit-allocation problem with the DP-based method, we represent the problem as an acyclic directed graph $G = (N, A)$, called a DP graph for short, where N is the set of nodes and the members of A are arcs. The arc from node i_k to node i_l is represented by $i_k \rightarrow i_l$ where i_k and i_l are the source node and the sink node of the arc respectively. A path can be represented as a concatenation of arcs.

Let seq be a bijection mapping from the subbands to the integer set from 0 to $|W| - 1$, where $|W|$ is the number of subbands; and let seq^{-1} be its inverse mapping from an integer to a subband. To construct the DP graph for the problem (P), we arrange the subbands z as a sequence $seq(z) \in \{0, \cdots, |W| - 1\}$, and divide b_{v-1} into $M = \lceil \frac{b_{v-1}}{\epsilon} \rceil$ components. For convenience, we set the bit constraint b_r with $r = 0, \cdots, v - 2$ as an integer multiple of ϵ. Then, we introduce the function q, which maps a node in the DP graph to its corresponding quality resolution.

The nodes in the DP graph are $\{(seq(z), k) |\ k = 0, 1, \cdots, M, z \in W\}$. If we let (a, b) be the source node of the arc $(a, b) \rightarrow (seq(z), k)$ to the sink node $(seq(z), k)$, then depending on the position of $(seq(z), k)$, (a, b) belongs to the set $\{(seq(z) - 1, i) | i \le k\} \cup \{(seq(z), k - 1)\}$, $\{(0, k - 1)\}$, or $\{(seq(z) - 1, 0)\}$.

Figure 5 shows the constructed DP graph. For the node (x, k), the corresponding subband is $seq^{-1}(x)$ and the corresponding quality resolution is $q(k) = r_{i+1}$. We can calculate the number of bits assigned to the subband associated with the sink node of each arc in the DP graph as well as the weighted distortion of the subband. For example, if the arc is $(u, k_u) \rightarrow (v, k_v)$, then the number of bits assigned to the subband $seq^{-1}(v)$ is $(k_v - k_u)\epsilon$. Accordingly, we can also calculate the number of bits assigned to each subband on any path, which consists of consecutive arcs, in the DP graph.

The DP approach uses $|W|$ passes to solve the problem (P) with the constraint that at the end of pass i, the optimal path to each node in the DP graph indexed by $(i, .)$ is found and recorded. At the first pass 0, we find the number of bits allocated to any node $(0, j)$ with $j \in \{0, \cdots, M - 1\}$. Then, based on that result, at pass 1, we find and record the optimal bit-allocation path (the path with the smallest weighted distortion among all the paths that end at the node) to each node $(1, .)$. Based on the result of the previous pass $i - 1$, we can repeat the process to derive the optimal bit-allocation path to any node $(i, .)$ and record the path to the node. After the pass $|W| - 1$, the bit-allocation corresponding to the optimal path from $(0, 0)$ to $(|W| - 1, k_l)$ with $k_l \epsilon = b_r$ for some b_r is the optimal bit-allocation to the quality resolution r; i.e., the optimal solution for problem (P_r) is derived. It can be shown that the DP approach ensures there is only one optimal path beginning at $(0, 0)$ to any node in the DP graph, but the proof is omitted due to the space limitation.

4.3. Min-max approach for unknown preferences

The optimization algorithms presented in previous sections require the subscriber's preference information. However, in many applications, the preference is not available to the encoder. Thus, we present a min-max approach that finds the optimal bit-allocation when the subscriber's preference is not known. The approach is a conservative strategy that ensures the worst performance of the algorithm is above a certain quality.

Let $\mu = [\mu_{(s,t,r)}]$ denote the subscriber's preference vector. In addition, let $\beta = [\beta_0, \cdots, \beta_{v-1}]$ and $b = [b_0, \cdots, b_{v-1}]$ be, respectively, the subband bit-allocation vector and the bit budget vector for all quality resolutions. The min-max approach for the problem (P) can be written as

$$\min_{b,\beta} \max_{\mu} \mathcal{D}(\beta_0, \beta_1, \cdots, \beta_{v-1}) \tag{38}$$

subject to $\sum_{z \in W} \beta_i[z] = b_i$, for $i = 0, \cdots, v - 1$,

and $\beta_{i-1}[z] \leq \beta_i[z]$, $b_{i-1} \leq b_i$ for $i = 1, \cdots, v - 1$.

In other words, the min-max approach finds the best bit-allocation vectors for the preference distribution that yields the largest distortion.

First, we show that the least favorable preference distribution μ^* is independent of the quality resolution r. For any subband bit-allocation β_r at the quality resolution r, the least favorable preference distribution maximizes the distortion $\mathcal{D}(\beta_0, \beta_1, \cdots, \beta_{r-1}, \beta_r, \beta_r, \cdots, \beta_r)$. From Equation (29), we have

$$\mathcal{D}(\beta_0, ..., \beta_{r-1}, \beta_r, ..., \beta_r) \leq \max_{s=0,...,\mathbf{p}-1} \max_{t=0,\cdots,\mathbf{q}-1} \max_{k=0,\cdots,r} \Theta(s, t, \beta_k), \tag{39}$$

$$= \Theta(\mathbf{p} - 1, \mathbf{q} - 1, \beta_0), \tag{40}$$

where Equation (39) is derived from $0 \leq \mu_{(s,t,r)} \leq 1$, and $\sum_{(s,t,r)} \mu_{(s,t,r)} = 1$; and Equation (40) is obtained because the maximum distortion can be obtained when the bits β_0 for the coarsest quality resolution are assigned to the subbands in the highest spatial and temporal resolutions. Thus, the least favorable preference μ^* occurs when all users have preference 1 for the resolution $(\mathbf{p} - 1, \mathbf{q} - 1, 0)$.

After deriving the least favorable preference μ^*, the problem can be solved easily by using the methods proposed previously. It is noteworthy that the above min-max problem finds the optimal bit-allocation for the codec containing only one spatial, temporal, and quality resolution. This result corresponds to allocating the bits optimally for a non-scalable wavelet codec.

5. Experiment results

We now evaluate the coding performance of the proposed bit-allocation methods on a 2D+t wavelet encoder. In the experiment, a GOP has 32 frames. First, each frame is decomposed by applying a three-level 2-D wavelet transform with the 9-7 wavelets; then, the five-level MCTF method is applied to each spatial subband. The metod uses the 5-3 wavelets for temporal decomposition of each spatial subband, as proposed in [17]. When MCTF is applied, we assume that the motion vectors are given. The motion estimation step uses a full search with integer-pixel accuracy. The block size is 16×16, and the search range is $[16, -15]$ both vertically and horizontally. Finally, the 2-D EZBC method [1, 8] is used to encode the wavelet coefficients of the 2D+t wavelet codec.

In the first two methods, the encoder knows each user's preference profile; and the third assumes that the preference profile is not available to the encoder. The first method is based on the Lagrangian approach, the second is based on the DP approach, and the third is based on the min-max approach.

We conduct four experiments on two video sequences: Foreman and Coastguard. Two of the experiments assume that there is only one quality resolution. The first experiment assumes that all the users subscribe to the same temporal resolution, but their spatial resolution preferences are different. Figure 6 shows the R-D curves of each sequence versus different spatial preference profiles. It is obvious that the scalable bit-allocation methods with known preferences achieve a better coding performance than the method that lacks the preference information. The DP method outperforms the Lagrangian method in all cases. Note that the DP method finds the optimal bit-allocation for the problem (P), while the Lagrangian method finds the optimal solution for the upper bound of the problem. In the second experiment, it is assumed that the only difference between the subscribers' preferences is the temporal resolution. That is, all users subscribe to the same spatial resolution. The experimental results shown in Figure 7 demonstrate that the DP method outperforms the Lagrangian method, and the min-max method has the worst performance in all cases. Note that the average $PSNR$ improvement of the DP method over the Lagrangian method in Figure 6 is higher than that in Figure 7, This indicates that knowing the preferences yields more $PSNR$ gain in the spatial resolution than in the temporal resolution.

The third experiment assumes that the users have three different spatial, temporal, and quality resolution preferences. In the experiment, there are three preference distribution settings. The preferences for the spatial, temporal, and quality resolutions are as follows: 1) temporal resolutions: 7.5 fps, 15 fps, and 30 fps; 2) spatial resolutions: $QuadCIF$, $QCIF$, and CIF; and 3) quality resolutions with bit constraints $b_0 = 2400$ kbps, $b_1 = 4600$ kbps, and $b_2 = 6200$ kbps.

Setting 1

$\mu_{r=2400kbit/GOP}$	7.5	15	30 (fps)
QuadQCIF	0.24	0	0
QCIF	0.06	0	0
CIF	0	0	0

$\mu_{r=4600kbit/GOP}$	7.5	15	30 (fps)
QuadQCIF	0	0.06	0
QCIF	0	0.24	0
CIF	0	0	0

$\mu_{r=6200kbit/GOP}$	7.5	15	30 (fps)
QuadQCIF	0	0	0
QCIF	0	0	0.08
CIF	0	0	0.32

Setting 2

$\mu_{r=2400kbit/GOP}$	7.5	15	30 (fps)
QuadQCIF	0.24	0.06	0
QCIF	0	0	0
CIF	0	0	0

$\mu_{r=4600kbit/GOP}$	7.5	15	30 (fps)
QuadQCIF	0	0	0
QCIF	0.06	0.24	0
CIF	0	0	0

$\mu_{r=6200kbit/GOP}$	7.5	15	30 (fps)
QuadQCIF	0	0	0
QCIF	0	0	0
CIF	0	0.08	0.32

Setting 3

$\mu_{r=2400kbit/GOP}$	7.5	15	30 (fps)
QuadQCIF	0.3	0	0
QCIF	0	0	0
CIF	0	0	0

$\mu_{r=4600kbit/GOP}$	7.5	15	30 (fps)
QuadQCIF	0	0	0
QCIF	0	0.3	0
CIF	0	0	0

$\mu_{r=6200kbit/GOP}$	7.5	15	30 (fps)
QuadQCIF	0	0	0
QCIF	0	0	0
CIF	0	0	0.4

The results are shown in Figure 8. Compared to Figures 6 and 7, there are no significant performance differences in the curves associated with the Lagrangian method and the min-max method.

6. Conclusion

We introduce the concept and the details of wavelet-based scalable video coding in this chapter. We also considers subscribers' preferred resolutions when assessing the performance of a wavelet-based scalable video codec. We formulate the problem as a scalable bit-allocation problem and propose different methods to solve it. Specifically, we show that the Lagrangian-based method can find the optimal solution of the upper bound of the problem, and that the dynamic programming method can find the optimal solution of the problem. We also consider applications where the subscribers' preferences are not known, and use a min-max approach to find a solution. Our experimental results show that knowing the users' preferences can improve the PSNR of the 2D+t wavelet scalable video codec. The average PSNR gain depends on the users' preference distribution. It can range from 1 db to 8 db at a fixed bit rate. There is a significant performance gap between when the preferences are known over when they are unknown. Hence, in our future work, we will reduce the gap or derive a method that enables use to estimate the preference patterns in the encoder.

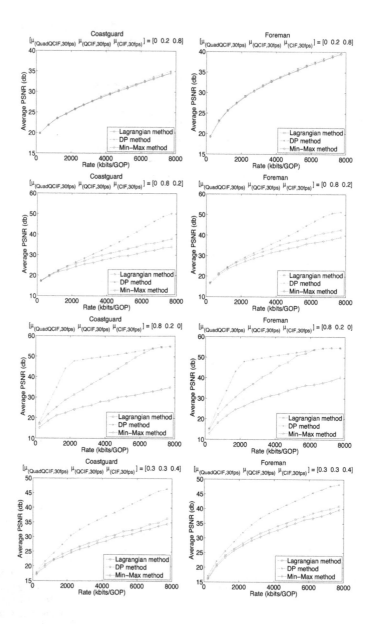

Figure 6. Comparison of the performance under different spatial preferences. Four preference patterns are used to subscribe to three spatial resolutions: QuadQCIF, QCIF, and CIF. Left: Coastguard. Right: Foreman. There is only one quality resolution and all users subscribe to 30 fps.

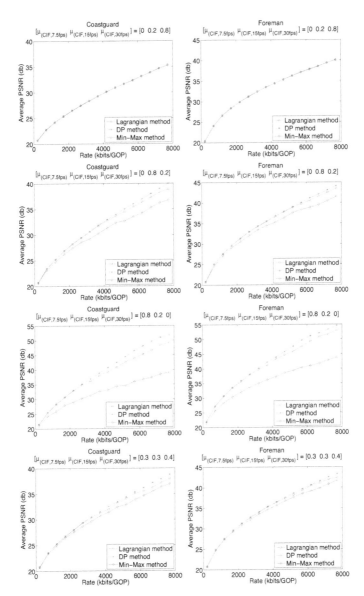

Figure 7. Comparison of the performance under different temporal preferences. Different preferences are used to subscribe to three temporal resolutions: 7.5 fps, 15 fps, and 30 fps. Left: Coastguard. Right: Foreman. There is only one quality resolution and all users subscribe to CIF.

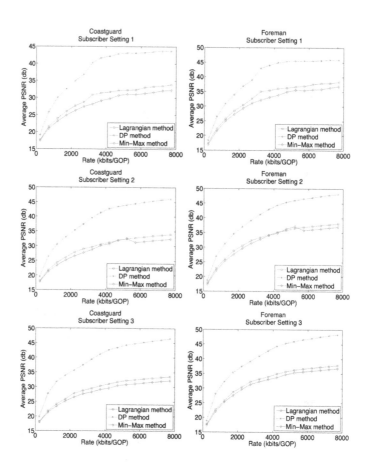

Figure 8. Comparison of the performance under different spatial, temporal, and quality preferences. Different preferences are used to subscribe to three temporal resolutions (7.5 fps, 15 fps, and 30fps), three spatial resolutions (QuadQCIF, QCIF, and CIF), and three quality resolutions (2400 kbps, 4600 kbps, and 6200 kbps). Left: Coastguard. Right: Foreman. Top row: the performance of setting 1; middle row: the performance of setting 2; and, bottom row: the performance of setting 3.

Author details

Guan-Ju Peng and Wen-Liang Hwang

Institute of Information Science, Academia Sinica, Nankang, Taipei, Taiwan

References

[1] Shih-Ta Hsiang and J. W. Woods. Embedded video coding using invertible motion compensated 3-D subband/wavelet filter bank. *Signal Processing: Image Communications*, 16:705–724, May 2001.

[2] J. Barbarien M. Van der Schaar J. Cornelis Y. Andreopoulos, A. Munteanu and P. Schelkens. In-band motion compensated temporal filtering. *Signal Processing: Image Communications*, 19:653–673, August 2004.

[3] Qian Zhang, Q. Guo, Qiang Ni, Wenwu Zhu, and Ya-Qin Zhang. Sender-adaptive and receiver driven layered multicast for scalable video over the internet. *IEEE Transactions on Circuits and Systems for Video Technology*, 15(4):482–495, April 2005.

[4] Heiko Schwarz, Detlev Marpe, and Thomas Wiegrand. Overview of the scalable video coding extension of the H.264/AVC standard. *IEEE Transactions on Circuits and Systems for Video Technology*, 17(9):1103–1120, 2007.

[5] Jens-Rainer Ohm. Three-dimensional subband coding with motion compensation. *IEEE Transactions on Image Processing*, 3(5):559–571, September 1994.

[6] Seung-Jong Choi and J. W. Woods. Motion-compensated 3-D subband coding of video. *IEEE Transactions on Image Processing*, 8(2):155–167, February 1999.

[7] K. Hanke T. Rusert and J.-R. Ohm. Transition filtering and optimized quantization in interframe wavelet video coding. *Proc. SPIE Visual Communications Image Processing*, 5150:682–694, 2003.

[8] Peisong Chen and John W. Woods. Bidirectional mc-ezbc with lifting implementation. *IEEE Transactions on Circuits and Systems for Video Technology*, 14(10):1183–1194, October 2004.

[9] Jens-Rainer Ohm, Mihaela van der Schaar, and John W. Woods. Interframe wavelet coding - motion picture representation for universal scalability. *Signal Processing : Image Communication*, 19(9):877–908, 2004.

[10] Daniel Lee Michael J. Gormish and Michael W. Marcellin. JPEG 2000: Overview, architecture, and applications. In *IEEE International Conference on Image Processing*, pages 29–32, Sepetember 2000.

[11] Kannan Ramchandran, Antonio Ortega, and Martin Vetterli. Bit allocation for dependent quantization with applications to multiresolution and MPEG video coders. *IEEE Transactions on Image Processing*, 3(5):533–545, 1994.

[12] Heiko Schwarz and Thomas Wiegrand. R-D optimized multi-layer encoder control for SVC. In *IEEE International Conference on Image Processing*, pages 281–284, September 2007.

[13] B. Usevitch. Optimal bit allocation for biorthogonal wavelet coding. In *Data Compression Conference*, pages 387 –395, March/April 1996.

[14] Cho-Chun Cheng, Guan-Ju Peng, and Wen-Liang Hwang. Subband weighting with pixel connectivity for 3-D wavelet coding. *IEEE Transactions on Image Processing*, 18(1):52–62, January 2009.

[15] Wen-Liang Hwang Guan-Ju Peng and Sao-Jie Chen. Fast implementation of the subband weighting for 3d wavelet coding. *ISRN Signal Processing*, 2011:Article ID 252734, 2011.

[16] David S. Taubman. High performance scalable image compression with EBCOT. *IEEE Transactions on Image Processing*, 9(7):1158–1170, 2000.

[17] Lin Luo, Jin Li, Shipeng Li, Zhenquan Zhuang, and Ya-Qin Zhang. Motion compensated lifting wavelet and its application in video coding. In *IEEE International Conference on Multimedia and Expo*, pages 365 – 368, August 2001.

Chapter 6

Error Resilient H.264 Video Encoder with Lagrange Multiplier Optimization Based on Channel Situation

Jian Feng, Yu Chen, Kwok-Tung Lo and
Xu-Dong Zhang

Additional information is available at the end of the chapter

1. Introduction

Robust delivery of compressed video in wireless packet-switched networks is still a chal-lenging problem. Video packets transmitted in wireless environments are often corrupted by random and burst channel error due to multi-path fading, shadowing, noise disturbance, and congestion in physical wireless channel.

To achieve an optimum transmission over a noisy wireless channel, both the source coding and network should be jointly adapted. An acceptable video quality in wireless environ-ment can be obtained by the adjustment of parameters in video codec and wireless network. For the former, people have proposed many error resilient video encoding algorithms to en-hance the robust performance of the compressed video stream in wireless networks. These algorithms can be divided into three categories: 1) error detection and error concealment al-gorithms used at video decoder of wireless receiver; 2) error resilient video encoding algo-rithms located at video encoder of wireless transmitter; 3) robust error control between video encoder and decoder based on 1) and 2). Fig.1 summarizes different techniques at dif-ferent parts of a wireless video transmission system.

Since error concealment algorithms are only used at video decoder in wireless receiver, they do not require any modification of video encoder and channel codec. Hence, there is not any increase of coding computing complexity and transmission rate. Therefore, error conceal-ment algorithms can be easily realized in present wireless video transmission system. How-ever, since error concealment algorithms make full use of spatial and temporal correlation in video stream to estimate the corrupted region of video frames, when the correlation be-tween corrupted region and correctly received frames is weak, error concealment algorithms

cannot achieve good effect so that there is apparent distortion in repaired reconstructed video frames. In addition, although error concealment algorithms can reduce the intensity of
temporal error propagation, it cannot reduce the length of temporal error propagation. As
we know, human visual system (HVS) is not very sensitive to short term obvious error
propagation while long term even slight error propagation will annoy the observation of
HVS impressively. Therefore, desirable error repaired effect should make the intensity and
length of error propagation minimum simultaneously.

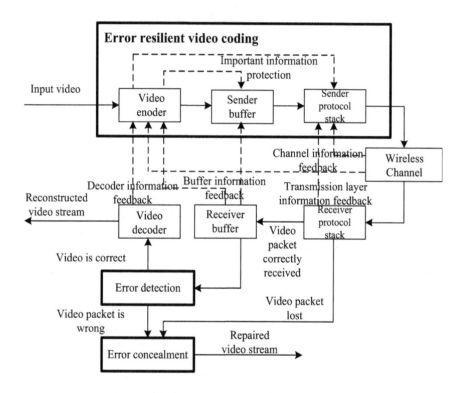

Figure 1. Error resilient methods used in packet-switched wireless networks

In a practical wireless video transmission system, one entire frame is normally encapsulated
into one video packet in order to make full use of limited wireless bandwidth. In this situation, any loss of one video packet would degrade image quality of successive frames in video decoder apparently since existing video standards utilize inter-frame prediction to make
high compression efficiency. Hence, many error resilient methods have been developed to
reduce the impacts of errors and improve the video quality in wireless video transmission in
recent years [1-4]. However, most of the previously developed algorithms mitigate coding
efficiency by adding redundancy to the video stream to enhance error resilient performance.

As mentioned, real time wireless video applications are very sensitive to the increase of coding overhead in [5], which may not only result in additional delay that makes correctly received video packets invalid, but also deteriorate the quality of service in wireless environment especially in ad hoc networks [6]. Therefore, it is necessary to make compressed video stream more resilient to errors at minimum expense of coding overhead.

In order to overcome the error propagation effect caused by video packet losses, long term memory motion-compensated prediction [7] is a reasonable way to suppress error propagation in the temporal domain at the cost of reducing the coding efficiency. In [8], the selection of reference frame in long-term motion compensated prediction is proposed for H.263 video with referring to the rate-distortion optimization (RDO) criteria. As a further work of [8], based on the original RDO model in error free condition, an error robust RDO (ER-RDO) method has been proposed in [9] for H.264 video in packet lost environment by redefining the Lagrange parameter and error-prone RD model. However, the ER-RDO method still requires a very high computational complexity to accurately determine the expected decoder distortion. To reduce the computational burden, Zhang et al. [10] developed a simplified version of the ER-RDO method by making full use of block-based distortion map to estimate the end to end distortion. Since the selected Lagrange parameters in these two methods are not precise enough to make corresponding rate distortion optimization, their cost for coding overhead for real time wireless video communication system is not desirable.

In the periodic frame method [11], a periodic frame is only predicted by previous l reference video frame, which is the previous periodic frame. l is the frame interval between neighboring periodic frames. When the frames between two periodic frames are lost, second periodic frame is still decoded correctly, so error propagation can be suppressed efficiently. However, the coding overhead of periodic frame increases obviously when the correlation between neighboring periodic frames is not high. To alleviate the heavy burden on wireless channel resulted by periodic frame, Zheng et al. also proposed the periodic macroblock (PMB) method [11] to reduce the increase of coding overhead by selecting only certain number of important MBs to be predicted by previous l reference video frame. PMB can effectively control the coding overhead with the sacrifice of the error reconstruction effect. Another effective way to constrain error propagation is to insert intracoded MBs. Compared to long term reference frame prediction, it needs more redundancy by adopting the intracoded mode. To obtain a better trade-off between the coding efficiency and error resilient performance, the methods based on accurate block-based distortion estimation model [12] [13] were developed for MPEG4 and H.261/3. The end-to-end approach in [12] generalized the RD optimized mode selection for point-to-point video communication by taking into account both the packet loss and the receiver's concealment method. In [13], the encoder computes an optimal estimate of the total distortion at decoder for a given rate, packet loss condition, and the concealment method. The distortion estimation is then incorporated within an RD framework to optimally select the coding mode for each macroblock. Both methods achieved better error resilient performance. However, their computational complexity and implementation cost are too high.

In this chapter, we develop a new channel based rate distortion (RD) model for error resilient H.264 video codec, which aims at minimizing the coding overhead increase while maintaining a good error resilience performance. In the new RD model, the practical channel conditions like packet lost rate (PLR) and packet lost burst length (PLBL), error propagation and error concealment effects in different reference frames are taken into consideration in analyzing the expected MB-based distortion at encoder. Moreover, for each reference frame, its corresponding Lagrange parameter is adjusted according to the variation of the channel based RD model, which can more accurately describe the relationship between coding rate and expected distortion at decoder in the sense of packet lost environment than other existing methods. Moreover, in our proposed new RD model, a proper intra-coded mode for error resilient performance is also considered. Therefore, more appropriate reference frame and encoding mode can be selected for each MB with the proposed method.

In the following of this chapter, a brief review on the error-robust rate-distortion optimization (ER-RDO) method is given in Section 2. The derivation of our proposed error resilient rate distortion (RD) optimization will be described in the same section. In section 3, the error resilient performance of the proposed method and some existing methods will be evaluated using computer simulations on H.264 video codec. Finally, some concluding remarks will be given in Section 4.

2. The proposed error resilience optimization method

As the latest video coding standard, H.264 has supreme coding performance by adopting lots of advanced techniques [14]. With the rate distortion optimization (RDO) operation, H.264 achieves a very good coding efficiency and a high PSNR simultaneously in error free condition. For encoding m^{th} MB in n^{th} frame, the RDO operation can find its most proper coding mode and reference frame by minimizing the cost as follows:

$$J_{org}(n,m,r,o) = D_s(n,m,r,o) + \lambda R(n,m,r,o) \tag{1}$$

where $D_s(n,m,r,o)$ and $R(n,m,r,o)$ are the source distortion and the coding rate when the MB is predicted by r^{th} reference frame and encoded with mode o. In an error free environment, the Lagrange parameter can be determined by the quantization parameter Q as follows [15]

$$\lambda = \begin{cases} 0.85 \times Q^2 & : (H.263) \\ 0.85 \times 2^{Q/3} & : (H.264) \end{cases} \tag{2}$$

However, the cost in (1) doesn't consider the distortion caused by error propagation and error concealment. Therefore, it cannot be directly used for finding the best reference frame and encoding mode in an error prone wireless packet-switched network if the channel condition is taken into consideration.

2.1. ER-RDO model

To take into account the packet lost effect, an error robust RDO (ER-RDO) method was developed in [11] by redefining the Lagrange parameter and error-prone RD model based on the practical wireless channel situation and potential decoded MB corrupted distortion. In the ER-RDO model, the expected overall distortion of mth MB in n^{th} frame is determined as

$$D_e(n,m,r,o) = (1-p)p_c D_s(n,m,r,o) + pD_{ec} + (1-p)(1-p_c)D_{ep} \qquad (3)$$

where D_{ec} is the error concealment distortion if this MB is lost, and D_{ep} represents the expected error propagation distortion in the case that this MB is received correctly but the reference frames are erroneous. p is the current wireless channel packet loss rate (PLR), and p_c is the probability that all reference frames are correct, which is computed by

$$p_c = (1-p)^k \qquad (4)$$

where k is the number of reference frames in the encoder buffer.

If we assume high-resolution quantization, the source distortion D_s depends on the rate (R) as follows [9]:

$$D_s(R) = \beta \times 2^{-\alpha R} \qquad (5)$$

where α and β parameterize the functional relationship between rate and distortion [13]. If uniform quantization is used, then we have

$$D_s(\Delta) = \Delta^2 / 12 \qquad (6)$$

where Δ is the quantization step size.

Referring to (5) and (6), the selected Lagrange parameter in ER-RDO model is computed as

$$\lambda_{ER-RDO} = -\frac{dD}{d\Delta}\frac{d\Delta}{dR} = (1-p)p_c\lambda \qquad (7)$$

With λ_{ER-RDO}, (3) and (4), the best reference frame r^* and encoding mode o^* for m^{th} MB in n^{th} frame selected as in [11] are determined as follows.

$$(r^*,o^*) = \arg\min(p_c D_s(n,m,r,o) + (1 - p_c)D_{ep}(n,m,r,o) + p_c \lambda R(n,m,r,o)) = \arg\min(p_c J_{org}(n,m,r,o) + (1 - p_c)D_{ep}(n,m,r,o)) \qquad (8)$$

From (4) and (7), we can find that the selected λ_{ER-RDO} in each reference frame is identical when the number of reference frame and PLR is known. That is to say, the correlation between the coding rate and expected overall distortion for all reference frames is equal. However, as we know, when the distance between the selected reference frame and the present encoding frame turns to be longer, the probability of correct reconstruction of this frame at receiver is higher with the degradation of the coding efficiency. Therefore, the term $(1 - p_c)D_{ep}$ in (8) is not accurate enough (a comprehensive interpretation will be given in next subsection). So in the sense of error resilience, the correlation between the coding rate and expected overall distortion for each reference frame at decoder should be different and be varied according to not only PLR and the range of reference frame, but also the distance between the selected reference predicted frame and the present encoding frame.

2.2. The proposed channel based RDO model

To overcome the problems of the ER-RDO model for H.264 video, we propose a new channel based RDO model to more accurately trade-off the coding efficiency and error resilient performance. For n^{th} video frame to be encoded, there are k reference frames in encoder buffer, namely $n-1$, $n-2$… $n-k$, as illustrated in Fig.2.

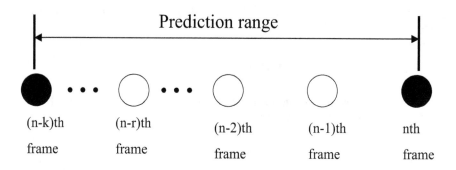

Prediction range

(n-k)th frame   (n-r)th frame   (n-2)th frame   (n-1)th frame   nth frame

Figure 2. Inter-coded prediction reference frame range

The estimated cost for n^{th} frame predicted by $n-r$ $(1 \leq r \leq k)$ reference frame is

$$J_p(n,n-r) = D_p(n,n-r) + \lambda_r R(n,n-r) \qquad (9)$$

where $R(n,n-r)$ is the coding overhead of nth frame predicted by n-r reference frame, and referring to (3),$D_p(n,n-r)$ is the expected overall distortion of nth frame at decoder in the proposed channel based RDO model with n-r reference frame. It is given by

$$D_p(n,n-r) = (1-p)^{k+1}(D_s(n,n-r) + D_{lep}) + (1-p)(1-(1-p)^k)D_{ep_r} + pD_{ec} \tag{10}$$

where $D_s(n,n-r)$ is the source distortion predicted by n-r reference frame in error free situation, D_{lep} is distortion caused by the long term error propagation when frames before reference frames are lost. And D_{ep_r} is the potential distortion caused by the frame loss in the range of reference frame when $n\text{-}r$ frame is the reference frame, which can be computed as followed.

$$D_{ep_r} = \sum_{j=r}^{k} D_{r_{j+1}} q_{ep}(r,j) + q_s(r)D_s(n,n-r) \tag{11}$$

For computing D_{ep_r} as in (11), it includes two parts: one is the error propagation distortion caused by $n\text{-}k$, $n\text{-}k\text{+}1\dots n\text{-}r$ reference frame. The term $D_{r_{j+1}}$ in (11) is error concealment reconstruction distortion when $n\text{-}j$ frame is lost $(r \le j \le k)$, and its corresponding occurrence probability is

$$q_{ep}(r,j) = p(1-p)^{k-j} \tag{12}$$

When the frames after present reference frame $n\text{-}r$ are lost, present encoding frame n can still be decoded correctly, this occurrence probability is computed as

$$q_s(r) = (1-p)^{k-r}(1-(1-p)^r) \tag{13}$$

So another part is the multiplying results of $q_s(r)$ and $D_s(n,n-r)$ as in (11).

With (9), (10) and (11), the final estimate cost for n^{th} frame predicted by $n\text{-}r$ reference frame is

$$
\begin{aligned}
J_p(n,n-r) &= (1-p)^{k+1}(D_s(n,n-r) + D_{lep}) + (1-p)(1-(1-p)^{k+1})D_{ep_r} + pD_{ec} + \lambda_r R(n,n-r) \\
&= (1-p)^{k+1}(D_s(n,n-r) + D_{lep}) + pD_{ec} + \lambda_r R(n,n-r) \\
&\quad + (1-p)(1-(1-p)^k)(\sum_{j=r}^{k} D_{r_{j+1}} q_{ep}(r,j) + q_s(r)D_s(n,n-r))
\end{aligned}
\tag{14}
$$

Finally, $J_p(n,n-r)$ is computed as

$$J_p(n,n-r) = ((1-p)^{2k+1} + (1-p)^{k-r+1} - (1-p)^{2k-r+1})D_s(n,n-r) + (1-p)^{k+1}D_{lep} + (1-p)(1-(1-p)^k)\sum_{j=r}^{k} D_{r_{j+1}} p(1-p)^{k-r} + pD_{ec} + \lambda_r R(n,n-r) \tag{15}$$

So with the derivatives of $J_p(n,n-r)$ for Δ as (7), the optimized Lagrange parameter for present encoding frame n predicted by reference frame n-r is obtained by

$$\lambda_r = -\frac{dD(n,n-r)}{d\Delta}\frac{d\Delta}{dR} = ((1-p)^{2k+1} + (1-p)^{k-r+1} - (1-p)^{2k-r+1})\lambda \qquad (16)$$

where we assume that the buffer length of reference frame k is larger than real-time PLBL obtained from the feedback of wireless channel situation.

2.3. Implementation of reference frame and mode selection algorithm

With the results obtained before, we apply the proposed channel based RDO model to select the best reference frame and encoding mode in an H.264 encoder as follows. For one MB in P frame, it has two categories of encoding modes: intracoded and intercoded. Intracoded modes include direct coding, *intra_4×4* and *intra_16×16*; intercoded modes include *inter_16×16*, *inter_16×8*, *inter_8×16* and *inter_P8×8* mode (this mode is composed of *inter_8×8*, *inter_8×4*, *inter_4×8* and *inter_4×4 sub 8×8* block modes). For each intercoded mode, the best reference predicted frame r^* for m^{th} MB in n^{th} frame in coding mode o is selected by finding the minimum cost of interceded mode$J_p(n, m, o, r)$.

$$J_p(n,m,o,r^*) = \arg\min(J_p(n,m,o,r))$$
$$= \arg\min(D_p(n,m,o,r) + \lambda_r R(n,m,o,r))$$
$$= \arg\min(((1-p)^{2k+1} + (1-p)^{k-r+1} - (1-p)^{2k-r+1})D_s(n,m,o,r) \qquad (17)$$
$$+(1-p)^{k+1}D_{lep} + (1-p)(1-(1-p)^k)\sum_{j=r}^{k} D_{r_{j+1}}p(1-p)^{k-r} + pD_{ec} + \lambda_r R(n,m,o,r))$$

where r^* is best reference predicted frame in coding mode o. Since $(1-p)^{k+1}D_{lep}$is same for any reference frame to predict n^{th} frame, andD_{ec} is independent of encoding modes and reference frame [8], (17) can be simplified to

$$J_p(n,m,o,r^*) = \arg\min(((1-p)^{2k+1} + (1-p)^{k-r+1} - (1-p)^{2k-r+1})D_s(n,m,o,r)$$
$$+(1-p)(1-(1-p)^k)\sum_{j=r}^{k} D_{r_{j+1}}p(1-p)^{k-r} + \lambda_r R(n,m,o,r)) \qquad (18)$$
$$= \arg\min(\alpha_r(D_s(n,m,o,r) + \beta_r \sum_{j=r}^{n} D_{r_{j+1}}p(1-p)^{n-j} + \lambda R(n,m,o,r)))$$
$$= \arg\min(\alpha_r(J_{org}(n,m,o,r) + \beta_r D_{referror}(r)))$$

$$a_r = \lambda_r / \lambda, \beta_r = \frac{(1-p)(1-(1-p)^k)}{\alpha_r} \tag{19}$$

$$D_{referror}(r) = \sum_{j=r}^{k} D_{r_{j-1}} p(1-p)^{n-r} \tag{20}$$

And then, the best encoding mode o^* in intercoded mode is

$$J_P(n,m,o^*,r^*) = \arg\min(J_P(n,m,o,r^*)) \tag{21}$$

For the best intracoded mode o^{**} for this MB, it can be determined as follows with the cost for intracoded mode $J_i(n, m, o, 0)$.

$$
\begin{aligned}
J_i(n,m,o^{**},0) &= \arg\min(J_i(n,m,o,0)) \\
&= \arg\min((1-p)D_s(n,m,o,0) + pD_{ec} + (1-p)\lambda R(n,m,o,0)) \\
&= \arg\min((1-p)J_{org}(n,m,o,0) + pD_{ec})
\end{aligned}
\tag{22}
$$

As the final results, the best encoding mode $\hat{o}$ and its potential best reference predicted frame $\hat{r}$ in the sense of optimized error resilience for m^{th} MB in n^{th} frame are found as

$$J_{best}(n,m,\hat{o},\hat{r}) = \arg\min(J_P(n,m,o^*,r^*), J_I(n,m,o^{**},0)) \tag{23}$$

3. Experimental results

In this section, we evaluate the performance of the proposed channel based RDO model in terms of video quality and coding efficiency in wireless packet lost environment. In our experiments, we use H.264 JM 8.2 codec as test platform where video stream structure is selected as IPPP.... Three standard QCIF video sequences, namely Salesman, Susie and Foreman, are used in the simulations. The range of tested intracoded frames in these sequences is from 10th to 100th frame. Their QP is set as 28, their frame rate in H.264 JM8.2 is 30 fps, and their buffer of reference frames includes previous five frames. In order to make full use of wireless channel bandwidth, each compressed video frame is transmitted by a single packet. A simple error concealment method is used to make analysis of potential error propagation and error concealment effect at video encoder. When a MB is assumed to be lost, it will be replaced by the MB at same position in the previous error free frame. As a comparison, we use the original H.264 JM8.2 codec, the periodic frame method, the PMB method [11] and ER-RDO method [8] as reference algorithms. In addition, for the PMB method, we use PMB (11%), and PMB (22%) and PMB (33%) to denote the corresponding performance when the proportions of periodic MB in video frame are 11%, 22% and 33% respectively.

We first look at the error resilience performance of the proposed method by considering the PSNR performance of the reconstructed video under a packet loss environment. Fig.3 shows the error reconstruction effect of three test sequences using different methods when PLR = 0.1 and PLBL < 5. At each point in Fig.3, it is an average PSNR result when any reference frame of present encoding frame is lost.

It is shown in Fig.3 that the proposed method always achieves the best reconstruction effect for the three test sequences when compared with other methods. In Fig.3 (a), for Salesman sequence with low motion scene, the proposed method outperforms H.264 JM8.2, PMB (11%), PMB (22%), PMB (33%) and ER-RDO with an average PSNR improvement of 1.18dB, 1.14dB, 1.04dB, 0.8dB and 0.2dB, respectively. In Fig.3 (b), for Susie sequence with moderate motion scene, the proposed method performs better than H.264 JM8.2, PMB (11%), and PMB (22%), PMB (33%) and ER-RDO with an average PSNR improvement of 2.48dB, 2.03dB, 1.43dB, 0.13db and 0.21dB, respectively. In Fig.3 (c), for Foreman sequence with high motion scene, the proposed method achieves better results than H.264 JM8.2, PMB (11%), and PMB (22%), PMB (33%) and ER-RDO with an average PSNR improvement of 3.61dB, 3.04dB, 2.45dB, 1.72db and 0.53dB, respectively. As a conclusion, the proposed method can achieve more robust error resilient performance in different video scenes.

For evaluating the coding efficiency of different methods, we consider their impacts on overall coding rate requirement and PSNR performance of reconstructed video in error free environment. The simulation results for the three test sequences are listed in Table 1, 2 and 3 respectively. It is seen that all of the error resilient methods have little effect on original video quality. For fair comparisons, the PSNR performance of the reconstructed video is more or less kept constant for different methods. We then compare the coding rate required for each method.

Method	PSNR-Y (dB)	PSNR-U (dB)	PSNR-V (dB)	Bit rate (kb/s)	Increase (%)
H.264 JM 8.2	35.57	39.6	40.14	56.83	0%
Periodic Frame FFFrame	35.54	39.61	40.19	60.08	5.72%
PMB (33%)	35.54	39.59	40.15	57.48	1.14%
PMB (22%)	35.59	39.61	40.17	57.05	0.39%
PMB (11%)	35.59	39.59	40.17	57.03	0.35%
ER-RDO	35.61	39.66	40.23	60.4	6.28%
The proposed method	35.57	39.6	40.15	57.14	0.54%

Table 1. Coding rate comparison of different methods in *Salesman* sequence

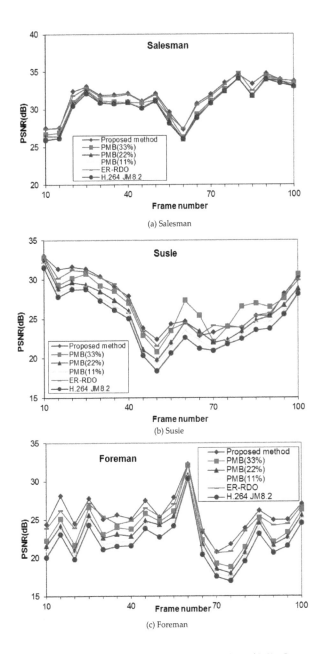

(a) Salesman

(b) Susie

(c) Foreman

Figure 3. Reconstruction effect comparison of different methods when PLR = 0.1 and PLBL < 5

Table 1 shows the coding rate requirement of different methods for *Salesman* sequence, in which there is high correlation between reference frames and encoding frame. It is noted that the coding redundancy resulted in all methods is smallest among the three test sequences. The coding rate increase of ER-RDO method is not desirable as it needs more bits than the periodic frame method, while the PMB method in different level of long term predicted MB can obtain less rate increase. The coding overhead increase of the proposed method is not obvious as it is only slightly larger than PMB (11%) and PMB (22%) and apparently smaller than PMB (33%).

Method	PSNR-Y (dB)	PSNR-U (dB)	PSNR-V (dB)	Bit rate (kb/s)	Increase (%)
H.264 JM 8.2	37.26	43.54	43.28	95.56	0%
Periodic Frame	37.24	43.59	43.37	108.91	13.97%
PMB (33%)	37.23	43.59	43.29	102.41	7.17%
PMB (22%)	37.26	43.62	43.27	99.76	4.39%
PMB (11%)	37.25	43.55	43.32	97.78	2.32%
ER-RDO	37.29	43.64	43.28	100.82	5.50%
The proposed method	37.26	43.56	43.24	95.75	0.2%

Table 2. Coding rate comparison of different methods in *Susie* sequence

For *Susie* sequence where the correlation between reference frames and encoding frame is moderate, the coding overhead is in general more than that of *Salesman* sequence, as shown in Table 2. It is noted that the coding rate of the periodic frame method has increased about 14%, which is a heavy burden for wireless channel. The coding rate increase of ER-RDO is smaller than PMB (33%), while it is still more than PMB (11%) and PMB (22%). The coding rate of the proposed method is just 0.2% higher than that of H.264 JM 8.2 but smaller than all other methods.

Method	PSNR-Y (dB)	PSNR-U (dB)	PSNR-V (dB)	Bit rate (kb/s)	Increase (%)
H.264 JM 8.2	35.72	39.04	40.72	109.17	0%
Periodic Frame	35.74	39.17	40.84	129.07	18.23%
PMB (33%)	35.69	39.14	40.78	116.41	6.63%
PMB (22%)	35.7	39.06	40.7	113.79	4.23%
PMB (11%)	35.71	39.03	40.75	112.46	3.01%
ER-RDO	35.73	39.04	40.75	116.62	6.82%
The proposed method	35.72	39.05	40.76	111.28	1.93%

Table 3. Coding rate comparison of different methods in *Foreman* sequenc

For *Foreman* sequence, as there is low correlation between reference frames and encoding frame, the required coding rate of all methods is largest in among the three test sequences, as shown in Table 3. Again, our proposed method achieves the best coding efficiency. The coding rate increase of the proposed method is only 1.93%, while that of PMB (11%), PMB (22%), PMB (33%), ER-RDO and the periodic frame method is 3.01%, 4.23%, 6.63%, 6.82% and 18.23%, respectively.

As a conclusion with the results of error resilient performance and the coding efficiency, the proposed method can obtain not only more satisfying video reconstruction effect but also smaller coding rate increase than the reference methods.

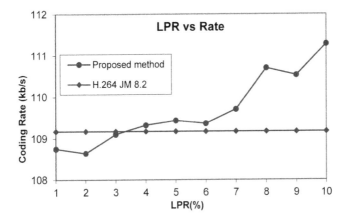

Figure 4. The coding rate (kb/s) of the proposed method with respect to original H.264 JM 8.2 codec in different PLR from 0.01% to 0.1%

Fig.4 shows the coding efficiency of the proposed method in different PLR from 0.01% to 0.1% of Foreman sequence. In Fig.4, we can find that the increase of coding rate using the proposed method is small when compared with that of H.264 JM 8.2 codec. Even in some instances of low LPR of Fig.4, the proposed method can achieve a slightly smaller coding rate than the original H.264 JM 8.2 codec.

As a further analysis on error resilient performance of the proposed method with respect to the PMB and ER-RDO method, Table 4, 5 and 6 give more detailed reconstruction PSNR (dB) effect comparison in Salesman, Susie and Foreman sequences when each of the reference frames in encoder buffer is lost. From the tables, we can find that the PMB method, especially PMB (33%) can achieve better results when the lost reference frame is far away from present encoding frame. On the contrary, ER-RDO can obtain better reconstruction effect when lost reference frame is near to present encoding frame. Our proposed method achieves a compromise between the two methods and obtains better average error reconstruction performance. In addition, it is always better than H.264 JM 8.2 when any reference frame in the encoder buffer is lost.

Lost reference frame	Proposed method	PMB (33%)	PMB (22%)	PMB (11%)	ER-RDO	H.264 JM8.2
1	34.04	32.63	32.41	32.31	34.06	32.29
2	32.56	31.65	31.37	31.27	32.49	31.21
3	31.54	30.83	30.5	30.37	31.34	30.31
4	30.7	30.17	29.78	29.67	30.4	29.58
5	29.99	29.57	29.57	29.57	29.6	29.57

Table 4. Reconstruction PSNR (dB) comparison of different methods in *Salesman* sequence

Lost reference frame	Proposed method	PMB (33%)	PMB (22%)	PMB (11%)	ER-RDO	H.264 JM8.2
1	31.74	30.03	28.37	27.65	32.48	26.99
2	28.42	28.31	26.59	25.84	28.98	25.15
3	26.2	27.1	25.41	24.63	25.73	23.96
4	24.86	26.29	24.58	23.82	23.87	23.16
5	23.92	23.07	23.07	23.07	23.07	23.07

Table 5. Reconstruction PSNR (dB) comparison of different methods in *Susie sequence*

Lost reference frame	Proposed method	PMB (33%)	PMB (22%)	PMB (11%)	ER-RDO	H.264 JM8.2
1	31.81	27.34	26.51	25.8	32.45	24.98
2	27.78	25.26	24.31	23.58	27.95	22.77
3	24.7	23.83	22.86	22.1	23.37	21.32
4	22.63	22.73	21.77	21.03	21.3	20.3
5	21.06	20.23	20.23	20.23	20.24	20.23

Table 6. Reconstruction PSNR (dB) comparison of different methods in *Foreman* sequence

4. Conclusions

In this paper, an error resilient method based on the feedback of wireless channel condition is proposed for robust H.264 video stream transmitted in wireless packet lost environment. The proposed method can smartly adjust Lagrange parameter for each reference frame at encoder buffer by adopting proposed channel based RDO model. The modified Lagrange parameter can better reflect the association between the expected distortion and coding efficiency of video streaming in the sense of error resilience in packet lost environments. Comprehensive experimental results show that the proposed method sufficiently absorbs the advantages of existing methods and achieves better error resilient performance with minimum increase of coding overhead.

Acknowledgements

The work of J. Feng was supported by the Hong Kong Baptist University under Grant Number RG2/09-10/080. The work of K.-T.Lo was supported by the Hong Kong Polytechnic University under Grant Number G-YH58 and G-YJ29.

Author details

Jian Feng[1], Yu Chen[2,3], Kwok-Tung Lo[3] and Xu-Dong Zhang[2]

1 Dept. of Computer Science, Hong Kong Baptist Uni., HK

2 Dept. of Electronic Eng., Tsinghua Uni., Beijing, China

3 Dept. of Electronic and Info. Eng., Hong Kong Polytechnic Uni., HK

References

[1] Wang Y., Wenger S., Wen J., and Katsaggelos K.K. Error resilient video coding techniques. IEEE Signal Processing Magazine 2000, 17(4), 61-82.

[2] Vetro A., Xin J., and Sun H.F. Error resilience video transcoding for wireless communication. IEEE Wireless Communication 2005., 12(4), 14-21.

[3] Stockhammer T., Hannuksela M.M., and Wiegand T. H.264/AVC in wireless environments. IEEE Trans. Circuits Syst. Video Technol. 2003, 13(7), 657-673.

[4] Hsiao Y.M., Lee J.F., Chen J.S. and Chu Y.S. H.264 video transmissions over wireless networks: Challenges and solutions. Computer Communications 2011, 34(14), 1661-1672.

[5] Katsaggelos A.K., Eisenberg Y., Zhai F., Berry R., and Pappas T.N. Advances in efficient resource allocation for packet-based real-time video transmission. Proceedings of the IEEE 2005, 93(1), 135-147.

[6] Zhu X.Q., Setton E., and Girod B. Congestion-distortion optimized video transmission over ad hoc networks. Signal Processing: Image Communication 2005, 20(8), 773-783.

[7]   Wiegand T., Zhang X., and Girod B. Long-term memory motion-compensated prediction. IEEE Trans. Circuits Syst. Video Technol. 1999, 9(2), 70–84.

[8]   T. Wiegand, Farber N., Stuhlmuller K., and Girod B. Error-resilient video transmission using long-term memory motion-compensated prediction. IEEE Journal on Selected Areas in Communications 2000, 18(3), 1050–1062.

[9]   T. Stockhammer, D. Kontopodis and T.Wiegand, "Rate-distortion optimization for JVT/H.26L coding in packet loss environment," Proc. PVW, Pittsburgh, PY, April 2002.

[10] Zhang Y., Gao W., Lo Y., Huang Q.M. and Zhao D. Joint Source-Channel Rate-Distortion Optimization for H.264 Video Coding Over Error-Prone Networks. IEEE Trans. Multimedia 2007, 9(3), 445-454.

[11] Zheng J.H. and Chau L.P. Error-resilient coding of H.264 based on periodic macroblock. IEEE Trans. Broadcasting 2006, 52(2), 223-229.

[12] Wu D., Hou Y.T., Li B., Zhu W., Zhang Y.Q. and Chao H.J. An end to end approach for optimal mode selection in Internet video communication. IEEE Journal on Selected Areas in Communications 2000, 18(6), 977-995.

[13] Zhang R., Regunathan S.L. and Rose K. Video coding with optimal inter/intra-mode switching for packet loss resilience. IEEE Journal on Selected Areas in Communications 2000, 18(6), 966-976.

[14] Wigand T., Sullivan G.J., Bjntegaard G., and Luthra A. Overview of the H.264/AVC video coding standard. IEEE Trans. Circuits Syst. Video Technol. 2003, 13(7), 560-576.

[15] Wiegand T. and Girod B. Lagrange multiplier selection in hybrid video coder control. Proc. ICIP '01, 2001: 542-545.

Chapter 7

Side View Driven Facial Video Coding

Ulrik Söderström and Haibo Li

Additional information is available at the end of the chapter

1. Introduction

Video compression is a task that is becoming more and more interesting as the use of video is growing rapidly. Video is today part of the daily life for anyone with a computer, e.g., video sites as Youtube [1] and video commercials on regular web sites. The network capacity is growing and one could assume that this would reduce the need for more efficient video compression. But since the use of video, and other types of data, is growing even faster than the capacity growth better ways for compression are needed. Furthermore, video is wanted for low capacity networks where high compression of video is essential for transmission so the need of efficient video compression is therefore also growing. The users are becoming used to a certain service and expects to have the same kind of service everywhere.

Video compression based on Discrete Cosine Transform (DCT) and motion estimation (ME) has almost reached its potential when it comes to compression ratio so to supply the users with the video capacity they want it is necessary to use different kinds of video coding techniques than the ones which are used today. These techniques function very well at reasonably high bitrates but when the bitrate is very low they fail to work properly. Of course, it is desirable to have a video compression scheme that works on arbitrary video but in this work we focus on facial video; video where the facial mimic is the most prominent and important information.

We have previously presented a coding scheme based on principal component analysis (PCA) [2] that make use of the fact that it is the facial mimic which is the most important part for facial video [3]. We have also calculated theoretical boundaries for the use of such a coding scheme [4]. We have extended the use of PCA into asymmetrical PCA (aPCA) [5] where a part of the frame is used for encoding and the entire frame is decoded. In this work we will show how aPCA can be used for encoding of one part of the frame while decoding uses a different part of the frame. More specifically we will use the side view or the profile of the side view of a face for encoding and decode the frontal view of this face.

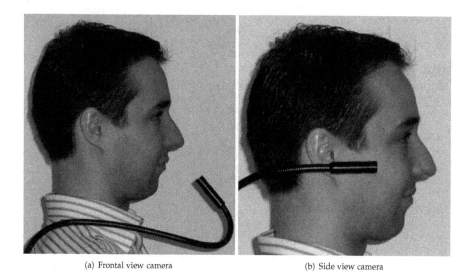

(a) Frontal view camera   (b) Side view camera

Figure 1. The face captured by cameras filming the frontal and side view of a person.

Encoding with the side view gives a huge benefit in usability since the user can wear a camera that films the side of the face instead of the front of the face. From a user point of view this turns video capturing into something which is performed without any inconvenience such as a camera in front of the face would mean. The differences are visualized in Fig. 1. For communication purposes you want to see the frontal view of a face. Humans usually wants to talk to someone who is facing them.

Communication with video where you can see the face of the person you are communicating with has not become the important application that is was predicted to be. Video telephone calls are used much less then it was thought. But still, the use of visual communication is growing over the Internet, with the use of popular communication applications, e.g. Skype. For this kind of communication the users usually sit in front of their computers with a fixed web camera; thus enabling hands-free usage. With aPCA hands-free usage can be realized even for mobile users. For all users the bitrate for transmitting the video can be drastically lowered so the scheme is not only beneficial for mobile users; low bitrate is wanted in all usage settings.

For some tasks video is superior to only voice since you can infer a lot of information from the facial appearance. If it can be provided when the user has both hands free and can move freely, it will improve the quality of communication. If the user has to hold a camera or be positioned in front of a camera you limit the users freedom to move as they have to be positioned in front of a fixed camera. The side view of a face can easily be filmed and this view can be used to encode video while the frontal view of the face is decoded.

The video coding that we present in this article describes a new way to encode video; the decoded part is not even used for encoding. This idea has been used for several other techniques (see section 2) but in these implementations real video is not decoded; they provide an avatar, an animation or a cartoon-like frame. aPCA coding creates real video frames (frontal view) from a video content that is not decoded (side view) but is much easier accessible for encoding.

Section 2 describes related work in very low bitrate video compression and section 3 describes PCA video coding. Section 4 explains how two views are used for encoding and decoding while section 5 show how only partial information from one view can be used for encoding while the entire second view is decoded. Section 6 show the results from practical experiments and the work is concluded in section 7.

2. Related work

Discrete Cosine Transform (DCT) is regarded as state-of-the-art for video compression and it is used together with motion estimation in most standard video codecs [6, 7]. But such a representation requires bitrates which are too high for low capacity networks, such as GSM. And as a consequence, video encoded with DCT does not have enough quality at very low bitrates. A previous technique that was aimed at videoconferencing at low bitrates based on DCT is called H.263 [8, 9]. Since this solution was based on DCT it didn't provide good enough quality when the bitrate was as low as over mobile networks. There are several other ways to represent facial images so that it can be transmitted over low capacity networks. Matching pursuit (MP) [10] is a technique that uses an alphabet where the encoder divides the video frames into features and the decoder assembles the features to a reconstructed frame. Very low bitrate is achieved by only transmitting information about which features that the frame consists of. A wireframe that resembles a face is used by several techniques, e.g., MPEG4 facial animation [11] and model based coding [12, 13]. The wireframe is texture-mapped with a facial image to give it a more natural appearance. Very low bitrate is achieved since only information about how to alter the wireframe is needed to make the face change shape between frames. The wireframe consists of several polygons; one of the most popular being the CANDIDE model, which comes in several versions [14]. Active Appearance Model (AAM) [15] relies on a statistical model of the shapes and pixel intensity of a face for video compression. AAM are statistical models; models of the shape of an object. The models are iteratively deformed so that they fit an object. For facial coding a model of the facial features are mapped onto a facial image. The model cannot vary in any possible way; it is constrained by the changes which occur within a training set. A comparative study of several AAM implementations can be found in [16]. Since the introduction of Microsoft Kinect sensor [17] which provide low-cost depth images solutions that use the Kinect to add quality to the extraction of facial features have been implemented. A better extraction of the facial features enable a much more accurate use of them for visualization purposes. An example of such an implementation is provided by Weise et al. [18] where they use facial animation as output and video recorded with the Kinect sensor as input.

The techniques which are noted above have at least one vital drawback when it comes to usage in visual communication. The face exhibits so many tiny creases and wrinkles that it is impossible to model with animations or low spatial resolution so high quality video is superior to animations [19]. To preserve the resolution and natural look of a face Wang and Cohen used teleconferencing over low bandwidth networks with a framerate of one frame each 2-3 seconds [20]. But to sacrifice framerate to preserve resolution is not acceptable either since they are both important for many visual tasks [21]. Any technique that want to provide video at very low bitrates must be able to provide video with high spatial resolution, high framerate and have natural-looking appearance. We have previously shown that PCA can overcome these deficits for encoding of facial video sequences [3]. Both Crowley [22] and Torres [23] have also made implementation where they use PCA to encode facial images. We have further improved PCA coding with asymmetrical PCA (aPCA) [5]. In the following sections we describe video coding based on PCA and aPCA. More extensive descriptions can be found in the references.

3. Principal component analysis video coding

Video coding based on Principal Component Analysis (PCA) is described in this section. A more detailed description and examples can be found in [3].

It is possible to decompose a video sequences into principal components and represent the video as a combination of these components. There are as many possible principal components as there are video frames N and each principal component is in fact an image. The space containing the facial images is called eigenspace Φ and this will be a space for a person's facial mimic when the eigenspace is extracted from a video where a person is displaying the basic emotions. Ohba *et.al.* provides a detailed explanation of such a personal mimic space [24]. The eigenspace $\Phi=\{\phi_1 \; \phi_2 \; ... \; \phi_N\}$ is constructed as

$$\phi_j = \sum_i b_{ij}(\mathbf{I}_i - \mathbf{I}_{\underline{0}})$$ (1)

where b_{ij} are eigenvalues from the eigenvectors of the covariance matrix $\{(\mathbf{I}_i - \mathbf{I}_{\underline{0}})^T(\mathbf{I}_j - \mathbf{I}_{\underline{0}})\}$. $\mathbf{I}_{\underline{0}}$ is the mean of all video frames and is constructed as:

$$\mathbf{I}_{\underline{0}} = \frac{1}{N} \sum_{j=1}^{N} \mathbf{I}_j$$ (2)

Projection coefficients $\{\alpha_j\}$ can be extracted from each video frame through projection:

$$\alpha_j = \phi_j(\mathbf{I} - \mathbf{I}_{\underline{0}})^T$$ (3)

It is then possible to represent a video frame as a combination of the principal components and the mean of all pixels. When all N principal components are used this representation is error-free:

$$\mathbf{I} = \mathbf{I}_{\underline{0}} + \sum_{j=1}^{N} \alpha_j \phi_j$$ (4)

The model is very compact and several principal components can be discarded with a very small error. A combination with fewer principal components M can be used to represent the image with a small error.

$$\hat{\mathbf{I}} = \mathbf{I}_{\underline{0}} + \sum_{j=1}^{M} \alpha_j \phi_j \qquad (5)$$

where M is a selected number of principal components used for reconstruction ($M < N$).

The sender and receiver use the same model for encoding and decoding and the only thing that needs to be transmitted between them are the projection coefficients. The sender extracts coefficients with the model and the receiver uses the coefficients with the model to recreate the video frames. This is very similar to the way that DCT-coding works since the sender and receiver uses the same model and only coefficients need to be transmitted.

The extent of the error incurred by using fewer components (M) than (N) is examined in [4]. With the model it is possible to encode entire video frames to only a few coefficients $\{\alpha_j\}$ and reconstruct the frames with high quality.

4. Asymmetrical principal component analysis video coding with encoding through the side view

There are two major drawbacks with the use of full frame encoding:

1. The information in the principal components are calculated from every pixel located in the frames. Pixels that aren't important for the facial mimic or belong to the background will have a large effect on the model if they have high variance.

2. The encoding and decoding complexity as well as the complexity for calculating the principal components are directly dependent on the number of pixels used in the calculations. High spatial resolution means a high complexity.

We have previously presented asymmetrical principal component analysis (aPCA) [5] where we use one part of a frame for encoding and decode the entire frame. This is possible to achieve through the use of pseudo principal components; information where not the entire frame is a principal component.

Previously we used foreground and the entire frame for aPCA. In this work we use a different kind of video sequences; where there are two facial views in the video. We have the side view of a face $\mathbf{I}^s$ and the frontal view of the face $\mathbf{I}^{fr}$ (Fig. 2).

We use the side view $\mathbf{I}^s$ for encoding and the frontal view $\mathbf{I}^{fr}$ for decoding. This is possible when there is a correspondence between the facial features in the two views. An eigenspace for the side view is constructed as:

$$\phi_j^s = \sum_i b_{ij}^s (\mathbf{I}_i^s - \mathbf{I}_{\underline{0}}^s) \qquad (6)$$

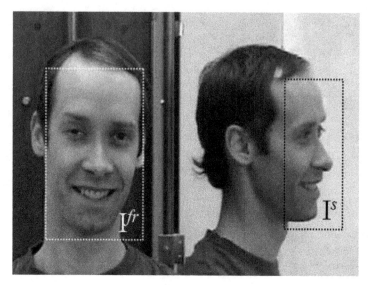

Figure 2. A video frame with the side $\mathbf{I}^s$ and front view $\mathbf{I}^{fr}$ shown.

where b_{ij}^s are eigenvalues from the eigenvectors of the covariance matrix $\{(\mathbf{I}_i^s - \mathbf{I}_{\underline{0}}^s)^T (\mathbf{I}_j^s - \mathbf{I}_{\underline{0}}^s)\}$ and $\mathbf{I}_{\underline{0}}^s$ is the mean of the side view. Encoding of video is performed as:

$$\alpha_j^s = (\mathbf{I}^s - \mathbf{I}_{\underline{0}}^s)^T \phi_j^s \qquad (7)$$

where $\{\alpha_j^s\}$ are coefficients extracted using information from the side view $\mathbf{I}^s$.

Since the frontal view should be decoded instead of the side view a space for decoding is needed. This is a space consisting of pseudo principal components where no no part of the components are orthogonal.

$$\phi_j^{p_{fr}} = \sum_i b_{ij}^s (\mathbf{I}_i^{fr} - \mathbf{I}_{\underline{0}}^{fr}) \qquad (8)$$

where $\mathbf{I}^{fr}$ is the frontal view of the frames and $\mathbf{I}_{\underline{0}}^{fr}$ is the mean image of the frontal view.

The coefficients from encoding with the side view are combined with this space for decoding.

$$\hat{\mathbf{I}}^{fr} = \mathbf{I}_{\underline{0}}^{fr} + \sum_{j=1}^{M} \alpha_j^s \phi_j^{p_{fr}} \qquad (9)$$

So, a decoded video of the frontal view can be created based only on information from the side view. The desired information is available through a much more easily-accessed information; this information is not even needed at the encode side. The side view is used for encoding and through the aPCA model the decoder can create the frontal view. The information that should be decoded is not needed for encoding.

aPCA models the correspondence between the views and it is easy to realize that such a correspondence exists. When, e.g., the mouth opens it gives rise to the same amount of change in the frontal and side view. The coefficients extracted from Eq. 7 are extracted from the change in the side view and it is the same change in the frontal view that is reconstructed in Eq. 9. Such reconstruction enables a easier use of hands-free equipment because it is more comfortable and easy to film the side of the face instead of the front of the face. The frontal view is always used for communication purposes so a decoded frontal view is fundamental for communication media. For communication through web cameras the sense of having eye-contact is often lost since the camera is not positioned in the screen; where the image(s) of the other(s) are shown. With a model where the eyes are looking at a screen this sense can be available since the information which is used for encoding does not affect the position of the decoded eyes.

The complexity for encoding is directly dependent on the spatial resolution of the frame that should be encoded. The important factor for complexity is $K * M$, where K is the number of pixels and M is the chosen number of eigenvectors. The complexity is reduced when two different views are used for encoding and decoding and there are fewer pixels in the view used for encoding.

5. Asymmetrical principal component analysis video coding with encoding through the profile

Instead of using the side view $\mathbf{I}^s$ for encoding we use the profile of the side view $\mathbf{X}^{pr}$. The profile of the side view is calculated as the pixel position of the edge between the face and the background in the side view and it is extracted through edge detection.

5.1. Edge detection

The profile is extracted from the side view through edge detection. Edge points are found by applying canny edge detection [25] to the image. The canny edge detector marks several edges in the picture (Fig. 3(a)) and the ones representing the edges between the side of the face and the background are selected by examining the pixel neighbors. The first pixel of the edge is chosen and each neighboring pixel which is an edge can be the next edge pixel. Clockwise pixels are selected ahead of counter-clockwise pixels and the selected edge for the entire side view is chosen. The facial mimic is dependent on changes in the area between the forehead and the mouth so the profile is calculated in this area. The pixel positions for the lip area are manually calculated as the edge of the lip instead of the edge between the face and the background. For each vertical position we extract one horizontal position (Fig. 3(b)). The side view $\mathbf{I}^s$ consists of the pixel intensities in the image:

$$\mathbf{I}^s = \begin{bmatrix} I(x_1, y_1) & I(x_2, y_1) & I(x_1, y_2) & \dots & I(x_h, y_v) \end{bmatrix} \tag{10}$$

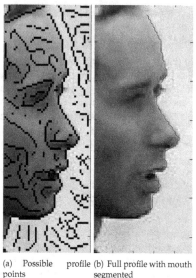

(a) Possible   profile (b) Full profile with mouth
points   segmented

Figure 3. Edge detection process. (a) Possible edges. (b) Chosen edge.

where $I(x,y)$ is the intensity for the specific pixel and h and v are the horizontal and vertical size of the images respectively. The profile only consist of the positions for the edges:

$$\mathbf{X}^{pr} = \left[x_{e_1}, y_{e_1}\ x_{e_2}\ x_{e_3}\ ...\ x_{e_T}\right] \tag{11}$$

where T is the number of points in the profile. The eigenprofile for encoding is calculated according to:

$$\phi_j^{pr} = \sum_i b_{ij}^{pr}(\mathbf{X}_i^{pr} - \mathbf{X}_{\underline{0}}^{pr}) \tag{12}$$

where $\mathbf{X}^{pr}$ are the profile of the side view, b_{ij}^{pr} are eigenvalues from the eigenvectors from the covariance matrix $\{(\mathbf{X}_i^{pr} - \mathbf{X}_{\underline{0}}^{pr})^T(\mathbf{X}_j^{pr} - \mathbf{X}_{\underline{0}}^{pr})\}$ and $\mathbf{X}_{\underline{0}}^{pr}$ is the mean image of the profile positions. $\mathbf{X}_{\underline{0}}^{pr}$ is shown in Fig. 4 and the first three eigenprofiles ϕ_j^{pr} are shown in Fig. 5.

A space for the frontal view is calculated similarly to when the profile is used for encoding as when the side view is used for encoding. The difference is that the eigenvectors from $(\mathbf{X}^{pr} - \mathbf{X}_{\underline{0}}^{pr})^T(\mathbf{X}^{pr} - \mathbf{X}_{\underline{0}}^{pr})$ are used instead of the eigenvectors from $(\mathbf{I}^s - \mathbf{I}_{\underline{0}}^s)^T(\mathbf{I}^s - \mathbf{I}_{\underline{0}}^s)$.

$$\phi_j^{p_{pr}} = \sum_i b_{ij}^{fr}(\mathbf{I}_i^{fr} - \mathbf{I}_{\underline{0}}^{fr}) \tag{13}$$

Figure 4. The mean profile $\mathbf{X}_{\underline{0}}^{pr}$.

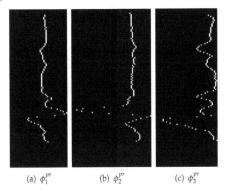

(a) ϕ_1^{pr} (b) ϕ_2^{pr} (c) ϕ_3^{pr}

Figure 5. The first three eigenprofiles ϕ_j^{pr} (Scaled for visualization).

Encoding is then performed according to:

$$\alpha_j^{pr} = (\mathbf{X}^{pr} - \mathbf{X}_{\underline{0}}^{pr})^T \phi_j^{pr} \tag{14}$$

and decoding is performed as:

$$\hat{\mathbf{I}}^{fr} = \mathbf{I}_{\underline{0}}^{fr} + \sum_{j=1}^{M} \alpha_j^{pr} \phi_j^{p_{fr}} \tag{15}$$

In this way the profile is used for encoding and the frontal view is decoded. The profile can be extracted through low-level processes such as edge detection which makes it fast to find. The success of edge detection may depend on the background so a template matching combined with edge detection is much more stable. For the experiments in this work we have manually corrected some edge detection errors.

Reconstruction quality (PSNR)			
ϕ	Y	U	V
5	34,9	39,3	41,9
10	37,4	39,4	42,2
15	38,6	39,4	42,3
20	39,6	39,4	42,3
25	40,3	39,4	42,3

Table 1. Reference results for frontal view encoding and decoding of the videos.

6. Practical results

In this section we present practical results for encoding with the side view and profile of the side view. The reconstructed video is always the frontal view. We use video sequences which contain both the side and frontal view of a person (Fig. 2). In these frames there is a correspondence between the facial features in the side view I^s and the frontal view I^{fr}. For example, when the mouth is opened it is visible in both views and the change in the side view is consistent with the change in the frontal view. For both experiments we use 10 video sequences. Each video sequence show one person when he/she is displaying Ekman's six basic expressions. The sequences are approximately 30 seconds long and the subjects starts with a neutral expression. After each basic expression the subject returns to the neutral expression. The reported results are averages for all the sequences.

The information that should be decoded is not needed for encoding since this information can be found by looking at information that has correspondence with it. The reconstruction quality is measured for the frontal view only and not the entire frame since it is only this view which is reconstructed. The reconstruction quality for encoding with the side view and the profile are compared to the quality of the frontal view when this is also used for encoding (regular PCA video coding). The quality for using regular PCA video coding is shown in Table 1. Table 2 and 3 show the reduction in quality there is compared to Table 1. The quality is measured in YUV color space since the video sequences are coded in this color space. The complexity reduction from using the alternative views for encoding instead of the frontal view is presented for the two different experiments.

6.1. Encoding with the side view, decoding with the frontal view

Table 1 show the quality of reconstructed frontal view for regular PCA encoding and Table 2 show the reduction in quality compared to this Table when the side view is used for encoding. From Table 2 it can be seen that the quality of the reconstructed frontal view is slightly lower for side view encoding compared to frontal view encoding (1,5 dB).But at the same time the encoding complexity is reduced. With a spatial size for the frontal view I^{fr} of 94x144 and a side view size of 48x128 (I^s) the complexity reduction is almost 55 %. However, the usefulness of this encoding is not found in quality or complexity since it provides a new idea for video coding. All previous methods aim at reconstructing the same video as the original video from a compressed version. Here it is possible to make use of a different video for encoding compared to decoding. This video is much easier to record and the usefulness of the video coding will be increased vastly.

Red. of rec. qual. (PSNR)			
ϕ	Y	U	V
5	0,8	0,1	0,0
10	1,4	0,1	0,1
15	1,6	0,0	0,1
20	1,7	0,0	0,1
25	1,6	0,0	0,1

Table 2. Reduction of reconstruction quality for encoding with side view compared to encoding with frontal view.

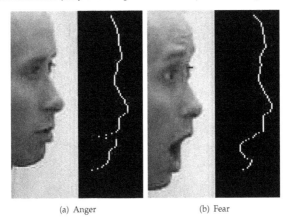

(a) Anger   (b) Fear

Figure 6. Example frames of profiles relating to the side view.

6.2. Encoding with the side view profile, decoding with the frontal view

Instead of using the side view I^s for encoding we use the profile of the side view X^{pr}. This profile is calculated according to section 5. Examples of how the profiles relate to the side views are shown in Fig. 6.

The amount of data that is needed for encoding is reduced from each pixel in the side view to only the positions of the profile points. In our experiments the profile consists of 98 points (T) so the encoding information is only 99 values. X values for all positions are needed but only the first y value since you only add one to the next (25 follows 24, 26 follows 25 and so on). The complexity reduction compared to encoding with the frontal view is more than 99%.

The objective quality reduction compared to encoding with the frontal view (Table 1) is presented in Table 3. A figure of the Y channel quality for the different encoding options is shown in Fig. 7. The reconstruction quality is significantly lower when the profile is used for encoding compared to using the side view. When the video is evaluated subjectively it can be seen that the video becomes jerky and loses its natural smoothness; something that is difficult to visualize with still images. In Fig. 8 a comparison between the original and reconstructed frames is shown together with the profiles. Most frames are reconstructed quite well but some video frames are not consistent with the rest of the video and this reduces the reconstruction quality. We have previously shown how this issue can be handled

Red. of rec. qual. (PSNR)			
ϕ	Y	U	V
5	2,5	0,1	0,1
10	3,8	0,2	0,2
15	4,2	0,2	0,2
20	4,5	0,2	0,2
25	5,0	0,2	0,3

Table 3. Reduction of reconstruction quality for encoding with profile compared to encoding with frontal view.

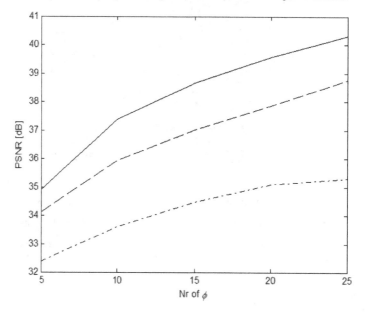

Figure 7. The Y-channel quality. – Encoding with the frontal view I^{fr} - - Encoding with the side view I^{s} ⋯ Encoding with the frontal view X^{pr}.

with Local linear embedding (LLE) [26, 27]. LLE is an unsupervised learning algorithm that computes low-dimensional, neighborhood-preserving embeddings of high-dimensional sources. By creating such an embedding for the reconstructed facial mimics it is possible to ensure that the frames share similarities with the surrounding frames and thus create a video with smooth transitions between the frames. The quality, measured in PSNR, will then be increased. Some frames are reconstructed with a blurry result and this also lowers the PSNR, but most of the quality loss depends on the difference in facial expression between the original and reconstructed frames.

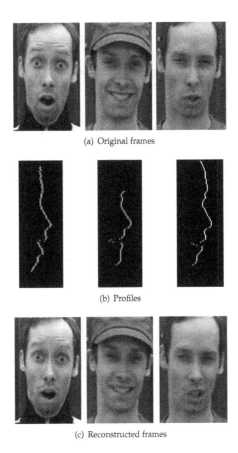

(a) Original frames

(b) Profiles

(c) Reconstructed frames

Figure 8. Example frames of original frames, profiles and frames reconstructed from encoding with the profiles.

7. Discussion

We have shown how Asymmetrical Principal Component Analysis (aPCA) is used for encoding and decoding of different facial parts. The importance is to have a correct correspondence between facial features in different views of the face. The use of the side view for encoding will increase the usefulness of aPCA since we can use video sequences which are easier to record for encoding but still decode the frontal view of the face. The side view is easier to film since a camera can be placed closely to the side of the face instead of in front of the face.

We have furthermore shown that it possible to use the position of the profile for encoding instead of the pixel values in the side view. The reconstructed video loses its natural transition between frames and the objective quality drops. This can be solved by incorporating local linear embedding and dynamic programming. The amount of data used for encoding is reduced with more than 99 % when the profile is used compared to using the frontal view.

Encoding from the side view and decoding of the frontal is a new kind of video coding since the decoded information is not even used in the encoding process. This enables the use of more user friendly video acquisition since the frontal view does not need to be recorded and the side view can be recorded with less user impact.

In the profile there is very little information about the eyes; it is difficult to model where the eye is looking. In the profile the left eyelid is visible so you can model opened or closed eyes but not where you are looking. As extra information to the profile it may be useful to add the pixel intensities for the eye region. This is easily solved by adding the pixels to the eigenprofile. The correspondences from both type of information are then modeled with aPCA.

Author details

Ulrik Söderström[1,*] and Haibo Li[2,3]

* Address all correspondence to: ulrik.soderstrom@tfe.umu.se

1 Digital Media Lab, Dept. of Applied Physics and Electronics, Umeå University, Umeå, Sweden
2 School of Communication and Information Technology, Nanjing University of Posts and Telecommunications, Nanjing, China
3 School of Computer Science and Communication, Royal Institution of Technology (KTH), Stockholm, Sweden

References

[1] Youtube. http://www.youtube.com/ (accessed 5 May 2012).

[2] Jolliffe I. Principal Component Analysis. New York: Springer-Verlag; 1986.

[3] Söderström U, Li H. Full-frame video coding for facial video sequences based on principal component analysis. In: Proceedings of Irish Machine Vision and Image Processing Conference (IMVIP); 2005. p. 25–32.

[4] Söderström U, Li H. Representation bound for human facial mimic with the aid of principal component analysis. International Journal of Image and Graphics. 2011;10(3):343–363.

[5] Söderström U, Li H. Asymmetrical principal component analysis for video coding. Electronics letters. 2008 February;44(4):276–277.

[6] Schäfer R, Wiegand T, Schwarz H. The emerging H.264 AVC standard. EBU Technical Review. 2003;293.

[7] Wiegand T, Sullivan GJ, Bjontegaard G, Luthra A. Overview of the H.264/AVC video coding standard. IEEE Trans Circuits Syst Video Technol,. 2003;13(7):560–576.

[8] Rijkse K. H.263: video coding for low-bit-rate communication. Communications Magazine, IEEE. 1996;34:42–45.

[9] Côté G, Erol B, Gallant M, Kossentini F. H.263+: Video coding at low bit rates. IEEE Transactions on Circuits and Systems for Video Technology. 1998;8:849–866.

[10] Neff R, Zakhor A. Very Low Bit-Rate Video Coding Based on Matching Pursuits. IEEE Transactions on Circuits and Systems for Video Technology. 1997;7(1):158–171.

[11] Ostermann J. Animation of Synthetic Faces in MPEG-4. In: Proc. of Computer Animation, IEEE Computer Society; 1998. p. 49–55.

[12] Aizawa K, Huang TS. Model-based image coding: Advanced video coding techniques for very low bit-rate applications. Proc of the IEEE. 1995;83(2):259–271.

[13] Forchheimer R, Fahlander O, Kronander T. Low bit-rate coding through animation. In: In Proc. International Picture Coding Symposium PCS$83; 1983. p. 113–114.

[14] Ahlberg J. CANDIDE-3 - An Updated Parameterised Face. Image Coding Group, Dept. of Electrical Engineering, Linköping University; 2001.

[15] Cootes T, Edwards G, Taylor C. Active appearance models. In: In Proc. European Conference on Computer Vision. (ECCV). vol. 2; 1998. p. 484–498.

[16] Cootes T, Edwards G, Taylor C. A Comparative Evaluation of Active Appearance Model Algorithms. In: 9th British Machine Vison Conference; 1998. p. 680–689.

[17] http://www.xbox.com/en-GB/kinect (accessed 15 June 2012).

[18] Weise T, Bouaziz S, Li H, Pauly M. Realtime Performance-Based Facial Animation. ACM Transactions on Graphics (Proceedings SIGGRAPH 2011). 2011 July;30(4).

[19] Pighin F, Hecker J, Lischinski D, Szeliski R, Salesin DH. Synthesizing Realistic Facial Expression from Photographs. In: SIGGRAPH Proceedings; 1998. p. 75–84.

[20] Wang J, Cohen MF. Very Low Frame-Rate Video Streaming For Face-to-Face Teleconference. In: DCC '05: Proceedings of the Data Compression Conference; 2005. p. 309–318.

[21] Lee J, Eleftheriadis A. Spatio-temporal model-assisted compatible coding for low and very low bitrate video telephony. In: Proceedings, 3rd IEEE International Conference on Image Processing (ICIP 96). Lausanne, Switzerland; 1996. p. II.429–II.432.

[22] Schwerdt K, Crowley J. Robust face tracking using color. In: Proc. 4th Int. Conf. on Automatic Face and Gesture Recognition; 2000. p. 90–95.

[23] Torres L, Prado D. High compression of faces in video sequences for multimedia applications. In: Proceedings. ICME '02. vol. 1. Lausanne, Switzerland; 2002. p. 481–484.

[24] Ohba K, Clary G, Tsukada T, Kotoku T, Tanie K. Facial expression communication with FES. In: International conference on Pattern Recognition; 1998. p. 1378–1378.

[25] Canny J. A Computational Approach to Edge Detection. IEEE Trans Pattern Anal Mach Intell. 1986 Jun;8(6):679–698.

[26] Le HS, Söderström U, Li H. Ultra low bit-rate video communication, video coding = facial recognition. In: Proc. of 25th Picture Coding Symposium (PCS); 2006.

[27] Chang Y, Hu C, Turk M. Manifold of Facial Expression. Analysis and Modeling of Faces and Gestures, IEEE International Workshop on. 2003;0:28.

Hardware-Efficient Architecture of Video Coder

Chapter 8

Implementation of Lapped Biorthogonal Transform for JPEG-XR Image Coding

Muhammad Riaz ur Rehman, Gulistan Raja and
Ahmad Khalil Khan

Additional information is available at the end of the chapter

1. Introduction

Advancements in digital image devices have culminated in increase in image size and quality. High quality digital images are required in different fields of life for example in medical, surveillance, commercials, space imaging, mobile phones, play stations and digital cameras. As a result, memory requirement for storing these high quality images has been increased enormously. Moreover, if we want to transmit these images over communication channel, it will require high bandwidth. Thus there is a need to develop techniques that reduces the size of image without significantly compromising the quality of digital image so that it can be stored and transmitted efficiently.

Compression techniques exploit redundancy in image data to reduce the required amount of storage for image. Different compression performance parameters such as compression ratio, computation complexity, compression / decompression time and quality of compressed image vary with different compression techniques. Most widely used image compression standard is JPEG (ISO/IEC IS 10918-1 I ITU-T T.81) [1]. It supports baseline, hierarchical, progressive and lossless modes and provides high compression at low computational cost. Figure 1 shows steps in JPEG encoding. It uses Discrete Cosine Transform (DCT) which is applied on 8x8 image block. However at low bit rate it produces blocking artifacts.

To overcome the limitations of JPEG, new standard i.e. JPEG2000 (ISO/IEC 15444-1 I ITU-T T.800) was developed [2]. JPEG2000 uses Discrete Wavelet Transform (DWT) and provides high compression ratio without compromising the quality of image quality even at low bit rates. It supports lossless, lossy, progressive and region of interest encoding. However, these advantages are achieved at the cost high computational complexity. Therefore there was a need for a compression technique that not only preserves the quality of high resolution images but also keep the storage and computational cost as low as possible.

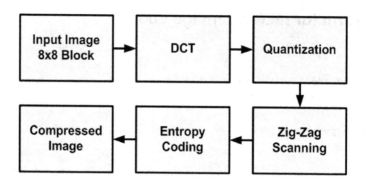

Figure 1. JPEG Encoding

A new image compression standard, JPEG eXtended Range (JPEG XR) has been developed which addresses the limitations of currently used image compression standards [3-4]. JPEG XR (ITU-T T.832 | ISO/IEC 29199-2) mainly targets to increase the capabilities of exiting coding techniques and provides high performance at low computational cost. JPEG XR compression stages are almost same at higher level as compared to existing compression standards but lower level operations are different such as transform, quantization, scanning and entropy coding techniques. It supports lossless as well as lossy compression. JPEG XR compression stages are shown in Figure 2.

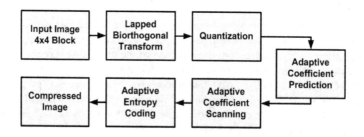

Figure 2. JPEG XR Encoding

JPEG XR use Lapped Biorthogonal Transform (LBT) to convert image samples into frequency domain coefficients [5-8]. LBT is integer transform and it is less computationally expensive than DWT used in JPEG2000. It reduces blocking artifacts at low bit rates as compared to JPEG. Thus due to less computational complexity and reduced artifacts, it significantly improves the overall compression performance of JPEG XR. Implementation of LBT can be categorized into software based implementation and hardware based implementation. Software based implementation is generally used for offline processing and designed to run on general purpose processors. Performance of software based implementation is normally less than hardware based implementation and mostly it is not suitable for real time applications. Hardware based implementation provide us superior performance and mostly suitable for real time embedded applications. In this chapter we will discuss LabVIEW based software implementation and Micro Blaze based hardware implementation of LBT. Next section describes the working of Lapped Biorthogonal Transform.

2. Lapped Biorthogonal Transform (LBT)

Lapped Biorthogonal Transform (LBT) is used to convert image samples from spatial domain to frequency domain in JPEG XR. Its purpose is the same as discrete cosine transform (DCT) in JPEG. LBT in JPEG XR is operated on 4x4 size image block. LBT is applied on blocks and macro blocks boundaries. Input image is divided into tiles prior to applying LBT in JPEG XR. Each tile is further divided into macro blocks as shown in Figure 3.

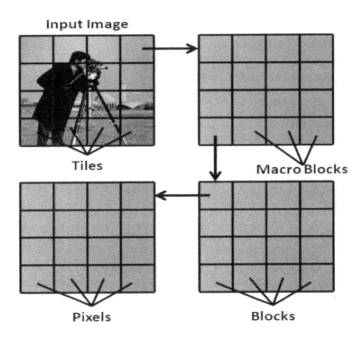

Figure 3. Image Partitioning

Each macro block is a collection of 16 blocks while a block is composed of 16 image pixels. Image size should be multiple of 16; if size is not multiple of 16, then we extend the height and or width of image to make it multiple of 16. This can be done by replicating the image sample values at boundaries. Lapped Biorthogonal Transform consists of two key operations:

1. Overlap Pre Filtering (OPF)

2. Forward Core Transform (FCT)

Encoder uses OPF and FCT operations in following steps as shown in Figure 4.

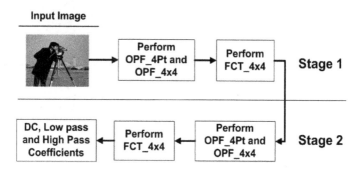

Figure 4. Lapped Biorthogonal Transform Stages [9]

OPF is applied on block boundaries, areas of sizes 4x4, 4x2 and 2x4 between block boundaries are shown in Figure 5.

The various steps performed in LBT are as follows:

1. In Stage 1, Overlap pre filter (OPF_4pt) is applied to 2x4 and 4x2 areas between blocks boundaries. Additional filter (OPF_4x4) is also applied to 4x4 area between block boundaries.

2. A forward core transform (FCT_4x4) is applied to 4x4 blocks. This will complete stage 1 of LBT.

3. Each 4x4 block has one DC coefficient. As macro block contains 16 blocks so we have 16 DC coefficients in one macro block. Arrange all 16 DC coefficients of macro blocks in 4x4 DC blocks.

4. In stage 2, Overlap pre filter (OPF_4pt) is applied to 2x4 and 4x2 areas between DC blocks boundaries. Additional filter (OPF_4x4) is also applied to 4x4 area between DC block boundaries.

5. Forward core transform (FCT_4x4) is applied to 4x4 DC blocks to complete stage 2 of LBT. This will results in one DC coefficient, 15 low pass coefficients and 240 high pass coefficients per macro block.

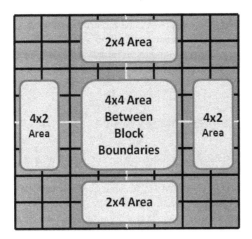

Figure 5. Image partitioning

The 2-D transform is applied to process the two dimensional input image. A 2-D transform is implemented by performing 1-D transform in rows and columns of 2-D input image. Matrix generated by Kronecker product is also used to obtain 2-D transform. Transform Y of 2-D input image X is given by Eq. (1) and Eq. (2):

$$Y = MX \tag{1}$$

$$M = Kron(T1,\ T2) \tag{2}$$

Where T1 and T2 are 1-D transform matrix for rows and columns respectively. Forward Core Transform is composed of Hadamard transform, Todd rotation transform and Toddodd rotation transform. Hadamard transform is Kronecker product of two 2-point hadamard transform Kron(Th, Th) where Th is given by Eq. (3):

$$Th = \frac{1}{\sqrt{2}}\begin{bmatrix} 1 & 1 \\ 1 & -1 \end{bmatrix} \tag{3}$$

Todd rotation transform is Kronecker product of 2-point Hadamard transform and 2-point rotation transform Kron (Th, Tr) where Tr is given by Eq. (4):

$$Tr = \frac{1}{\sqrt{4 + 2\sqrt{2}}}\begin{bmatrix} 1+\sqrt{2} & 1 \\ 1 & -\left(1+\sqrt{2}\right) \end{bmatrix} \tag{4}$$

Toddodd rotation transform is Kronecker product of two 2-point rotation transform Kron (Tr, Tr). Overlap pre filtering is composed of hadamard transform Kron (Th, Th), inverse hadamard transfom, 2-point scaling transform Ts, 2-point rotation transform Tr and Toddodd transform Kron (Tr, Tr). Inverse hadamard transform is Kronecker product of two 2-point inverse hadamard transform Kron (inverse (Th), inverse (Th)).

3. LabVIEW based Implementation of LBT

LabVIEW is an advanced graphical programming environment. It is used by millions of scientists and engineers to develop sophisticated measurement, test, and control systems. It offers integration with thousands of hardware devices. It is normally used to program, PXI based system for measurement and automation. PXI is a rugged PC-based platform for measurement and automation systems. It is both a high-performance and low-cost deployment platform for applications such as manufacturing test, military and aerospace, machine monitoring, automotive, and industrial test. In LabVIEW, programming environment is graphical and it is known as virtual instrument (VI).

LabVIEW implementation of LBT consists of 10 sub virtual instruments (sub-VIs). LBT implementation VI hierarchy is shown in Figure 6.

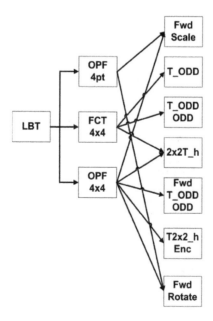

Figure 6. LBT VI Hierarchy

These sub-VIs are building blocks of LBT. Operations of these sub-VIs are according to JPEG XR standard specifications [3]. OPF 4pt, FCT 4x4, OPF 4x4 are main sub-VIs and are used in both stages of LBT. OPF 4pt further uses FWD Rotate and FWD Scale VIs. Similarly FCT 4x4 and OPF 4x4 require T_ODD, 2x2T_h, T_ODD ODD, T2x2h_Enc, FWD_T ODD ODD sub-VIs.

Figure 7 shows main block diagram of LBT implementation in LabVIEW that performs sequence of operations on the input image.

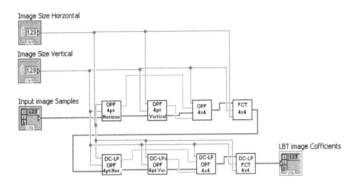

Figure 7. LBT Block Diagram

In stage 1, image samples are processed by OPF 4pt in horizontal direction (along width) of the image. This operation is performed on 2x4 boundary areas in horizontal direction. Figure 8 shows block diagram of OPF 4pt.

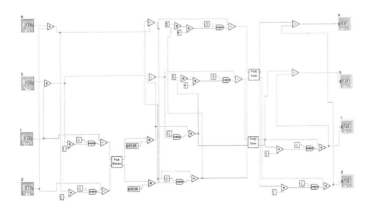

Figure 8. OPF 4pt Block Diagram

Each OPF 4pt performs addition, subtraction, multiplication and logical shifting on four im-age samples. The OPF 4pt requires four image samples and process them in parallel. For ex-ample, addition of samples a, d and b, c are performed in parallel as shown in Figure 8. Data is processed simultaneously when it is available to operators: addition, subtraction, multipli-cation or logical shifter. This parallel computation speeds up the overall execution time. It uses two additional sub-VIs i.e., Fwd Rotate and Fwd Scale. These sub-VIs require two im-age samples and can be executed in parallel. In OPF 4pt, two Fwd Scale sub VIs are executed in parallel. Two OPF 4pt sub-VIs are required for 2x4 and 4x2 block boundaries areas. Fig-ure 9 shows processing of OPF 4pt.

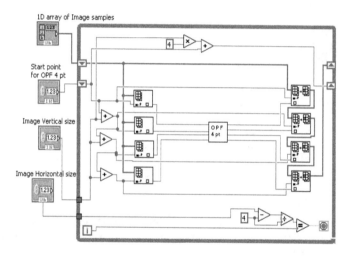

Figure 9. Block Diagram for OPF 4pt Processing

OPF 4pt operation is also performed in vertical direction (along height) of the image. For processing in both directions OPF 4pt requires 1D array of input image samples, starting point for the operation of OPF 4pt and dimensions of input image.

After the operation of OPF 4pt, OPF 4x4 is performed on 4x4 areas between block bounda-ries to complete overlap pre filtering. Figure 10 shows block diagram of OPF 4x4.

OPF 4x4 operates on 16 image samples. It uses T2x2_Enc, FWD Rotate, FWD Scale, FWD ODD and 2x2T_h sub-VIs. Here these sub-VIs are also executes in parallel. Four T2x2h_Enc and 2x2T_h sub-VIs are executing in parallel. Similarly FWD Rotate, FWD Scale and FWD ODD are also executed in parallel. OPF 4x4 starts processing on 16 image samples at once and outputs all 16 processed image samples at same time. Figure 11 shows block diagram for processing of OPF 4x4.

For processing of image samples for OPF 4x4 operation: start point of OPF 4x4 and image dimensions are required along with input images samples. After the processing of OPF 4x4, FCT 4x4 is performed on each 4x4 image block. Figure 12 shows block diagram of FCT 4x4.

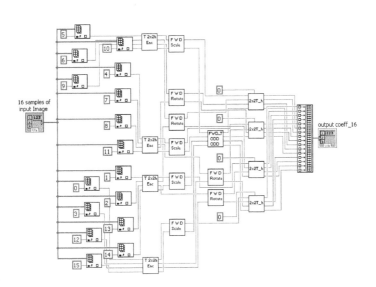

Figure 10. Block Diagram of OPF 4x4

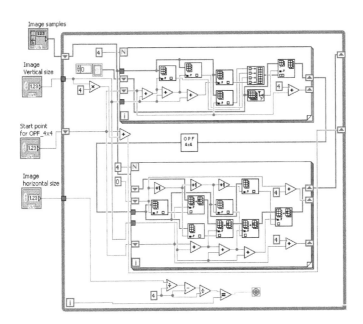

Figure 11. Block Diagram for OPF 4x4 Processing

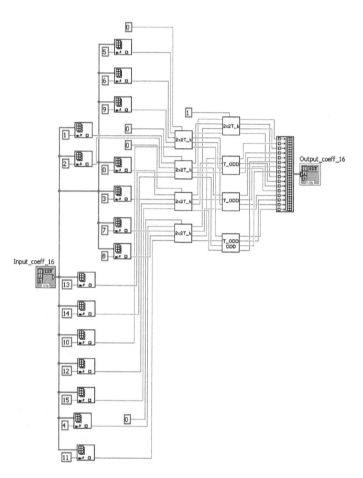

Figure 12. Block Diagram of FCT 4x4

FCT 4x4 operation requires 2x2T_h, T_ODD and T_ODDODD sub-VIs. These sub-VIs are also executed in parallel to speed up the operation of FCT 4x4. It is operated on 16 image samples that are processed in parallel. This completes the stage 1 of LBT. This will result one DC coefficient in each 4x4 block. In stage 2, all operations will be performed on these DC coefficients of all blocks. DC coefficients will be considered as image samples and arranged in 4x4 blocks. OPF 4pt is performed in horizontal and vertical directions on DC coefficients block boundaries with 4x2 and 2x4 areas. OPF 4x4 is also applied on 4x4 areas between DC blocks boundaries. FCT 4x4 is performed on each DC 4x4 blocks to complete stage 2 of LBT. At this stage, each macro block contains 1 DC, 15 low pass coefficients and 240 high pass coefficients.

We tested LabVIEW implementation on NI-PXIe 8106 embedded controller. It has Intel 2.16GHz Dual core processor with 1GB RAM. It takes 187.36 ms to process test image of size 512x512. We tested LBT in lossless mode. Functionality of implementation is tested and verified with JPEG XR reference software ITU-T T835 and standard specifications ITU-T T832.Memory usage by top level VI is shown in Table 1.

Resource Type	Used
Front panel Objects	22.6 KB
Block Diagram Objects	589.4 KB
Code	73.7 KB
Data	66.6 KB
Total	752.2 KB

Table 1. Memory Usage

Important parameters of implementation of top level VI and sub-VIs are shown in Table 2.

VI	No. of Nodes	Wire Sources	Connector Inputs	Connector Outputs
LBT.vi	561	641	0	0
OPF 4pt.vi	61	60	4	4
OPF 4x4.vi	56	90	1	1
FCT 4x4.vi	48	71	1	1
Fwd Scale.vi	28	26	2	2
Fwd Rotate.vi	14	12	2	2
2x2 T_h.vi	19	15	5	4
FWD T_ODD ODD.vi	41	37	4	4
T2x2h Enc.vi	25	21	4	4
T_ODD ODD.vi	45	41	4	4
T_ODD.vi	58	54	4	4

Table 2. VIs Parameters

4. Soft processor based hardware design of LBT

To use Lapped Biorthogonal transform in real time embedded environment, we need its hardware implementation. Application specific hardware for LBT provides excellent performance but up-gradation of hardware design is difficult because it requires remodeling of whole hardware design. Pipeline implementation of LBT also provides outstanding performance but due to sequential nature of LBT, it requires large amount of memory usage [10-12]. In this section, we describe a soft embedded processor based implementation of LBT. The proposed architecture design is shown in Figure 13.

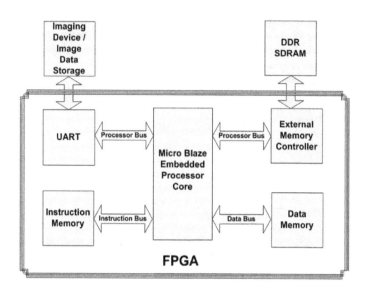

Figure 13. Proposed Architecture Design

Soft embedded processor is implemented on FPGA and its main advantage is that we can easily reconfigure or upgrade our design. The processor is connected to UART and external memory controller through processor bus. Instruction and data memories are connected to soft embedded processor through instruction and data bus respectively. The instructions of LBT processing are stored in instruction memory that will be executed by the proposed soft embedded processor core. Block RAM (BRAM) of FPGA is used as data and instruction memory.

For the processing of LBT, digital image is loaded into DDR SDRAM from external source like imaging device through UART. Image is first divided into fix size tiles i.e. 512x512. Tile data is fetched from DDR SDRAM into the data memory. Each tile is processed independently. OPF_4pt and OPF_4x4 operations are applied across blocks boundaries. After that FCT_4x4 operation is applied on each block to complete first stage of LBT. At this stage, each block has one DC coefficient.

For second stage of LBT, we consider these DC coefficients as single pixel arranged in DC blocks of size 4x4 and same operations of stage 1 are performed. After performing OPF_4pt, OPF_4x4 and FCT_4x4, stage 2 of LBT is completed. At this stage, each macro block has 1 DC coefficient, 15 low pass coefficients and 240 high pass coefficients. We send these coefficients back to DDR SDRAM and load new tile data into data memory. DDR SDRAM is just used for image storage and can be removed if streaming of image samples from sensor is available. Only data and instruction memory is used in processing of LBT. Flow diagram in Figure 14 gives summary of operations for LBT processing.

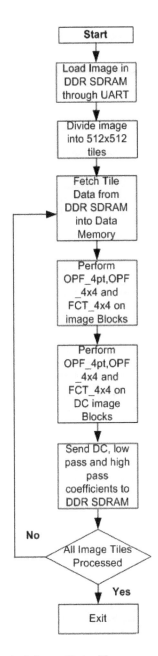

Figure 14. Flow Diagram of LBT Processing in Proposed Design [9]

The proposed design is tested on Xilinx Virtex-II Pro FPGA and verified the functionality of design according to standard specifications ITU-T T832 and reference software ITU-T T835. Test Image is loaded into DDR SDRAM through UART from computer. Same test image is also processed by reference software and compares the results. Both processed images were same when indicates correct functionality of our design. FPGA resources used in implementation are shown in Table3.

Resource Type	Used	% age of FPGA
Number Slice Registers	3,742	13%
Number of occupied Slices	3,747	27%
Number of 4 input LUTs	2,962	10%
Number of RAMB16s	25	18%
Number of MULT18X18s	3	2%

Table 3. FPGA Resource Utilization

Processor specifications of design are listed in Table 4.

Processor Speed	100MHz
Processor Bus Speed	100MHz
Memory for Instruction and Data	32KB

Table 4. Processor Resources

Memory required for data and instruction in our design is 262,144 bits. As the input image is divided into fix size tiles i.e. 512x512, design can process large image sizes. Minimum input image size is 512 x 512. Due to less memory requirements, easy up-gradation and tile based image processing. It is suitable for low cost portable devices. Test image is used of size 512x512 and in unsigned-16 bit format. Execution time to process test image is 27.6ms. Compression capability for test image is 36 frames per second. Figure 15 shows original and decompressed image which was compressed by proposed design. Lossless compression mode of JPEG XR is used to test the implementation so recovered image is exactly same as original image.

(a)   (b)

Figure 15. Figure (a) shows original image. Figure (b) shows decompressed image which was compressed by proposed LBT implementation.

5. Conclusion

In this chapter we have discussed the implementation of Lapped Biorthogonal Transform in LabVIEW for state of art image compression technique known as JPEG XR (ITU-T T.832 | ISO/IEC 29199-2). Such implementation can be used in PXI based high performance embedded controllers for image processing and compression. It also helps in research and efficient hardware implementation of JPEG-XR image compression. Moreover we also proposed an easily programmable, soft processor based design of LBT which requires less memory for processing that's makes this design suitable for low cost embedded devices.

Author details

Muhammad Riaz ur Rehman, Gulistan Raja and Ahmad Khalil Khan

Department of Electrical Engineering, University of Engineering and Technology, Taxila, Pakistan

References

[1] Wallace and G K. The JPEG still picture compression standard. IEEE Transactions on Consumer Electronics 1992; 38(1) xviii - xxxiv.

[2] Taubman and D S. JPEG2000: standard for interactive imaging. Proceedings of the IEEE 2002; 90(8) 1336 – 1357.

[3] ITU-T JPEG XR image coding system – Image coding specification. ITU-T Recommendation T.832; 2009.

[4] Frederic Dufaux, Gary Sullivan and Touradj. Ebrahimi. The JPEG XR Image Coding Standard. IEEE Signal Processing Magazine 2009; 26(6) 195-199.

[5] Malvar and H S.The LOT: transform coding without blocking effects. IEEE Transactions on Acoustics, Speech and Signal Processing 1989; 37(4) 553 – 559.

[6] Malvar and H S.Biorthogonal and nonuniform lapped transforms for transform coding with reduced blocking and ringing artifacts. IEEE Transactions on Signal Processing 1998; 46(4) 1043 – 1053.

[7] J Z Xu, F Wu, J Liang and W Zhang. Directional Lapped Transforms for Image Coding. IEEE Transactions on Image Processing 2010; 19(1) 85-97.

[8] Maalouf, A Larabi and M C. Low-complexity enhanced lapped transform for image coding in JPEG XR / HD photo. In: 16th IEEE International Conference on Image Processing (ICIP), 7-10 Nov. 2009, 5 – 8.

[9] M R Rehman and G Raja. A Processor Based Implementation of Lapped Biorthogonal Transform for JPEG XR Compression on FPGA. The Nucleus 2012; 49(3)

[10] Ching Yen Chien, Sheng Chieh, Huang, Chia Ho Pan, Ce Min Fang and Liang-Gee Chen. Pipelined arithmetic encoder design for lossless JPEG XR encoder. In: 13th IEEE International Symposium on Consumer Electronics, 25-28 May. 2009, 144 – 147.

[11] Groder, S H Hsu and K W. Design methodolgy for HD Photo compression algorithm targeting a FPGA. In: IEEE International SOC Conference, 17-20 Sept. 2008, 105 – 108.

[12] Ching Yen Chien, Sheng Chieh Huang, Shih-Hsiang Lin, Yu-Chieh Huang, Yi-Cheng Chen, Lei-Chun Chou, Tzu-Der Chuang, Yu-Wei Chang, Chia-Ho Pan and Liang-Gee Chen. A 100 MHz 1920×1080 HD-Photo 20 frames/sec JPEG XR encoder design.In: 15th IEEE International Conference on Image Processing (ICIP), 12-15 Oct. 2008, 1384 – 1387.

[13] Chia Ho Pan, Ching Yen Chien, Wei Min Chao, Sheng Chieh Huang and Liang Gee Chen. Architecture Design of Full HD JPEG XR Encoder for Digital Photography Applications. IEEE Transactions on Consumer Electronics 2008; 54(3) 963 – 971.

Algorithm and VLSI Architecture Design for MPEG-Like High Definition Video Coding-AVS Video Coding from Standard Specification to VLSI Implementation

Haibing Yin

Additional information is available at the end of the chapter

1. MPEG-like and AVS Video Coding Standard

In multimedia system, there are several video coding standards such as MPEG-1/2/4 [1]-[3], H.264/AVC [4], VC-1 [5], they are the source coding technology basis for digital multimedia applications. Despite of the emerging HEVC standard [6], H.264/AVC is the most mature video coding standard [4] [9]. China Audio and Video Coding Standard (AVS) is a new standard targeted for video and audio coding [7]. Its video part (AVS-P2) had been formally accepted as the Chinese national standard in 2006 [7]. Similar with MPEG-2, MPEG-4 and H. 264/AVC, AVS-P2 adopts block-based hybrid video coding framework. AVS achieves equivalent coding performance with H.264/AVC. There are different coding tools and features in different standards. However, the crucial technologies they employed are very similar with coincident framework. These similar standards are MPEG-like video standards.

In MPEG-like video encoders, motion estimation (ME) and motion compensation (MC) give a temporal prediction version of the current macroblock (MB). Intra prediction (IP) gives the spatial prediction version. Simultaneously, the predicted MB is coded and followed by transform (DCT), quantization (Q), inverse transform (IDCT), and inverse quantization (IQ). The distorted image is reconstructed with in-loop deblocking (DB) filter. Entropy coding (EC) adopts variable length coding to exploit symbol statistical correlation.

AVS-P2 is also a MPEG-like standard similar with H.264/AVC [4]. Its major coding flow is similar with those of other MPEG-like standards. There are also some differences between AVS and H.264/AVC. There are five luminance and four chrominance intra prediction modes on the basis of 8x8 blocks in AVS. Also, only 16x16, 16x8, 8x16, and 8x8 MB inter partition modes are used in AVS, in which quarter pixel motion compensation with 4-tap fractional pixel interpolation is adopted. Being different from H.264/AVC baseline profile, the Jizhun profile in AVS supports bidirectional prediction in B frames using a novel "symmetric" mode [7]. Combined with forward, backward, symmetric, and direct temporal prediction modes, there are more than fifty MB inter prediction modes. The industrialization for the AVS standard is being on and leaded by the AVS industry alliance. Efficient AVS video encoder design is important for AVS standard industrialization to dig the standard compression potential.

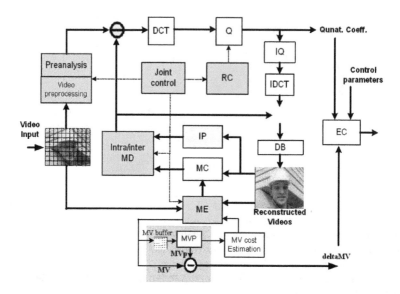

Figure 1. The modules to be jointly optimized in MPEG-like video encoder framework.

With the technology development and video quality requirement increment, consumer demand is being generated for larger picture sizes and more complex video processing [8]-[10]. High definition (HD) video application has become the prevailing trends. A wide range of consumer applications require the ability to handle video resolutions across the range from 720P (1280x720) and full high definition (full-HD, 1920x1080) to quad full high definition (QFHD, 3840x2160) and even Ultra HD (7680x4320) [15]-[22].

HD applications result in higher bit rate and complex video coding [15] [21]. Achieving higher video compression is one important task for video coding expert group and related corporations, especially for HD and super HD applications. Efficient HD MPEG-like video encoder implementation is a huge challenge.

H.264/AVC and AVS standards offer the potential for high compression efficiency. However, it is very crucial to design and optimize video encoder to fully dig and explore the compression potential, especially for the HDTV applications. In this chapter, we discuss the design considerations for HD video encoder architecture design, focusing on algorithm and architecture design for crucial modules, including integer and fractional pixel motion estimation, mode decision, and the modules suffering from data dependency, such as intra prediction and motion vector prediction.

2. High Definition Video Encoder Hardware Implementation

2.1. VLSI Implementation

AVS and H.264/AVC video encoders may be implemented on platforms such as general CPU or DSP processor, multi-core processor, or hardware platforms such as FPGA (Field Programmable Gate Array) and ASIC (Application Specific Integrated Circuit). For efficient HD video encoder, FPGA and ASIC are well-suited platforms for VLSI implementation. These platforms offer huge hardware computation (macrocells or hardware gate) and on-chip storage (SRAM) resources, which are both important and indispensible for professional HD MPEG-like video encoder implementation.

The hardware architectures for MPEG-4 video encoders were reviewed in [11]. Also, there are several only intra-frame encoder architectures reported in [12]-[14]. The predominating VLSI architectures for HD H.264/AVC encoder architectures were reported in the literature. However, algorithm and architecture further optimization is still important and urgent.

2.2. Design Challenges

There are several challenges as for HD video encoder architecture design, including ultra high complexity and throughput, high external memory bandwidth and on-chip SRAM consumption, hardware data dependency, and complex prediction structures. Moreover, multiple target performance trade-off should be taken into consideration.

The first challenge is complexity and throughput. H.264 and AVS requires much higher computation complexity than the previous standards, especially for HDTV applications. There are some coding tools that contribute to performance improvement, however resulting in high computation complexity, such as complex temporal prediction with multiple reference frame (MRF), fractional motion vector (MV) accuracy, and variable block size motion estimation (VBSME), intra prediction with multiple prediction modes, Lagrangian mode decision (MD), and context-based adaptive binary arithmetic coding (CABAC). As a result, the processing throughput is dramatically high. Taking 1080P@30Hz as an example, there are 8160 macroblocks (MB) in one frame, and the MB pipelining throughput is 244800 MBs per second. In QFHD@ 30fps format, the throughout is as four time as that in 1080P@30fps. In the-state-of-the-art architectures [15]-[21], the average MB pipeline interval generally varies from 100 to 500 cycles. Under this constraint, the architecture designs, for IME with large search range and FME with multiple modes, are both huge challenges.

The second challenge is the processing sequential flow and data dependency. There are frame, MB, and block level data dependencies. The frame-level dependencies due to I, P, and B frames contribute the considerable system bandwidth. The MB-level sequential flows include intra/inter prediction, MB reconstruction (REC), EC, and DB filter. At the block level, one block intra prediction (IP) is context-dependent with the up, left, and up right blocks. In the reconstruction loop, DCT, Q, IQ, and IDCT are processed in turn. The motion vector prediction (MVP) is context-dependent with the up, left, and up right blocks. These hierarchical data dependencies are harmful for hardware pipelining. It is important to efficiently map the sequential algorithms to parallel and pipelined hardware architectures to improve the hardware utilization and the throughput capacity.

Third, high SRAM consumption and external memory bandwidth are major challenges. Local SRAM buffers are necessary to achieve data communication among adjacent pipeline stages in pipelined architecture. Reference pixel SRAM buffers for IME and FME are the largest buffer due to the large size search window. Buffer structure and data organization are highly related with hardware architecture. As a result, on-chip buffer structure and data organization are important consideration factors for hardware architecture design.

External memory bandwidth is another challenge. There are huge data exchanges between external memory and on-chip SRAM buffer for real-time video coding. The reference pixel access operations are the largest bandwidth consumers with almost 80% consumption. MRF motion estimation directly doubles the bandwidth consumption and aggravates the bandwidth burden greatly.

Fourth, multiple target performance optimization is another challenge. In terms of hardware architecture efficiency, there are multiple target parameters concerned. Typical target performance parameters are R-D performance, hardware cost, on-chip SRAM consumption, processing throughput, external memory bandwidth, and system power dissipation, etc.

How to achieve trade off is critical for architecture design. Multiple target performance parameters are all factors to be considered for architecture design. It is very difficult to satisfy all these constraints and reach optimal trade-off. It is very necessary to make in-depth research at algorithm and architecture level optimization to tradeoff multiple mutually exclusive factors.

2.3. Algorithm and Architecture Joint Design

As analyzed above, HD video encoder architecture design is a multiple target optimization problem, and challenged by several factors. Among these multiple target parameters, on-chip SRAM size and external memory bandwidth are very crucial. These two targets have important influences on data organization and on-chip buffer structure [23] [24]. Fig.1 gives the inter-relationship among algorithm, architecture, data organization, and buffer structure.

The hardware oriented algorithm is customized under the hardware architecture constraint, with data organization and data flow considered. Hardware architecture is designed with the buffer structure considered according to the algorithm characteristics constraint. Data organization and on-chip buffer structure are jointly designed to achieve efficient data reuse and regular control flow for massive data streaming. On the one hand, efficient data reuse alleviates high memory bandwidth burden and decrease the SRAM consumption. On the other hand, regular control flow simplifies the architecture RTL (Register-Transfer-Level) code implementation.

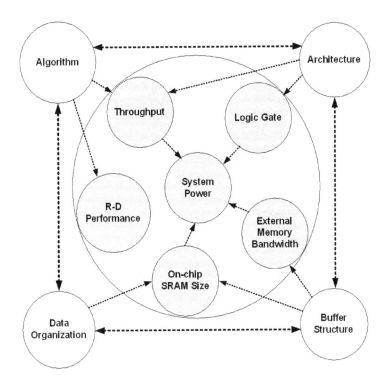

Figure 2. Algorithm, architecture, data organization, and buffer structure

The multiple target performance parameters are complex. The hardware oriented algorithm directly determines the R-D performance. The hardware architecture determines the logic gate consumption. The buffer structure determines the external memory bandwidth consumption, and determines the on-chip SRAM consumption jointly with the data organization. The system power dissipation is more complicate, and determined by the throughput capacity, logic gate, memory bandwidth, and SRAM size. Also, it is directly and indirectly related with algorithm, architecture, data organization, and buffer structure.

According to above analysis, algorithm and architecture should be jointly designed under the multiple target performance trade off consideration. Data organization and on-chip buffer structure are highly related with algorithm and architecture. They should be focused on during the mapping process from algorithm to architecture.

2.4. Multiple Target Parameter Optimization

In order to achieve multiple target performance optimization, it is necessary to explore the inter-function mechanism among the multiple targets. Also, how to make exact and fair comparison among multiple target performance parameters is a basic but important problem. It is difficult to build appropriate multiple target performance evaluation models to guide algorithm and architecture joint design. The following factors jointly contribute to this dilemma.

First, different profile and level combination, as well as the video specification are targeted in prevailing architectures [12]-[21]. There are different advanced coding tools in different profiles. As a result, it is not easy to evaluate the multiple target performance of the architectures in different profile and level combinations.

Second, there is complex inter-relation among multiple target performance parameters. Logic gate and on-chip SRAM consumption are mutually interdependent, and highly related with the throughput and architecture. System power dissipation is related with logic gate, SRAM, and system clock frequency (throughput). The external memory bandwidth is related with the system throughput and on-chip SRAM. These target performance parameters are all inter-dependent, and it is not easy to accurately measure the inter-influence mechanism for multiple target performance evaluation.

Third, R-D performance fair comparison is very difficult. On the one hand, R-D performance results reported in the architectures [15]-[21] are derived with different benchmark algorithms. On the other hand, different test sequences are used for R-D performance simulation. Even the same PSNR results reported may correspond to different algorithm performance. PSNR is not the most suitable criterion for accurate video quality assessment.

Fourth, different architectures target for different applications. Some works focus on professional high-end video applications, such as digital TV and broadcasting, in which the compression efficiency is the first target with the highest priority. Some works focus on portable applications, in which power dissipation is the first important target. Different target performance parameters cherish different priority levels in different application targets. This factor is preferred to be considered for multiple target performance evaluation.

The above multiple target performance parameters, with different applications, different profile and levels, are the design constraints for multiple target performance optimization.

3. Hardware Oriented Algorithm Customization

3.1. Multiple Module Joint Algorithm Optimization

In AVS and H.264/AVC video encoder, there are several normative modules whose algorithms are deterministic and not allowed for customization. They are transformation (DCT), quantization (Q), inverse quantization (IQ), inverse transformation (IDCT), intra prediction (IP), motion vector prediction (MVP), motion compensation (MC), deblocking (DB) filter, and entropy coding (EC). Among them, DCT, Q, IQ, and IDCT jointly form the reconstruction (REC) loop. There are other four modules whose algorithms are customizable according to the application targets. They are video preprocessing or video preanalysis, motion estimation (ME), mode decision (MD), and rate control (RC). Fig.1 gives the video coding framework with these two types of module partition.

The modules with customizable algorithms are very important for architecture design. In VLSI architectures, the REC and IP are usually combined and embedded with the MD module to break the block level data dependency. The MC module is usually combined and embedded with the FME module to reuse the interpolation hardware circuit. As a result, we mainly focus on the four critical modules: IME, FME with MC, MD with IP and REC, and MVP for data dependency in this work. The architectures of the DB and EC modules also influence the throughput, hardware efficiency and power dissipation. Nevertheless, we mainly focus on the modules with customizable algorithm.

3.2. Integer and Fractional Motion Estimation

Motion estimation (ME), including integer-pel ME (IME) and fractional-pel ME (FME), is the most complex module in MPEG-like video encoder. HD ME implementation is highly challenged due to not only large search window, but also new tools such as variable block size ME (VBSME) and multiple reference frames. Moreover, data dependency in block level motion vector prediction (MVP) should be considered for rate distortion optimized ME. Thus, hardware friendly ME algorithm modifications are very important [25] [26]. MVP is combined with the IME and FME modules for algorithm and architecture design.

3.2.1. IME Algorithm Analysis

Full search algorithm is usually adopted due to its good quality and high regularity [25] [26], and it is well-suited for hardware implementation. However, it is challenged due to large search range. Hardware friendly ME algorithm customization is necessary for co-optimization [25]. Fast algorithms can be classified into several categories [15]-[21]: predictive search, hierarchical search, and reduction in search positions and algorithm simplification techniques.

The first category is the predictive ME algorithm. If a predictive MV is estimated using MV field correlation, local search can be employed instead of global search. These types of algorithms achieve small SRAM and logic consumption with high throughput. Predictive ME algorithms achieve almost no performance loss in the sequences with smooth motion. However, R-D performance loss is unavoidable in the sequences with complex motion due to MV prediction malfunction.

Hierarchical multi-resolution ME algorithm is efficient for HD video coding with large search window [18] [24]. Its idea is to predict an initial MV estimate at the coarse level images and refine the estimate at the fine level images. These algorithms are well-suited for hardware implementation due to control regularity and good performance. Relatively, hierarchical search algorithms achieve better tradeoff between R-D performance and hardware cost.

Under the assumption that the matching cost monotonically increases as the search position moves away from the one with minimum cost, convergence to the optimal position still can be achieved without matching all candidates. Consequently, computation is reduced by decimation of search positions. The type algorithms are well-suited for software based video encoder with tradeoff between computation and performance. However, they are ill-suited for hardware implementation due to high irregularity. Also, this method usually traps in local minima resulting in performance degradation due to frequent failure of monotonically distribution assumption in sequences with complex motion.

Simplification techniques are proposed and combined with IME algorithms, especially for full search, to alleviate the high complexity in HD cases. Typical methods include simplification of matching criterion and bit-width reduction [15].

3.2.2. FME Algorithm Analysis

FME contribute to the coding performance improvement remarkably, but the computation consumption is dramatically high. The optimal integer pixel motion vectors (MV) of different size blocks are determined at the IME stage by SAD reuse. At the FME stage, half and quarter pixel MV refinements are performed centered about these integer pixel MVs sequentially.

Although the factional candidate motion vectors are no more than 49 points, FME complexity is very high due to complex interpolation calculation and VBSME support. The FME algorithm is customizable. Typical hardware oriented FME algorithms include five categories [15]-[21]: candidate reduction, search order, criterion modification, interpolation simplification, and partition mode reduction.

First, shrinking the search range is efficient to reduce the search candidates. There are 49 candidates, comprising of one integer-pixel, eight half-pixel, and 40 quarter-pixel candidates. As shown in Fig.3, 49 candidates may be reduced to 17 candidates, 25 candidates, and 9 candidates, and 6 candidates respectively.

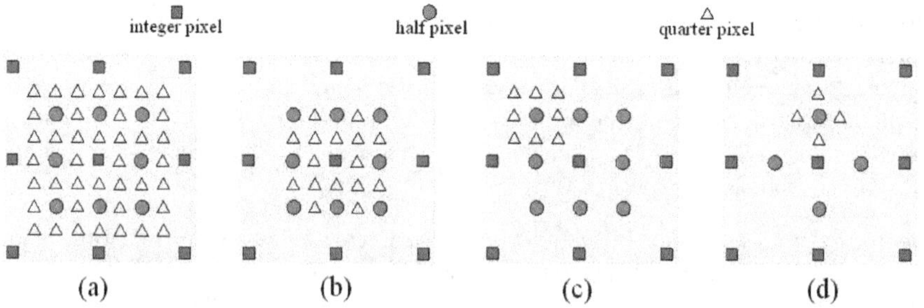

Figure 3. Candidate MVs in different FME algorithms.

Second, search order is important in FME due to data flow design consideration in fraction pixel interpolation. Single-iteration and two-iteration search order are two typical techniques. Full search is usually in single-iteration within 49 or 25 candidates as shown in (a) and (b) in Fig.3, with high data reuse efficiency. Two-iteration is usually employed to search optimal half-pixel MV at the first iteration stage, as shown in (c) and (d) in Fig.3, then quarter-pixels are refined at the second iteration stage. Relatively, data reuse efficiency in two-iteration is lower than that in single-iteration method.

Third, matching criterion modification is employed in some works. SATD + λR_{MV} is the typical criterion, and Hadamard transformation is used to calculate the SATD from inter-prediction residue. R_{MV} is the coding bit cost of the MV residue. λ is the Lagrangian multiplier for rate distortion optimized motion estimation.

Fourth, interpolation simplification is employed in some works to alleviate the computation burden. Six-tap and two-tap interpolation filters are used for standard half and quarter pixel interpolations. The interpolation used for fraction pixel MV motion search is allowed for simplification at the cost of R-D performance degradation.

Fifth, variabe block size (VBS) partition preselection technology is usually combined with FME algorithm to alleviate the data processing burden accounting for multiple partition modes. In HD video encoders, block partition preselection is acceptable. In some works, only blocks larger than 8x8 are supported to alleviate the throughput burden [15] [26]. Some heuristic measures are employed to exclude some partition modes [16] [20] [21].

3.2.3. The Proposed IME Algorithm

Accounting for the design challenges, they are two types of IME architectures. The first type of architectures are based on zero motion vector (MV) centered search algorithm [15] [17]-[19]. All reference pixels in the search window are buffered in on-chip buffer with large size SRAM consumption. The other types of architectures are based on predefined MV centered local search algorithm [16] [21] [27]. In these works, local search is performed within local search window centered about the predefined center MV (MVc), for example a predicted MV (MVp). As a result, only partial reference pixels are buffered into on-chip SRAM buffer. These architectures achieve small SRAM consumption and fast search speed, however suffering from search accuracy degradation due to inefficient MVc estimation.

The center MV based local search algorithm is the most suitable solution for HD and ultra HD applications. It is crucial to improve the MVc accuracy to sustain this type algorithm's advantage. Traditional MV prediction algorithms utilize the motion filed correlation to estimate the center MV. It is efficient for the sequences with regular motion. However, they may malfunction in sequences with complex motion.

According to the predominating IME architectures [15]-[22], multi-resolution algorithms are well-suited for HD encoder implementation with good tradeoff between performance and complexity. In this work, we tends to employ multi-resolution search algorithm to search an appropriate candidate center MV to compensate the malfunction due to conventional MV prediction algorithm. Multiple center MV selection is employed to estimate the MVc.

The proposed predictive based motion estimaiton algorithm is shown in Fig.4. Multi-resolution coarse presearch is employed to presearch a candidate center MV (MV_p). Spatial and temporal domain MV median predictions are employed to determine two predictive center candidates (MV_s and MV_t). The MV of skip mode, MV_{skip}, is also taken as one candidate. As a result, these four candidate center MVs are selected to estimate the center MVc. This measure is adopted to improve the MVc prediction accuracy.

The proposed multi-resolution algorithm is performed from the coarsest level L_2 (16:1 downsampled), and the middle level L_1 (4:1 down-sampled), to the finest level L_0 (undownsampled) sequentially. The 256 pixels in one MB (at level L_0) are shown in Fig.5-(a). They are 4:1 down-sampled to four 8x8 blocks (level L_1) indexed by m and n, respectively marked using different symbols:×(mn=00),●(mn=01),▲(mn=10), and ■(mn=11). Similarly, each 8x8 block at level L_1 is 4:1 down-sampled to four 4x4 subblocks (level L_2) indexed by p and q, respectively marked using red, blue, green and black colors. The three-level down-sampling and the indices (m~q) are shown from (a) to (c) in Fig.5. Similarly, all reference pixels are also down-sampled into sixteen interlaced reference sub-search windows.

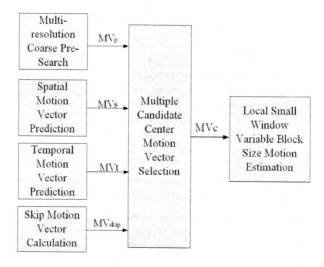

Figure 4. The proposed multiple candidate multi-resolution IME algorithm.

The control flows of the proposed IME algorithm are illustrated in Fig.6. Suppose the whole integer pixel search window is $\pm SR_X \times \pm SR_Y$. Here $\pm 32 \times \pm 32$ is used as an illustration example accounting for page limitation. Motion vector refinement is processed by three successive hierarchical stages as follows.

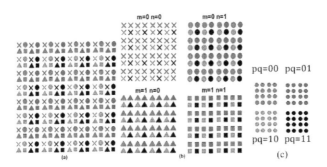

Figure 5. Pixel organization and illustration for multi-resolution IME algorithm.

First, full search is done at level L_2 to check all downsampled candidate motion vectors (black points) in the whole search window shown in Fig.6-(a). To accelerate search speed, four-way parallel searches are employed using four downsampled pixel samples (mn=01). As shown in Fig.6-(a), there are four-way parallel matching operations issued. Each way searches four horizontally adjacent candidates by this four-way parallelism. As a result, the proposed algorithm achieves the throughput of sixteen candidates at each cycle at level L_2.

Second, motion vector refinement at level L_1 is shown in Fig.6-(b). Only the pixels marked with ●(mn=01) attend in SAD calculation for L_1 level refinement. Four refinement centers are shown with four red circles as shown in Fig.6-(a). Four-way local searches at level L_1 are simultaneously performed within local search window $\pm SR_{XL1} \times \pm SR_{YL1}$ centered about four center candidates respectively. One optimal MV (MVp) is finally selected. Then, the final center MVc is estimated from MV_p, MV_s, MV_t, and MV_{skip} using median estimation.

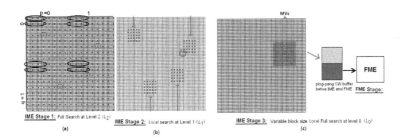

Figure 6. Structure of the proposed multi-resolution IME algorithm.

Third, variable block size IME is performed at stage 3 at level L_0 only within local search window with size of $\pm SR_{XL0} \times \pm SR_{YL0}$. The resulting R-D performance degradation is small due to the high MV correlation existing in different size blocks of one MB if the local search window is large enough [21].

If the system throughput is not enough for real-time coding, for example in QFHD format, N-way hardware parallelism may be employed at L_0 level for variable block size IME refinement. N is an integer and determined according to the system throughput. The search window size parameters are as follows: $SR_X=128$, $SR_Y=96$, $SR_{XL1}=10$, $SR_{YL1}=8$, and $SR_{XL0}=16$, $SR_{YL0}=12$. These parameters are all customizable according to the application targets and video specification.

Corresponding to the algorithm modification, the MB level pipeline structure should be modified. To improve the throughput efficiency for HD video coding, we deepen the pipeline structure and separate the conventional one-stage IME into three pipeline stages: integer pixel presearch, local search window reference pixel fetch, and local integer pixel motion estimation. The system level pipeline structure will be given in the forthcoming section (system pipeline structure).

The reference pixels are buffered twice, during the presearch stage and the local integer pixel motion estimation stage. At the presearch stage, only quarter-downsampled reference pixels are buffered into on-chip buffer. At the local integer pixel stage, only the reference pixels in the local small search window centered about MVc are buffered into on-chip buffer.

3.2.4. The Proposed FME Algorithm

FME contributes to the coding performance improvement remarkably, but the computation consumption is also very high. The optimal integer pixel MVs of VBS blocks are determined at the IME stage by SAD reuse. At the FME stage, half and quarter pixel MV refinements are performed centered about these integer pixel MVs sequentially. We adopt two-iteration FME algorithm framework as shown in Fig.3-(c).

On-chip SRAM consumption for the reference pixels in HD video encoder is dramatically high. To decrease the on-chip SRAM consumption for reference pixels buffering, we propose an efficient buffer share mechanism between IME and FME with algorithm simplification. Only the local search window centered about MVc are buffered in ping-pong structed buffer for IME and FME data reuse.

There are strong correlations existing in the MVs of different size blocks in the same MB [26]. As a result, there exists a local search window (LSW) which contains almost all displaced blocks needed in the whole window case for FME refinement. Thus, FME only needs to be performed within this LSW.

Another important problem in hardware oriented FME algorithm is the huge bidirectional interpolation consumption burden. In AVS Jizhun profile, a novel bidirectional prediction, "symmetric" mode, is adopted. In this mode, only forward MV (mvFw_Sym) is coded in syntax stream, while backward MV (mvBw_Sym) is predicted from mvFw_Sym by

$$mvBw\_Sym = -(\frac{mvFw\_Sym \times BlockDistanceBw}{BlockDistanceFw}) \tag{1}$$

Here, BlockDistanceFw and BlockDistanceBw are the temporal distances between the current block and its forward and backward reference frames. mvBw_Sym and mvFw_Sym are all quarter pixel MV. To obtain the fractional pixel displaced block, we need to perform half and quarter pixel interpolation successively. If symmetric mode is adopted in both IME and FME, the interpolation computation cost will be very high, and the normal FME pipeline rhythm is also disturbed. So, simplification for symmetric mode FME is necessary.

At the IME stage, although the mvFw_Sym is integer pixel accuracy, its corresponding mvBw_Sym is quarter pixel accuracy. Some cycles are desired to finish the quarter pixel interpolation, so this extra cycle consumption will lower the throughput efficiency of the IME module. Thus, symmetric mode is not supported in IME in this work.

Symmetric mode FME refinement is followed after forward and backward individual FME refinements. mvFw_Sym is initialized as the quarter pixel accuracy MV (mvFw_normal) of normal forward FME to calculate the corresponding backward MV in the symmetric mode. There are eight half-pixel and eight time quarter-pixel candidate MVs to be refined in FME. As a result, only eight times half-pixel and quarter-pixel interpolation are needed respectively for forward reference MB, and totally sixteen times half-pixel and quarter-pixel interpolation are needed respectively for the backward displaced blocks. This extra interpolation computation is acceptable and has no conflict with symmetric FME refinement.

3.3. Rate Distortion Optimized Mode Decision

3.3.1. Data Processing Throughput Burden Analysis

Intra prediction (IP) incurs block level data dependency and makes efficient mode decision (MD) algorithm and architecture design more difficult. In general, the reconstruction loop (REC) is combined with MD. IP is usually arranged with MD at the same pipeline stage. MD algorithm is customized with IP jointly considered.

To maximize the R-D performance, the most commonly used method is the rate-distortion optimization (RDO) based MD algorithm. It evaluates the cost function (RDcost) of all candidate modes, and the mode with the minimal RDcost is selected for final coding. In some architectures, simplified MD criterion is used instead of RDcost. Three typical simplified criterions are SAD, SATD, and WSAD (weighted SAD). By employing Lagrangian optimization technique, WSAD criterion achieves superior performance than SAD or SATD criterions.

Suppose S and S' are the original MB and the reconstructed one, and P is the predicted version of a certain mode. Qp and λ are the quantization step and the Lagrange multiplier. Two typical mode decision criterions RDcost and WSAD are described by

$$RD_{cost}(mode, Qp) = SSD(S,S',mode,Qp) + \lambda \times R_{MB}(S,S',mode,Qp) \qquad (2)$$

$$WSAD(mode,\lambda) = SAD(S,P,mode,Qp) + \lambda \times R_{MBheader}(S,P,mode,Qp) \qquad (3)$$

SSD is the sum of the squared difference between S and S', while SAD or SATD is the SAD or SATD value between S and P. R_{MB} is the bits of all syntax elements in the MB. $R_{MBheader}$ is the coding bit of the syntax elements in the MB header.

RDO based MD achieves superior performance due to Lagrangian optimization. In the case of RDcost criterion, genuine distortion is measured with SSD, and genuine rate is used and measured with R_{MB}. Comparatively, only rate is considered in WSAD, in which rate is estimated with SAD and $R_{MBheader}$. It is the measure simplifications of rate and distortion in WSAD that result in the performance degradation compared with RDcost.

RDO based MD contribute to coding performance considerably. However, the resulting complexity is very high due to abundant candidate modes. SSD between S and the reconstructed block S' is computed for distortion measure. Rate R is computed by entropy coding (EC). In the end, RDcost is obtained according to R and SSD. The mode with the minimal RDcost is finally selected. The computation costs of R and D for all candidate modes are high. As a result, RDO based MD is computationally intensive. It is challenging to implement architecture design for genuine RDO based MD. Almost all H.264/AVC encoder architectures adopt simplified MD criterion. WSAD, SATD or SAD criterion is used instead of RDcost [15]-[21].

RDO off based MD achieves considerable complexity reduction at the cost of performance degradation. In some works [28], RDO off based mode preselection technique is employed to select partial intra and inter candidate modes, and these candidate modes are further selected using the RDO MD criterion, and the mode with the minimal RDcost is taken as the final coding mode. This combined algorithm achieves better trade off in terms of multiple target performance optimization [28].

Relatively, challenges of RDO based MD in AVS is relatively lower than that of H.264/AVC. It is possible to implement RDO based MD by adopting mode preselection to alleviate the throughput burden. RDO based MD for hardware implementation is challenged by two factors, data dependency and throughput burden.

In AVS Jizhun profile, five luminance and four chrominance modes are adopted for 8x8 block intra prediction. Thus, there are totally $5 \times 4 + 4 \times 2 = 28$ blocks to be checked for RDO based intra mode decision in 4:2:0 format videos.

There are five inter modes: P_skip, 16×16, 16×8, 8×16, and 8×8 in P frames. Comparatively, the inter prediction modes of B frames are more complex. An inter prediction mode of B frame is the combination result of two factors. One is the temporal prediction direction such as forward, backward, and bidirectional (symmetric). The other factor is the MB partition mode such as 16x16, 16x8, 8x16, and 8x8. The temporal prediction direction and MB partition mode combination results in abundant inter coding modes in B frames.

In this work, mode preselection mechanism is used for throughout burden alleviation.

3.3.2. Mode Preselection and Algorithm Simplification

We take two measures to alleviate the serious throughput burden. On the one hand, genuine RDO based MD is adopted for intra mode selection in I frames to sustain the fidelity of anchor frame of the whole GOP, while WSAD based MD is used for intra mode selection in P, B frames based on two considerations. One is that there are many candidate modes to be checked, so candidate mode elimination is highly expected. Another is that the percentages of intra modes is low in P and B frames, so simplified WSAD based intra mode decision in P/B frames results in negligible performance degradation.

On the other hand, two factors in MB inter prediction modes are separately selected for mode decision. Temporal prediction direction measures the temporal correlation. FME searches the quarter pixel MV justly based on this measure. So, temporal prediction direction is pre-selected at the FME stage using the WSAD criterion. The selected temporal prediction mode may be forward, backward or symmetric (f/b/s). While MB partition mode is to describe the motion consistency of one MB. If four blocks in a MB have consistent motion, the optimal MB partition mode will be 16×16. If four blocks in a MB have highly irregular motion, the optimal MB partition mode will be 8×8. The MB partition mode selection is chosen by the RDO based MD algorithm.

With the above two simplified measures, candidate modes of P and B frames are largely reduced. The worst case occurs in B frames. The temporal prediction (f/b/s) of each 8x8 mode (B_8x8) in B frames is selected using the WSAD criterion. Then, there are still two modes in each block in B_8x8 partition mode, i.e. direct mode (B_8x8_direct) and f/b/s mode (B_8x8_f/b/s). As a result, there are seven candidate modes to be selected. They are respectively skip/direct, 16x16, 16x8, 8x16, 8x8_f/b/s, 8x8_direct, and the intra mode pre-selected based on the RDO off criterion WSAD.

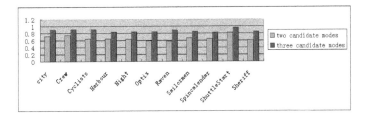

Figure 7. The mode matching probability between two and three candidate modes and the optimal mode using the RDO criterion.

There is intrinsic relationship between WSAD distribution of all modes and the optimal mode selected by RDO based MD. We find that the mode with the smallest WSAD value is usually the optimal mode selected with RDcost criterion. Certainly, these two modes mismatch sometimes. If we can preselect partial modes based on the WSAD criterion, what about the matching probability between these preselected modes and the optimal mode in the case of RDcost criterion? We had made investigation on the mode matching statistics using ten standard 720P test sequences. Fig. 7 gives the mode matching probability between two and three candidate modes and the optimal mode, which are selected by WSAD criterion and the RDcost criterion respectively. According to Fig.7, the matching probability varies from 0.6 to 0.8 in the case of two candidate modes; while the probability varies from 0.8 to 0.99 in the case of three candidate modes.

With this conclusion, we can preselect three inter modes with higher probabilities based on the WSAD criterion to further alleviate the throughput burden. Then, the selected three inter modes, the selected intra mode, and the skip/direct mode are checked using the RDO based mode decision. The simplified algorithm achieves fast decision speed by mode pre-selection and breaking the dependency between prediction direction and MB partition mode.

3.4. Data Dependency Immune Motion Vector Prediction

Residue coding is adopted for MV coding to utilize the motion field correlation. Thus, a predicted MV is desired for MV coding bit estimation for rate distortion optimized matching cost calculation. Moreover, this MV prediction is simultaneously desired at IME, FME, MD, and EC stages.

Quarter pixel accuracy MVs of the left, up, up-right, and up-left adjacent blocks in the optimal MB coding modes are employed for MV prediction. In general, IME, FME, and MD are arranged at adjacent pipeline stages. Thus, quarter pixel accuracy MVs of the blocks in the optimal modes are unavailable for MV prediction in IME and FME. This block level data dependency in spatial MV prediction disturbs the normal pipelining rhythm.

Ideally, quarter pixel MVs are desired for MV prediction at all pipelining stages. This can be easily implemented in software based encoder with sequential processing. However, it is challenged in hardware case with pipeline structure. As shown in Fig.8-(a), MV prediction for RDO based IME for current block (C00) needs quarter pixel MV of its left block (MVA) in the left MB, however it is being on the FME stage, also the MB partition mode is still unknown until FME stage has finished. Similar problem exist in the case of MV prediction for RDO based FME. Thus, algorithm simplification is desired to break this dependency.

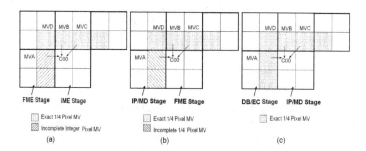

Figure 8. Dependency in MV predictor and simplified algorithm, (a): MV predictor for IME, (b): MV predictor for FME, (c): MV predictor for MD.

As shown in Fig.8-(a), incomplete integer pixel MV of the left block in the case of 8x8 MB partition mode is use for C00 MV prediction for IME. Similarly, incomplete quarter pixel MV of the left block is used for C00 MV prediction for FME. Here, the incomplete MV of 8x8 MB partition mode is used because the MB is being at the MD stage. Exact quarter pixel MVs of the neighboring blocks are used for MV prediction of the MD and EC stages.

4. Hardware Architecture

4.1. System Pipeline Structure and System Architecture

Pipeline structure is crucial for system architecture design. In H.264 and AVS encoder architectures, four-stage MB pipeline structure was adopted in the architectures [15] [16] [19] [20]. The sequential coding modules are arranged into four stages, and they are IME, FME, MD with IP, as well as EC and DB.

Three-stage MB-pipeline architecture was proposed to decrease the pipeline latency, and save on-chip memory buffer. The architectures in [17] [18] adopted this pipeline structure. FME and IP are combined at the same stage. However, brutal algorithm and high parallelism are desired for algorithm simplification on mode decision to satisfy the system throughput constraint.

The proposed system architecture with improved six-stage MB level pipeline structure is shown in Fig.9. In accordance with the predictive MV based local motion estimation algorithm in this work, the IME module in conventional four-stage pipeline structure is separated into three stages: IME presearch, local search window reference pixel fetch, and integer pixel VBSME.

As shown in Fig.9, the forward and backward SW reference pixels are stored in Forw. Luma Ref. Pels SRAMs and Back. Luma Ref. Pels SRAMs. Luma Ref, Reg Array and Back. Luma Ref. Reg Array, whose size is very small. Multi-resolution IME predict the center MV (MVp) first, then variable block size ME (VBSME) is performed and the local small Luma SW is transferred simultaneously into the dual-port Local Luma Ref. Pels SRAMs, by which efficient data share between IME and FME is achieved.

The chrominance (Chrom) components do not attend in matching cost calculation in IME and FME, thus it is unnecessary to load the whole Chrom SW into on-chip buffer. According to MVp, we can only load the corresponding local small chrom SW, i.e. Local Forw. Chrom Ref. Pels SRAM and Local Back. Chrom Ref. Pels SRAM. Similarly, the Forw. Chrom Reg. Array and Back. Chrom Reg. Array are employed to perform data format transform and buffering. Thus, this local SW buffer saves 80% Chrom SW SRAM consumption compared with the unoptimized case.

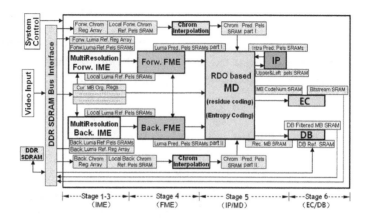

Figure 9. The proposed pipeline structure and system architecture in MPEG-like video encoder

The quarter pixel interpolation versions in the displaced blocks of all possible inter mode are buffered in the Luma Pred. Pels SRAMs (part I and II) and Chom Pred. Pels SRAM (part I and II) to implement data share between FME and IP/MD stages.

To achieve circuit reuse of the residue coding and the EC loops between IP/MD and EC/DB stages, the MB CodeNum SRAM is employed to store the CodeNum fields of all coefficients in the blocks of the selected optimal mode. Thus, bitstream can be easily generated at the following EC stage according to the CodeNum using Golomb exp-coding, and the coded bitstream is buffered in the Bitstream SRAM to wait for external SDRAM bus transactions.

4.2. Motion Estimation Architecture with MVP

In HD and ultra HD video encoders, multiple parallel processing element (PE) arrays are usually desired to improve throughput. Three-level hierarchical sequential MV refinement is employed to improve the search accuracy. So, it is preferred to adopt reconfigurable PE array structure to achieve efficient PE reuse at adjacent levels.

4.2.1. Integer Pixel Presearch

Integer pixel presearch performs successive refinements from level L_2 to level L_1. The block diagram of the proposed IME presearch architecture is given in Fig.10. It should be mentioned that integer pixel presearch only target for the center MV (MVc) estimation, and variable block size motion estimation is not adopted here.

The basic unit for motion estimation is processing element (PE), which performs SAD (sum of absolute difference) calculation for one pixel. Sixteen parallel processing element units are combined as a group i.e. processing element array (PEA). The task of processing element array (PEApq) is to calculate SAD for 4x4 block indexed by p and q shown in Fig.5-(c), which is 16:1 down-sampled from level L_0. Four-way parallel processing element array, consisting of 64 parallel processing elements, work as a group as a processing element array subset (PEAS), accounting for SAD calculation of one 8X8 block (mn=01). Search luminance reference pixels and current MB are fetched from external memory and inputted to the luminance reference pixel buffer (LRPB) and current Sub-MB register (CSMR) respectively.

IME presearch controller accepts encoding parameters from MB controller and main processor, and coordinates all sub-modules for multi-resolution MV refinements. SAD values and MV costs are inputted to the WSAD adder tree and four-input WSAD comparator for SAD reuse and MV selection. Four-way PEAS parallelism structure is employed to achieve 4X speed to cover large search window for real-time HD video coding.

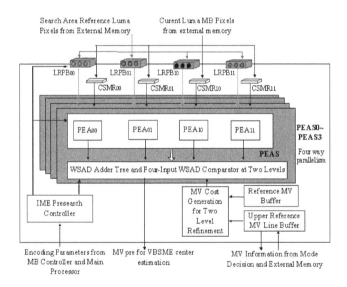

Figure 10. The architecture for integer pixel presearch.

At the level L_2 stage, four-way parallelism is employed with 4x4 processing element arrays, totally 256 processing element (PE) units. This two-dimension PE arrays achieve the throughput of sixteen candidates each cycle at level L_2 as shown in Fig.6-(a).

At the level L_1 stage, four PE array modules (PEA_{00}~PEA_{11}) are combined to implement one PE array subset (PEAS). As a result, sixteen parallel PEA units are mapped to four-way PEAS units to achieve 4-way parallel local refinement at level L_1, as a result achieving the throughput of four candidate MVs each cycle at level L_1.

4.2.2. Local Integer Pixel Motion Estimation Stage

Local integer pixel variable block size IME is at the third pipeline stage. Only block size no smaller than 8x8 is considered due to the observation that smaller block size partition achieves trivial performance improvement in HD cases with high complexity [17] [22].

Fig. 11 gives the whole structure for integer pixel variable block size IME. Triple-buffered SRAM is employed to store the luminance reference pixels centered around MVc. This structure supports simultaneous access for three clients: next MB reference pixel refreshment, current MB variable block size IME, previous MB FME.

Here, the 256-PE array is the basic unit for block matching cost calculation, and it calculates the SAD value for one candidate motion vector, 256 original and reference pixels attend in SAD calculation. In general, the larger the local search window size, the higher rate distortion performance achieved. In this work, local search window with size of 32 x 24 is used for local refinement. If only one-way 256-PE array is employed, the throughput is only one candidate MV each cycle. That means that at least 768 cycles are desired for one MB processing. In order to achieve high throughput capability, N-way parallelism may be employed. In this work, N=2 and N=3 are adopted for 1080P and QFHD format respectively.

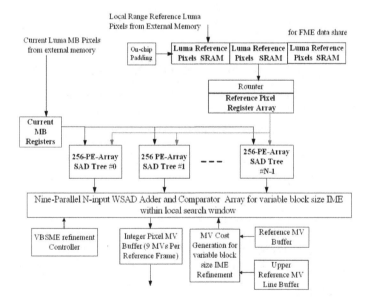

Figure 11. The structure for integer pixel variable block size motion estimation.

In order to support variable block size IME, 8x8 block is taken as the basic processing unit. Variable block size IME is implemented by employing SAD reuse [25]. Thus, 256-PE array is combined with SAD adder tree for SAD reuse to implement variable block size IME, i.e. 256-

Algorithm and VLSI Architecture Design for MPEG-Like High Definition Video Coding-AVS Video
Coding from Standard Specification to VLSI Implementation

189

PE Array SAD Adder Tree, as shown in Fig. 11. There are nine possible MB partition modes, and N adjacent motion vectors are simultaneously searched. Here, nine partition blocks are respectively 16x16, 16x8_1, 16x8_2, 8x16_1, 8x16_2, 8x8_1, 8x8_2, 8x8_3, and 8x8_4. As a result, nine SAD values of N adjacent motion vectors are simultaneously inputted into the module, titled as Nine-parallel N-input WSAD Adder and Comparator, to select nine optimal motion vectors for nine partition blocks. This architecture is similar with work in reference [15]. Variable block size mode partition is determined at the FME stage.

4.3. The Architecture of Mode Decision with IP

4.3.1. Data Dependency Removal in VLSI Architecture

An important problem in mode decision VLSI architecture design is the block level data dependency due to intra prediction. This data dependency breaks the normal pipeline rhythm for intra prediction and mode decision. An intelligent mode decision scheduling mechanism is proposed in Fig.12 and Fig.13 to eliminate the data dependency in P/B and I frames respectively.

Inter mode decision scheduling in P and B frames is used as the illustration example shown in Fig.12. First, intra modes of B_{00}, U and V blocks are successively fed to the pipeline for RDcost estimation. Then four luminance blocks and U, V blocks of the skip/direct modes are followed. Suppose T is the block level pipeline period in the MD architecture. At the time of 6T, the intra mode of B_{00} has finished the pipelining and the reconstructed pixels are ready. During the period from 7T to 8T, the intra modes of B_{01} is preselected based on WSAD criterion and then intra mode RDcost calculation for B_{01} can initiate at the time of 10T. Using the same mechanism, intra mode RDcost calculation of B_{10} and B_{11} are inserted between luminance blocks and initialized at the time of 17T and 24T. With this intelligent pipeline scheduling strategy, the data dependency problem of intra prediction is solved in P and B frames with 100% hardware utilization efficiency.

Similarly, the intra mode decision scheduling mechanism in Fig.13 is implemented with inevitable utilization discount, in which the period from 15T to 18T is idle to wait for pixel reconstruction. The RDO based intra mode decision for I frames can achieve 85.7% hardware utilization efficiency.

Figure 12. The pipeline scheduling strategy for intra and inter mode decision in P and B frames.

Figure 13. The pipeline scheduling strategy for intra mode decision in I frames.

4.3.2. The MD VLSI Architecture

The proposed VLSI architecture for RDO based mode decision is given in Fig.14. Seven prediction versions of the current MB are buffered in the Ping-pang buffers for data share between FME, IP, and MD. Seven prediction MB buffers (Pred. Pels. Buf.) from no. 1 to no. 7 store the predictions of the 16x16_f/s/b, 16x8_f/s/b, 8x16_f/s/b, 8x8_f/s/b, 8x8_direct, intra_preselected and direct/skip modes in P and B frames, In each mode, there are six blocks $B_{00} \sim B_{11}$, U, and V. Also, the current MB is also buffered for fluent MD pipelining.

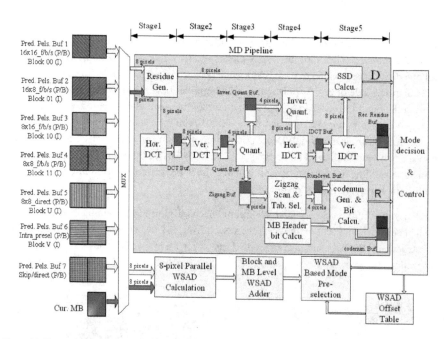

Figure 14. The proposed VLSI architecture of RDO based mode decision.

To achieve the desired throughout at MB level mode decision pipeline, eight pixels of one line in the original block and its predicted block are fetched from the buffers in each cycle and fed into the residue generation (residue Gen.) module to calculate the residue in parallel. The integer DCT in AVS is based on 8x8 block. Horizontal DCT (Hor. DCT) and vertical DCT (Ver. DCT) should be processed in turn to implement the butterfly based fast DCT. Thus, Hor. DCT and Ver. DCT are arranged into adjacent block level pipeline stages to achieve high throughput with the transpose DCT buffer. Eight residue pixels in one line are fed into the Hor. DCT module in parallel.

Quantization (Quant) in AVS needs two multipliers with wide bit width. If eight-way parallel structure is employed. The circuit consumption of multiplexers will be high. Thus, Four-way parallel structure is adopted for the Quant module. Different data throughput rate between Ver. DCT and Quant are buffered and balanced by the Quant buffer. The quantized coefficients are buffered to the inverse quantization (Inver. Quant) module and zigzag buffers simultaneously with necessary data store and format transform for the following zigzag scan and Inver Quant modules. Inverse quantization is very simple, thus it is combined with Hor. IDCT at the same stage. Hor. IDCT and Ver. IDCT are similar with those of DCT. The Ver. IDCT module produces the reconstructed residue, which is fed to SSD calculation (Calcu.) module for SSD calculation and MB reconstruction by the reconstructed residue buffer.

The other parallel data processing loop is the mode preselection. The intra mode in P and B frames and the inter modes are preselected based on WSAD criterion. During the MD stage, mode pre-selection is simultaneously done by employing the eight-pixel parallel WSAD calculation, block and MB level WSAD adder, and the WSAD based mode preselection modules. WSAD offset table interface is used for algorithm optimization for WSAD based mode preselection in the future.

The codenum fields of one MB of the optimal mode are buffered in the codenum buffer for data share between MD and the following entropy coding (EC), which generates the final bitstream simply according to codenum fields instead of quantized coefficients using Exp-Golomb coding. Redundant run-level, table selection, VLC table are eliminated by codenum data share between MD and EC instead of quantized coefficients.

5. Experiment and Simulation Results

5.1. Algorithm Rate Distortion Performance

The whole modified video coding algorithms are developed and evaluated with hardware implementation consideration for Jizhun profile AVS video encoder. The modifications includes the proposed hierarchical ME algorithm, the simplified MV prediction and symmetric FME algorithms, the simplified WSAD based intra mode decision in P and B frames, the simplified inter mode decision algorithm. The modified whole video encoder is compared with the anchor algorithm, which is the standard RM52J with full search and fully RDO based MD (RM52J+FS). RM52J was developed only for syntax compliance test and verification. The source code efficiency is low. Its C model version was developed with efficient data structure and coding style. The simulation results are given in Fig.15.

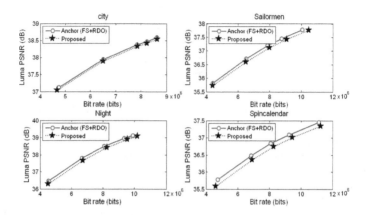

Figure 15. The rate distortion curves of typical 720P test sequences.

Compared with the optimal anchor without any simplification, the average PSNR degradation of the proposed algorithms is generally smaller than 0.1dB. The worst case occurs in the case of the "Spincalendar" sequence with complex motion and prediction modes. The worst PSNR degradation is smaller than 0.15dB. The major PSNR degradation is derived from the IME and MD algorithm simplifications. It should be emphasized that the reference benchmark is optimal algorithm with full search motion estimation and fully RD optimized mode decision. This quality loss is achieved with considerably hardware implementation convenience. The subject visual quality in HD case is almost negligible.

5.2. Hardware Cost

The proposed architecture was implemented with Verilog-HDL language and synthesized by Design complier with SMIC 130nm 1P9M standard cell library. Table 1 shows the hardware cost of the proposed architecture and comparisons to other typical reference designs. The profile and level, video format, reference frame number, variable block partition mode, pipeline structure, throughput, system frequency, gate count, and SRAM consumption are also taken as comparison factors.

According to the results in table 1, the system throughput efficiency is only lower than that of the architecture in [21]. The logic cost and SRAM consumption of this work is competitive to other reference works.

AVS Jizhun profile is equivalent to the main and high profile of H.264/AVC. B frame is supported in the proposed architecture. Two reference frame motion estimation is supported in P frame coding. As a result, the computation and throughput burden is 2X as the works with only one reference motion estimation.

	T.C. Chen [15]	H.C.Chang [16]	Z. Y. Liu [17]	Y. K. Lin [18]	Yi. H. Chen [19]	L.F. Ding [20]	Proposed
Profile/level	Baseline@ Level3.1	Baseline@ Level 3.1	Baseline@Le vel4	High@ Level4	High/ SVC	Multiview/ High	Jizhun
Video format	720p@ 30fps	720p@ 30fps	Full HD	Full HD	Full HD	FullHD / QFHD	Full HD @60i
Ref. frame	1/4	1	1	1	3	1	2
VBS Mode	All	All	above 8x8	All	All	All	above 8x8
Intra Mode	All	All	All	All	All	All	All
Pipeline	4 stage	4 stage	3 stage	3 stage	4 stage	8 stage	6 stages
Throughput (cycles/MB)	1000	1000	820	592	678	312	600
frequency	108Mhz	108MHz	200Mhz	145Mhz	166Mhz	280Mhz	150Mhz
Logic Gate	923K	470K	1140K	593K	2079K	1732K	1230
SRAM Size	35KB	13.3KB	108.3KB	22KB	81.7KB	20.1KB	29KB
Power	785mW	183mW	1409mW		411mW	522mW	764mW
CMOS Technology	UMC .18um 1P8M	TSMC 0.13um	0.18um 1P6M	UMC 0.13um	UMC 90nm	TSMC 90nm	UMC .13um 1P8M

Table 1. Comparison of the High Definition Encoder Chips and Architectures

Fair R-D performance is not easy. Different reference codes and different test sequences are used for rate distortion performance comparison. Comparison is expected using the same test sequences with the same benchmark. More important, the frame level average PSNR results are used in current works. PSNR may not be accurate for perceptual video quality. As a result, the PSNR comparison to reference works are not provided in this work due to the fact that fair comparison.

Multi-resolution motion estimation and partial RDO based mode decision are employed in this work. As a result, the coding performanc of this work is competitive to other works with brunt algorithm simplifications on motion estimation and mode decision.

6. Conclusion and Future Works

6.1. Conclusions

In this chapter, we propose systematic works for efficient high definition MPEG-like, such as AVS, video encoder VLSI implementation. VLSI Implementation challenge, algorithm and architecture joint design, and multiple target performance optimizations are reviewed and analyzed. Hardware oriented algorithm customizations are made for the crucial algorithm customizable modules, including integer pixel and fractional pixel motion estimation, mode decision, intra prediction, and motion vector prediction. Then, hardware architectures of the crucial modules, motion estimation with motion vector prediction, mode decision with intra prediction and reconstruction loop, are proposed. Algorithm performance and multiple target performance are respectively reported. This work targets for high definition AVS video encoder architecture. However, the algorithms and architectures are well-suited for H.264/AVC, even HEVC video encoder design.

6.2. Future Trends

Perspectives and future trends in video encoder architecture design may focus on the following factors. First, low-power video encoder architecture is desired for in mobile systems or portable applications. Low power algorithm and architecture design are one emerging issue. Second, professional video encoder architecture is preferred in the high-end applications such as the broadcasting enterprises. Third, algorithm and architecture joint design will be an important trend for HD video encoder architecture. Fourth, algorithm and architecture design for ultra HD and HEVC video encoder will become one research trend.

Acknowledgements

This work was supported by NSFC 60802025, ZJNSF Y1110114 LY12F01011, S&T project of Zhejiang province 2010C310075, and the open project of State Key Laboratory of ASIC&System of Fudan University 10KF010, and the open project of SKL of Novel Soft Technology, Nanjing University (KFKT2012B09).

Author details

Haibing Yin*

Address all correspondence to: yinhb@cjlu.edu.cn

Jiliang University, China

References

[1] ISO/IEC. (1993). Information technology- Coding of moving pictures and associated audio for digital storage media at up to about 1.5 Mbit/s- Part 2: Video.

[2] ISO/IEC13818-2. (2000). Information technology- Generic coding of moving pictures and associated audio information: Video.

[3] ISO/IEC. (2004). Information technology-Coding of audio-visual objects- Part 2: Visu-
     al. *ISO. Retrieved 2009-10-30.*

[4] ITU-T (2005). Recommendation and International Standard of Joint Video Specifica-
     tion. ITU-T Rec. H.264/ ISO/ IEC AVC, Mar.., 14496-10.

[5] SMPTE 421M. VC-1 Compressed Video Bit stream Format and Decoding Process.
     http://www.smpte.org/smpte_store/standards/pdf/ s421m.pdf.

[6] Documents of the first meeting of the Joint Collaborative Team on Video Coding
     (JCT-VC)- Dresden, Germany. (2010). 15-23 April,ITU-T. 23 April. Retrieved 21 May.

[7] Information technology- Advanced coding of audio and video- Part 2: Video. (2005).
     AVS Standard Draft.

[8] Wiegand, T., Sullivan, G. J., Bjontegaard, G., & Luthra, A. (2003). Overview of the H.
     264/AVC video coding standard. IEEE Trans. Circuits Syst. Video Technol Jul.., 13,
     560-576.

[9] http://en.wikipedia.org/wiki/x264.

[10] MSU Seventh MPEG-4 AVC/H.264 Video Codecs Comparison. http://compres-
     sion.ru/video/codec_comparison/h264_2011/.

[11] Po-Chin, Tseng., Yung-Chi, Chang., Yu-Wen, Huang., Hung-Chi, Fang., Chao-Tsung,
     Huang., & Liang-Gee, Chen. (2005). Advances in Hardware Architectures for Image
     and Video Coding-A Survey. Proceeding of IEEE January,., 93(1), 184-197.

[12] Yu-Wen, Huang., Bing-Yu, Hsieh., Tung-Chien, Chen., & Liang-Gee, Chen. (2005).
     Analysis, fast algorithm, and VLSI architecture design for H.264/AVC intra frame
     coder. *in IEEE Transactions on Circuits and Systems for Video Technology,* 15(3), 378-401.

[13] Yu-Kun, Lin., Chun-Wei, Ku., De -Wei, Li., & Tian-Sheuan, Chang. (2009). A 140-
     MHz 94 K Gates HD1080p30s Intra-Only Profile H.264 Encoder. IEEE Trans. Cir.
     Syst. Video Tech March., 19(3)

[14] Chun-Wei, Ku., Chao-Chung, Cheng., Guo-Shiuan, Yu., Min-Chi, Tsai., & Tian-
     Sheuan, Chang. (2006). A High-Definition H.264/AVC Intra-Frame Codec IP for Digi-
     tal Video and Still Camera Applications. IEEE Trans. Cir. Syst. Video Tech August.,
     16(8)

[15] Huang, W. Y., et al. (2005). A 1.3 TOPS H.264/AVC single-chip encoder for HDTV ap-
     plications. in IEEE ISSCC Dig. Tech. Papers, Feb., , 128-129.

[16] Hsiu-Cheng, Chang., Jia-Wei, Chen., Bing-Tsung, Wu., Ching-Lung, Su., Jinn-Shyan,
     Wang., & Jiun-In, Guo. (2009). A Dynamic Quality-Adjustable H.264 Video Encoder
     for Power-Aware Video Applications. IEEE Trans. Cir. Syst. Video Tech Dec, 19(12),
     1739-1754.

[17] Zhenyu, Liu., Yang, Song., & Satoshi, Goto. (2009). HDTV 1080P H.264/AVC Encoder Chip Design and Performance Analysis. IEEE Journal of Solid-state Circuits Feb,., 44(2)

[18] Yu-Kun, Lin., Chia-Chun, Lin., Tzu-Yun, Kuo., & Tian-Sheuan, Chang. (2008). A Hardware-Efficient H.264/AVC Motion-Estimation Design for High-Definition Video. IEEE Trans. Cir. Syst. Video Tech July,., 55(6)

[19] Yi-Hau, Chen., Tzu Der, L. G., & Chuang , Chen. (2008). An H.264/AVC Scalable Extension and High Profile HDTV 1080p Encoder Chip. 2008 Symposium on VLSI Circuits Digest of Technical Papers Jun., 104-105.

[20] Yu-Han, Chen., Tung-Chien, Chen., Chuan-Yung, Tsai., Sung-Fang, Tsai., & Liang-Gee, Chen. (2009). Algorithm and Architecture Design of Power-Oriented H. 264/AVC Baseline Profile Encoder for Portable Devices. IEEE Trans. Cir. Syst. Video Tech August,., 19(8), 1118-1128.

[21] Li-Fu, Ding., Wei-Yin, Chen., et al. (2010). A 212 MPixels/s 4096 2160p Multiview Video Encoder Chip for 3D/Quad Full HDTV Applications. IEEE Journal of Solid-State Circuits Jan,., 45(1), 46-58.

[22] Hai, bing., Yin, Hong., gang, Qi., Huizhu, Jia., Don, Xie., & Wen, Gao. (2010). Efficient Macroblock Pipeline Structure in High Definition AVS Video Encoder VLSI Architecture. *IEEE International Symposium on Circuits and Systems, Paris, France, 30 May-2 June*.

[23] Tuan, C. J., Chang, S. T., & Jen, C.W. (2002). On the data reuse and memory bandwidth analysis for full-search block-matching VLSI architecture. IEEE Trans. Circuits Syst. Video Technol Jan., 12(1), 61-72.

[24] Ching-Yeh, Chen., Chao-Tsung, Huang., Yi-Hau, Chen., & Liang-Gee, Chen. (2006). Level C+ Data Reuse Scheme for Motion Estimation With Corresponding Coding Orders. IEEE Trans. Circuits Syst. Video Technol April., 16(4)

[25] Yu-Wen, Huang., Ching-Yeh, Chen., et al. (2006). Survey on Block Matching Motion Estimation Algorithms and Architectures with New Results. *Journal of VLSI Signal Processing*, 42, 297-320.

[26] Haibing, Yin., Huizhu, Jia., & Wen, Gao. (2010). A Hardware-Efficient Multi-resolution Block Matching Algorithm and its VLSI Architecture for High Definition MPEG-like Video Encoders. IEEE Trans. Circuits Syst. Video Technol September, 20(9), 1242-1254.

[27] Tsung-Han, Tsai., & Yu-Nan, Pan. (2011). High Efficiency Architecture Design of Real-Time QFHD for H.264/AVC Fast Block Motion Estimation. IEEE Trans. Circuits Syst. Video Technol Nov., 21(11), 1646-1658.

[28] Hai bing., Yin, Honggang., Qi, Zhu, Hui., Chuang, Jia., Xiao, Zhu., & Xie, Dong. (2010). Algorithm Analysis and Architecture Design for Rate Distortion Optimized

Mode Decision in High Definition AVS Video Encoder. Signal Processing: Image Communication October, 25(9), 633-647.

[29] Heng-Yao, Lin., Kuan-Hsien, Wu., Bin-Da, Liu., & Jar-Ferr, Yang. (2010). An Efficient VLSI Architecture for Transform-Based Intra Prediction in H.264/AVC, IEEE Trans. Circuits Syst. Video Technol June, 20(6), 894-906.

[30] Chih-Hung, Kuo., Li-Chuan, Chang., & Kuan-Wei, Fan. (2010). Hardware/Software Codesign of a Low-Cost Rate Control Scheme for H.264/AVC, IEEE Trans. Circuits Syst. Video Technol Feb, 20(2), 250-261.

[31] Xiang, Li., Norbert, Oertel., et al. (2009). Laplace Distribution Based Lagrangian Rate Distortion Optimization for Hybrid Video Coding, IEEE Trans. *Circuits Syst. Video Technol*, 19(2), 193-205.

[32] Lian, C. J., Chien, S. Y., Lin, C. P., Tseng, P. C., & Chen, L. G. (2007). Power aware multimedia: Concepts and design perspectives. *IEEE Circuits Syst. Mag.*, 7(2), 26-34.

[33] Zhou, J. D., Zhou, X., He, J., Zhu, J., Kong, P., & Liu, S. Goto. (2011). A 530 Mpixels/s 4096 2160@60 fpsH.264/AVC high profile video decoder chip. *IEEE J. Solid-State Circuits*, 46(4), 777-788.

[34] Kim, H., & Park, I. (2001). High-performance and low-power memory interface architecture for video processing application. IEEE Trans. Circuits Syst. Video Technol Nov., 11(11), 1160-1170.

Permissions

The contributors of this book come from diverse backgrounds, making this book a truly international effort. This book will bring forth new frontiers with its revolutionizing research information and detailed analysis of the nascent developments around the world.

We would like to thank Yo-Sung Ho, for lending his expertise to make the book truly unique. He has played a crucial role in the development of this book. Without his invaluable contribution this book wouldn't have been possible. He has made vital efforts to compile up to date information on the varied aspects of this subject to make this book a valuable addition to the collection of many professionals and students.

This book was conceptualized with the vision of imparting up-to-date information and advanced data in this field. To ensure the same, a matchless editorial board was set up. Every individual on the board went through rigorous rounds of assessment to prove their worth. After which they invested a large part of their time researching and compiling the most relevant data for our readers. Conferences and sessions were held from time to time between the editorial board and the contributing authors to present the data in the most comprehensible form. The editorial team has worked tirelessly to provide valuable and valid information to help people across the globe.

Every chapter published in this book has been scrutinized by our experts. Their significance has been extensively debated. The topics covered herein carry significant findings which will fuel the growth of the discipline. They may even be implemented as practical applications or may be referred to as a beginning point for another development. Chapters in this book were first published by InTech; hereby published with permission under the Creative Commons Attribution License or equivalent.

The editorial board has been involved in producing this book since its inception. They have spent rigorous hours researching and exploring the diverse topics which have resulted in the successful publishing of this book. They have passed on their knowledge of decades through this book. To expedite this challenging task, the publisher supported the team at every step. A small team of assistant editors was also appointed to further simplify the editing procedure and attain best results for the readers.

Our editorial team has been hand-picked from every corner of the world. Their multi-ethnicity adds dynamic inputs to the discussions which result in innovative outcomes. These outcomes are then further discussed with the researchers and contributors who give their valuable feedback and opinion regarding the same. The feedback is then collaborated with the researches and they are edited in a comprehensive manner to aid the understanding of the subject.

Apart from the editorial board, the designing team has also invested a significant amount of their time in understanding the subject and creating the most relevant covers. They scrutinized every image to scout for the most suitable representation of the subject and create an appropriate cover for the book.

The publishing team has been involved in this book since its early stages. They were actively engaged in every process, be it collecting the data, connecting with the contributors or procuring relevant information. The team has been an ardent support to the editorial, designing and production team. Their endless efforts to recruit the best for this project, has resulted in the accomplishment of this book. They are a veteran in the field of academics and their pool of knowledge is as vast as their experience in printing. Their expertise and guidance has proved useful at every step. Their uncompromising quality standards have made this book an exceptional effort. Their encouragement from time to time has been an inspiration for everyone.

The publisher and the editorial board hope that this book will prove to be a valuable piece of knowledge for researchers, students, practitioners and scholars across the globe.

List of Contributors

Jung-Ah Choi and Yo-Sung Ho
Gwangju Institute of Science and Technology (GIST), 261 Cheomdan-gwagiro, Buk-gu, Gwangju, Republic of Korea

Ben-Shung Chow
Department of Electrical Engineering, National Sun Yat-Sen University, Lienhai Rd., Kaohsiung, Taiwan, R.O.C.

Ehsan Akhtarkavan and M. F. M. Salleh
Universiti Sains Malaysia, Malaysia

Holger Meuel, Julia Schmidt, Marco Munderloh and Jörn Ostermann
Institut für Informationsverarbeitung, Leibniz Universität Hannover, Germany

Guan-Ju Peng and Wen-Liang Hwang
Institute of Information Science, Academia Sinica, Nankang, Taipei, Taiwan

Jian Feng
Dept. of Computer Science, Hong Kong Baptist Univ., HK

Xu-Dong Zhang
Dept. of Electronic Eng., Tsinghua Uni., Beijing, China

Kwok-Tung Lo
Dept. of Electronic and Info. Eng., Hong Kong Polytechnic Univ., HK

Yu Chen
Dept. of Electronic Eng., Tsinghua Uni., Beijing, China
Dept. of Electronic and Info. Eng., Hong Kong Polytechnic Univ., HK

Ulrik Söderström
Digital Media Lab, Dept. of Applied Physics and Electronics, Umeå University, Umeå, Sweden

Haibo Li
School of Communication and Information Technology, Nanjing University of Posts and Telecommunications, Nanjing, China
School of Computer Science and Communication, Royal Institution of Technology (KTH), Stockholm, Sweden

Muhammad Riaz ur Rehman, Gulistan Raja and Ahmad Khalil Khan
Department of Electrical Engineering, University of Engineering and Technology, Taxila, Pakistan

Haibing Yin
Jiliang University, China

Printed in the USA
CPSIA information can be obtained
at www.ICGtesting.com
JSHW011403221024
72173JS00003B/406